East Meets Black

East Meets Black

Asian and Black Masculinities in the Post–Civil Rights Era

Chong Chon-Smith

University Press of Mississippi Jackson

www.upress.state.ms.us

The University Press of Mississippi is a member of the Association of
American University Presses.

First printing 2015
∞
Library of Congress Cataloging-in-Publication Data available
British Library Cataloging-in-Publication Data available

For My Oma

.

Contents

Acknowledgments   ix

Introduction: *Racial Magnetism* in Post–Civil Rights America   3

1. The Asian American Writing Movement and Blackness: Race and Gender Politics in Asian American Anthologies   35

2. Yellow Bodies, Black Sweat: Yao Ming, Ichiro Suzuki, and Global Sport   55

3. "I'm Michael Jackson, You Tito": Kung-Fu Fighters and Hip-Hop Buddies in Martial Arts Buddy Films   84

4. Afro-Asian Rhythms and Rhymes: The Hip-Hop and Spoken Word Lyricists of I Was Born with Two Tongues and the Mountain Brothers   115

Conclusion: Critical Reflections on Race, Class, Empire, and the "Pains of Modernity"   138

Notes   143

Works Cited   169

Index   184

Acknowledgments

There is a community of people who, having the gift of encouragement and sacrifice, generously gave their time and energy for this book to be completed. I hope they see, inside these pages, evidence of their inspiration and support. Judith Halberstam, Shelley Streeby, Nayan Shah, Tak Fujitani, and Lisa Yoneyama always offered me an open door and a warm smile, and helped me fundamentally to rethink the project into a book. Lisa Lowe provided unwavering guidance and intellectual freedom. Words are not enough to express my gratitude for her brilliance and kind spirit. I am deeply indebted to other valued mentors, colleagues, and interlocutors who came along just at the right time: June Johnston, Kathryn McPherson, Coach Malone, Lisa Sánchez González, Helena Woodard, Cindy Franklin, Candice Fujikane, Ruth Hsu, Laura Lyons, Hagen Koo, Chung-Hoon Lee, Rosemary Marangoly George, Don Wayne, Camille Forbes, Jin-Kyung Lee, Patrick Velasquez, Cecilia Ubilla, Quincy Troupe, George Lipsitz, Dylan Rodríguez, Setsu Shigematsu, James Kyung-Jin Lee, Ayo Shanti Oum, Iris Morales, and the late Fred Ho.

Much of the success of this book I attribute to Wesley Stone, Chris Bible, Gilberto Porter, JoonHyun Choi, Norman Ho, Jason James, and Agustinas Suhardja. They have been loyal comrades throughout the journey of writing and revising. The Newman Center at the University of Texas at Austin, Emmanuela Hong, Manilay Khamphanh, Arvind Santhanam, Tra My Evelyn Huyhn, Sergio Palacios Coyote, OASIS at the University of California, San Diego, the Scientific Soul Sessions collective, and the World Martial Arts Center have provided fellowship and laughter when I needed it most! For my fellow graduate students who helped me survive and thrive in perfect weather, bureaucratic institutions, tennis courts, and potluck dinners, I thank Kulvinder Arora, Aimee Bahng, Emily Cheng, David Carroll, Yu-Fang Cho, David Coyoca, Margaret Fajardo, Lilia Fernandez, May Fu, Hellen Lee-Keller, Gregory Lobo, Natchee Blu Narnd, Nga Nyugen, Gabriela Nunez, Theo Verinakis, and Chuong Dai Vo. For helping me make my institutional home at Hunter College of the City University of New York, I thank my remarkable colleagues in the Departments of English and Asian American

Studies: Tanya Agathocelous, Jeff Allred, Meena Alexander, Mark Bobrow, Sarah Chinn, Michael Dowdy, Jeremy Glick, Jennifer Hayashida, Gavin Hollis, Candice Jenkins, Leigh Jones, Peter Kwong, Harriet Luria, Ramesh Mallipeddi, Donna Masini, Mark Miller, Janet Neary, Sonali Perera, Angela Reyes, Amy Robbins, Dow Robbins, Trudy Smoke, Neal Tochin, Barbara Webb, and David Winn. I will always be grateful to my department chair, Cristina León Alfar, for her steadfast support and judicious leadership. At the University Press of Mississippi, I thank my editor, Vijay Shah, who has navigated this project with superb guidance and pertinent advice throughout the publishing process. Craig Gill has directed the book with enthusiasm, and Walter Biggins initially saw promise in this project at the early stages of development. I also thank Norman Ware for his expert copyediting and good cheer.

For my father, Donald Smith, I hope that this book represents some lessons you have instilled in me. For Yu-Chong Kim, my older sister and my mother hen, thank you for always being there for me and giving me sage advice. Your strength and faith in our battle with cancer inspires us. My thanks and appreciation to Robert Kim, niece Natilee, and nephew Nathan for making her happy and loved. To the Kamita family, thank you for the warm welcome into your family, especially the fresh crabs and vacations we shared. For my daughter Hana, one day I hope you may read this dedication to you. Your eyes are the keys that unlock my own fears—what a whole new world you have shown me. And for my beloved mother, Yong Son Chon, your hard work and sacrifice allowed me to follow my own dreams.

My deepest love and appreciation I save for Aki. Two continents and One Love—I could not have finished this book without you making me laugh every day and showing me the intimacy of happiness.

East Meets Black

Introduction

Racial Magnetism in Post–Civil Rights America

> Much of the history of African/Asian and Black American/Asian American inter-actions is not as well known as it should be. All peoples of whatever race or color have criss-crossed into each other's lives more than we think.
> —Yuri Kochiyama, in *Shades of Power*, the newsletter of the Institute for MultiRacial Justice

In post–civil rights America, the making of race and masculinity has been a moralizing project. During this era of economic and racial realignment, Asian and black men have been represented by white supremacy as oppositional humans in U.S. national culture. Inasmuch as black masculinity summons biological stereotypes of athletic supremacy and bankrupt intelligence, Asian masculinity invokes cultural myths of scholastic dominance and emasculated bodies. Whereas Asian American men are viewed as obedient and meek, black men are seen as subversive, violent, and threatening. In popular perception and private conversation, Asian American masculinity is illegitimate vis-à-vis U.S. national manhood while black masculinity represents the total antithesis and repudiation of it.[1] Asian men supposedly perform Isaac Asimov's laws of robotics, performing an inanimate interior with a Yellow Peril work ethic, while black men harbor the dark continent of Africa with its imagined stain of self-imposed poverty and unruly corruption. Since the mid-1960s, Asian American men have been labeled as model minorities, politely assimilating buffers between white supremacy and black revolution, while black men have been identified as public enemy number one, requiring the discipline of law and order. Under this rubric of racial cannibalism, black and Asian masculinity negate each other, polarized within a binary spectrum of positive and negative moral attribution necessary for the management of class and racial crises in the post–civil rights era.

In the racial architecture of post–civil rights America, Asian and black men are positioned along binary axes that define a system of social meanings in symmetrical contrast to each other—brain/body, hardworking/lazy, nerd/criminal, culture/genetics, acceptability/monstrosity, submissive/aggressive, self-reliant/government dependent, student/convict, feminization/hypermasculinization, technocrat/athlete, and solution/problem—which I term *racial magnetism*. In this sense, the structural design of racial magnetism is a captivating field formed by institutions that control the means of representation through moral prescriptions of attraction and repulsion (opposites do attract, don't they?). The term "racial" denotes, of course, a mythic category, a scientific and cultural construction that has no validity in biology or anthropology. Fundamentally, race is a social construct; it operates in the United States as a regulatory concept to organize a pyramidal structure of wealth, property, status, and life opportunities in a complex negotiation with gender, class, sexuality, and nation that sustains a social order founded upon commonsense notions of visual and biological difference. I employ the noun "magnetism" to stress an ideological field of signification, a "magnetic state" that reduces the infinite diversity of humanity expressed by Asian and black masculinities into a simple dichotomy of rivalry and competition. This reification through division prescribes a host of political and cultural meanings onto the body of Asian and black masculinity. For example, at elite universities and in popular sports, the disproportional representation between Asian and black men visually reinforces racial magnetism's biological precepts of black men as all bodies and no brains, and Asian men as all brains and no bodies.[2]

Examining how we make sense of these differences, cultural scholar Stuart Hall discusses how popular ideas become articulated into common sense:

> Images, concepts and premises . . . provide frameworks through which we
> represent, interpret, understand and "make sense" of some aspect of social
> existence. . . . [I]deologies do not consist of isolated and separate concepts,
> but in the articulation of different elements into a distinctive set or chain of
> meaning.[3]

Through "images, concepts and premises" of symmetrical opposition, the legibility of racial magnetism demonstrates a zero-sum relationship for U.S. citizenship and secures the grammar of signification chains found in popular stereotypes of the male body in U.S. national culture. Situational, and often oppositional, race and stereotypes are forces of bodily control. That is, minority masculinities cannot surpass the universal power center of white national manhood, and black vis-à-vis Asian stereotypes articulated in certain combinations reinforce this architecture codified onto the Asian and black male body. Through plus and minus reinforcement, these oppositions arrange a neat relationship of push (-) and pull (+) that gives coherence to racial and economic maneuvers situated in the reproduction of hegemonic relations. An element of this racialized symmetry is the construction of the white power center both everywhere and nowhere, a center with Teflon capability that easily slides off two-dimensional stereotyping and that disavows the centrality of race in everyday life.

Further, magnetism suggests a sense of allure, a kinetic pull that is at once invisible yet powerful and desirable. The narrative fluency of racial magnetism allows for its interpretive strength: we feel it and believe in it because the grammar of racial interpretation has the ability to push or pull our folk wisdom based on racialized fictions, achieved through epistemologies of knowing through unknowing. Consequently, racial illiteracy is a fundamental feature of American life, a powerful drug that diverts the needed will and energy for the elimination of modern racism. There is a certain attractiveness in placing human bodies in categories of differential understanding; this is rationality, the science of the Enlightenment and the feeling of progress through typology. This dominant coupling of Asian and black masculinity constitutes an interesting symmetry and forms tidy systems of containment with origins in the state bureaucracy, the media, and academia, which together compose a morality tale of Light and Dark suitable for a Dickens novel.

East Meets Black: Asian and Black Masculinities in the Post–Civil Rights Era explores the inspiring, contradictory, hostile, resonant, and unarticulated ways in which Afro-Asian racialization has developed in the post–civil rights era. It is the first book-length, interdisciplinary examination of Asian and black masculinities in American literature and popular culture. Beginning with the Moynihan Report and journalistic reports about Asian Americans as "model minority," black and Asian men were racialized together, bonded as if "racially magnetized." In order to suture the citizen-subject to the ideology of market democracy and white supremacy, the comparative racialization of Asian and black masculinity would be paramount to the project of reproducing the "mathematical precision" of class and racial power in the United States.[4] This need to conjoin racialized men in a binary framework delineating bad versus good citizenship, as problem or solution, subversive or obedient, unruly or docile, illustrated the anxieties of capitalism and whiteness at a moment of revolutionary critique, mainly led by Black Power and the Black Panther Party.

Through the concept of racial magnetism, my book examines both dominant and emergent representations of Asian and black masculinities as mediating *figures* for the contradictions of race, class, and gender in post–civil rights America. The post–civil rights era marks the neoliberal and multicultural parameters for U.S. citizenship and class advantage, when the growing immigration of technically trained Asians and the decline of black industrial labor helped usher in a new period of class reconstruction and racial rearticulation. In addition, while the state abandoned social programs at home and expanded imperial wars overseas, national, sociological, economic, and media discourses posited that the post–civil rights moment was a period of imminent racial danger because social movements like Black Power and the Asian American movement challenged the understanding that social equality through civil rights had been achieved. *East Meets Black* both studies the dominant discourses that "pair" Asian and black racialized masculinities together, and examines the Asian American counterdiscourses—in literature, film, popular sport, hip-hop music, and performance arts—that link social movements and Afro-Asian cultural expressions as active critical responses to this dominant formation.

Two influential works have informed us about Asian American masculinity and Asian-black relationships in literature. First, David Eng's *Racial Castration: Managing Masculinity in Asian America* surveys Asian American male writers including Frank Chin, David Henry Hwang, Lonny Kaneko, and Louis Chu within the disciplinary boundaries of psychoanalysis and literary criticism.[5] Chapters are motivated by a central endeavor to showcase the theoretical possibilities of Sigmund Freud, Jacques Lacan, and queer psychoanalytic scholarship. Subsequently, he poses the question: "Can psychoanalysis be as useful to Asian American and ethnic studies as it has been to feminist and queer studies?"[6] He persuasively argues that gender and sexuality must be understood in the process of racial formation. Certainly, my work has been influenced by Eng's original analysis of Asian American masculinity, and I consider his framework to be an important window to understanding the interiority of the "human" within structures of dominance and resistance. However, *East Meets Black* departs from *Racial Castration* in several important respects. First, I diverge from the central theoretical and archival premises of *Racial Castration* because my intellectual biases lean toward understanding the relationship between capitalism and race as well as between social movements and cultural production. Following Michael Omi and Howard Winant's *Racial Formation in the United States*, I assess the role of the state in shaping comparative racialization and the conditions required for Asian American citizenship that pivot upon white capitalist assimilation and antiblack politics.[7] One may consider another question: can Asian American masculinity be fully theorized and understood without understanding uneven racial hierarchy and the workings of capitalism as defining features of U.S. identity politics? While employing psychoanalysis especially in examining homosocial bonds in cinema, *East Meets Black* is also attentive to the *relational* and *statist* conditions that produce minority masculinities in this era of globalization.

Second, Daniel Kim's *Writing Manhood in Black and Yellow: Ralph Ellison, Frank Chin, and the Literary Politics of Identity* is an important contribution to Asian American and African American literary criticism and comparative race studies.[8] Kim posits that the genre of narrative fiction by minority masculinities, specifically Ellison and Chin, allows men of color access to national manhood by using the rhetoric of cultural nationalism and homophobia. By framing postcolonial psychoanalysis as his theoretical foundation, Kim discusses the emasculation of the "native" writer in American literature. Chin's and Ellison's responses to emasculation through queering literature establish a "minority discourse" of literary masculinities that illustrates the complications of critique through a contradictory homophobia. Supple in textual analysis and nuanced intersectional theorization, *Writing Manhood in Black and Yellow* is the first sustained study of Asian American and African American writers in literature. Yet it focuses on two writers and one sphere of cultural production, which limits its scale and scope. For example, we see the difficulties of employing the colonial mindset to compare Ellison's masterful 1952 novel *Invisible Man*, still embedded in the Fordism of Cold War America, and the 1970s writings of Frank Chin, published *after* the emergence of Black Power, the Asian American movement, and neoliberal restructuring. One can see the significance of tracing different literary traditions and themes in order to understand their mutuality and difference for literary cogency. However, *East Meets Black* interrogates, borrowing from Michel Foucault's *The Order of Things*, the "strategic apparatus" of racial magnetism in the post–civil rights era, which, as my literature chapter attests, became the context for the Afro-Asian literary collaborations between Ishmael Reed and Frank Chin.[9]

Third, my study of Asian and black masculinities is not limited to the study of literature. Rather, *East Meets Black* is the first examination to broaden the discussion of Asian and black masculinities in relation to U.S. popular culture, where much of our commonsense meanings of national manhood and masculinity are organized, regulated, and reproduced. For example, in my sports chapter, I explore the spectacle and physical performance of Major League Baseball figures such as Ichiro Suzuki within the discourse of global multiculturalism and highlight the racially coded controversy between Yao Ming and Shaquille O'Neal in transnational sport. In my film chapter, I assess the prominence of martial arts buddy films such as *Romeo Must Die* and

Rush Hour, which present Afro-Asian homosociality in mainstream cinema and examine Asian-black spectatorship as an "oppositional gaze" in U.S. visual culture. Finally, my music chapter links the possibilities of Afro-Asian cultural fusions in hip-hop for the creation of alternative post–civil rights subcultures and theorizes about the little-understood cultural evolution now occurring among Asian American youth, particularly on the Internet.

As a response to most studies of masculinity in gender studies, such as R. W. Connell's *Masculinities*, *East Meets Black* does not presuppose the conceptual centrality of whiteness, namely the white/nonwhite methodology that preoccupies most scholars who attempt to explain the social construction of masculinity and the arrangement of racial power.[10] In particular, the linearity between whiteness and nonwhiteness does not consider the complex exchanges between minority masculinities that illuminate the ways in which men of color create broad and particular social relations. In this way, this book circumvents most scholarship that centers the white bourgeois subject as the filter through which racial meanings activate. In *Female Masculinity*, Judith Halberstam observes: "All too many studies that currently attempt to account for the power of white masculinity recenter this white male body by concentrating all their analytic efforts on detailing the forms and expressions of white male dominance."[11] In light of this preponderance of focus upon the white male body, let us now turn to how the comparative racialization of Asian and black masculinity has helped to structure the organization of race, gender, and capital in the post–civil rights era.

Materially, comparative racialization is a response to sublate the inequalities of the property system and conditions of work.[12] In her remarkable book *Immigrant Acts*, Lisa Lowe clarifies the contradictions inherent between the "capital imperative" and "political imperative" as responsible for a fundamentally flawed process of organizing the relations of production through "racialized gendered relations."[13] Capital utilizes racial difference as one variable in its profit accumulation process through racialized labor stratification, exemplified by African chattel slaves, Chinese coolies, Asian/Latina garment workers, Filipina nurses, Caribbean nannies, Indian engineers, and white CEOs. She argues that "as the state legally transforms the Asian *alien* into the Asian American *citizen*, it institutionalizes the disavowal of the history of racialized labor exploitation and disenfranchisement through the promise of freedom in the political sphere."[14] Although the nation-state formally guarantees political emancipation through universal equality, the imperative of capital for cheap exploitable labor produces "a racially segmented and stratified labor force," which profits from the gulf between the ideological promise of abstract citizenship and the everyday practice of infinite accumulation in civil society.[15] She historicizes the period after World War II and the 1970s as indicative of this inherent contradiction between the economic and political spheres but fails to comment upon *how* a "strong, hegemonic nation-state [regulates] the terms of that post-war economic internationalism."[16] In addition, Lowe mentions only two strategies the nation-state employed to service the capital imperative: the globalization of production and the incorporation of new labor supplies. Later in this introduction, I will specify other strategies deployed by the nation-state, the university, and the media to consolidate the capital imperative through a strong hegemonic narrative of crisis management discursively framed around black and Asian male bodies, labor, and sex.

More recently, scholars such Christine So and erin Khuê Ninh have analyzed the relationship between the capital imperative and the articulation of racial difference. In *Economic Citizens*, So relates, "Asians have historically symbolized economic imbalance, an association that reveals certainly that racialized identities are constructed through the machine of capital but also that economics itself is racialized."[17] For So, Asian American communities that assimilate into the logic of economic exchange from "images of money, commodities, buying, lending, banking, and selling," produce a certain racial surplus due to the racial anxieties of the nation-state and the inherent contradictions of capital accumulation and abstract citizenship.[18] Therefore, their incorporation into the capital imperative produces racial excess and complicates the viability of full incorporation, which the cultural sphere has to expel due to racialized gendered relations. In such a repulsion, economic assimilation leads to cultural alienation in which black Americans experience redoubled alienation in both economic exchange and cultural citizenship.

Similarly, in her book *Ingratitude*, Ninh explains that the Asian immigrant family is a production unit within the capital imperative that asks members to replicate the good, capitalist subject, consequently straining relationships between disciplining mothers and "debt-bound" daughters. By examining the privatizing or internalizing narrative of oppression from the capital imperative to the family structure, Ninh locates the vectors of power within the racialized family unit an important institution to comprehend the axis of "multivalent power."[19] Her analysis reveals the web of power relations that link the reproduction of capitalist activity and the cross-generational experience of the Asian family unit, ultimately leading to trauma, alienation, and silence between mothers and daughters. Such recent scholarship in Asian American studies conveys the primacy of understanding the relationship between hegemonic economic engines and the articulation of racial difference. After acknowledging the relationship between race and capitalism, I now turn to how the crises of racial revolutions and neoliberal realignment created the necessary conditions for managing the legitimacy and cogency of market democracy and white supremacy.

The perfect storm of black revolution, identity-based social movements, student strikes, urban unrest, the Vietnam War, and falling corporate profits created crises for market democracy and white power that would redefine U.S. national culture and set the table for a new social contract and new national fictions to validate those projects. Trinidadian theorist C. L. R. James illustrates that the sparks of revolutionary awakening, whether intended to overthrow absolute monarchism or bourgeois society, contain the seeds not only of revolution but also of conservative backlash.[20] Theorizing Afro-Asian comparative racialization as a crisis management tool for market democracy's conservatism, this section explores the ways in which Asian Americans' transformation into model minority citizens, as obedient subjects in comparison to subversive black subjects, mediated the crossfire between white capitalist reproduction and black-led revolutionary critique.

How did the making and remaking of race and masculinity through Afro-Asian difference help to sharpen the legibility of narratives shaping urban poverty, the viability of the American Dream, a postracial society, and notions of marketplace "freedoms" in a time that saw decisive restructuring to adapt to the modern-world system? How has the post–civil rights promise of a fundamental shift in American life actually been manifested in greater economic inequality, a category in which the United States is now a world leader, and simultaneously in the ubiquitous self-internalization of racial inferiority in the post–Michael Jordan and post–Michael Jackson age of multiculturalism, lucidly captured in Kiri Davis's 2005 film *A Girl Like Me*?[21] In the post–civil rights era, after the promise of the Great Society and the rise of multiculturalism, how do we still have a pyramidal structure for the distribution of economic and racial power? Observing the ebb and flow of how Asian American masculinity is constituted by discourses of black masculinity helps us understand this hegemony, and why the establishment of a modern Asian American citizenry requires an antiblack sensibility. Therefore, the national narratives that I analyze below are *legible* for "common sense" in order to maintain the glamour of market democracy in the "golden hour" of racial revolutions and neoliberal murmuring.

In *Racial Formation*, Omi and Winant discuss the notion of "trajectory" to describe the relationship between social movements and the state within a historical period: "Thus, 'reform,' 'reaction,' 'radical change,' or 'backlash'— indeed every transformation of the racial order—is constructed through a process of clash and compromise between racial movements and the state."[22] Omi and Winant discuss the process of *how* a "trajectory" is formed through multiple power struggles and their consequences within the terrain of Hall's theory of ideology. On the one hand, the concept of racial magnetism helps us understand the relationship between social movements and the role of the state, university, and media in responding to imminent threats through model minority and black pathology discourses. On the other hand, I extend the formulation of trajectory to synthesize the relationship between white supremacy and black revolution, and how representations of Asian Americans became a safeguard for the containment of such black radicalism and antisystemic critique. In no small measure, these tales of Afro-Asian racialization are tales of American modernization.

In *Race for Citizenship*, comparative race scholar Helen Jun argues that Afro-Asian narratives elucidated by the state were "central to the reproduction of U.S. neoliberal episteme that has radically transformed conceptions of both citizenship and the state."[23] Geographer Laura Pulido has formulated that differential racialization means that "racial meanings are attached to different racial/ethnic groups that not only affect their class position and racial standing but also are a function of it. Thus there is a dialectic between the discursive and the material."[24] The state, academia, and the media had made society legible: the more the U.S. public could read it, the greater those ideological apparatuses' capacity to control an unsure and panicked citizenry undergoing rapid processes of class and racial realignment. The theory of racial magnetism references the applied power of the racial state to make such claims and suggests the use of comparative racialization as a technology or tool to manage the ascendancy of various radicalisms that had erupted from and challenged such biopolitical assertions. In a market democracy, the overriding yardstick of white-black race relations defines Asian American racialization. The theory of racial magnetism ultimately tells a parable about state biopower and moral panic, the monopolization of wealth and the inequitable traffic of suffering, and the relationship between the making of "masculinity" and the legitimation crisis of U.S. economic and racial power centers.

To be sure, the comparative racialization of Asian and black men is a disavowal of structural inequality in the post–civil rights era, and its representational power becomes truth of being for those interpellated from state apparatuses. It is located within the rhetoric of colorblind white supremacy and reformist white liberalism, and in the multicultural and neoliberal vision that emerged after the Civil Rights Movement. Much of the post–civil rights era has figured Asians to be in between the perplexed power dynamics of white superiority over and against black inferiority. Perhaps James Baldwin said it best, with his usual eloquence: "The American Dream is at the expense of the American Negro."[25] In short, how could the tenets of antiblackness be a rite of passage and compliance for citizenship and capital reproduction from Asian alien outsider to Asian American insider?

Situated within a Gramscian moment of racial, economic, and imperial "crisis," the watershed year—1965—marks a major political and cultural shift in U.S. race talk. One hundred years after the Civil War, panethnic Asian America would emerge from the echo of another racial revolution and the realignment of Fordism to neoliberal capitalism. In August 1965, Bell 204B helicopters, paramilitary equipment deployed in Vietnam, hovered above the concrete ablaze in Watts, Los Angeles. Two weeks later, the Hart-Celler Act would open "third world" immigration from the decolonizing world to the United States and profoundly transform a generation of Asian lives in America from inassimilable aliens to model minorities. The clarion call of black urban America occurred chronologically in precision with Asian American dreams for a better life through war-weary diasporas in motion. During this crucible between urban immobility and immigrant renewal, the grand experiment of race and citizenship in the United States would undergo a fundamental transformation in national dialogue, ideological recruitment, and martial enforcement.

From 1965 to 1972, more than 350 urban rebellions erupted, instantiating the Black Power era of militant male revolt. Urban black masculinity had arrived—vociferous, unafraid, and organized. In Oakland, Bobby Seale, Huey Newton, and Richard Aoki theorized about radical politics; they hustled Little Red Books on the Berkeley campus, forming a historic Afro-Asian alliance in the Bay Area. Questioning the Civil Rights Movement doctrine of ahimsa or nonviolence, black men of different radical stripes, including Malcolm X, Robert Williams, Stokely Carmichael, and Eldridge Cleaver, inaugurated an era of social movement masculinities, in the process frightening white national manhood as national security threats. From ahimsa passivity to Black Power militancy, in a movement that historian Gerald Horne observed as the emerging generation of "hearing children of deaf parents," black urban freedom dreams for social transformation animated a *second civil war* across dynamics of race, class, gender, sexuality, and nation.[26] Commemorated in Left academia, these identity-based social movements by women, Asians, Latino/as, farm workers, American Indians, the LGBT community, antiwar students, free-love hippies, established communists, and antiestablishment punks recalibrated the extant social contract. Synchronically, market democracy had been in an existential imbroglio over falling profits, the influence of unions, the social cost of labor, and international perceptions of racial apartheid.

In *The New Asian Immigration in Los Angeles and Global Restructuring*, Paul Ong, Edna Bonacich, and Lucie Cheng state that "a crisis within a capitalist system means a breakdown in productive expansion and accumulation. . . . The current crisis in capitalism began to emerge in the advanced capitalist countries in the 1960s."[27] In *The Condition of Postmodernity*, geographer David Harvey remarks: "In retrospect, it seems there were signs of serious problems with Fordism as early as the mid-1960s."[28] The Fordist Compromise, a seesaw Keynesian negotiation between owners of capital and labor unions, shifted to a neoliberal orientation toward cheaper labor costs during this time. In his later work, *A Brief History of Neoliberalism*, Harvey details the central premises of neoliberal doctrine in which privatization, global markets, deregulation, monetary manipulation, and the dismantling of social safety nets underwrite a conservative theory of individual freedom and happiness through the principles of the market. He concludes that neoliberal "creative destruction" was put into motion "as a political project to re-establish the conditions for capital accumulation and to restore the power of economic elites."[29] Helen Jun identifies the principal role of University of Chicago Nobel economists, whose neoliberal principles gained intellectual weight and the ear of future U.S. presidents, including Ronald Reagan and his secretary of state, George Shultz.[30] Finally, to understand the shift from Fordism to neoliberalism in the mid-1960s, one need only remember what Kwame Nkrumah once said: "Class struggle is a fundamental theme of recorded history."[31] As such, this specific moment between race and capital converged in hyperbolic fashion, and the outcome was *crisis*, in the heart of the Cold War and in the throes of history being made from below, a century after the Civil War.

Crisis theorists Stuart Hall, Michael Denning, and Toni Negri have explained the function of crises in realigning the relations of production and the role of state power in managing the panicked citizenry.[32] They hallmark specific episodes or periods in history such as the AFL-CIO Popular Front, Margaret Thatcher's Britain, U.S. militarism in the 1960s, and the Keynesian New Deal to punctuate that perpetual crisis and moral panic, the creation of a "condition, episode, person or groups [that] become defined as a threat to societal values and interest," are endemic and necessary to market stability.[33] For Denning, Antonio Gramsci's concept of a "conjuncture" helps to explain crisis periods such as during the Popular Front, when "the political forces which are struggling to conserve and defend the existing structure itself are making every effort to cure them, within certain limits, and to overcome them. These incessant and persistent efforts . . . form the terrain of the 'conjunctural,' and it is upon this terrain that the forces of opposition organise."[34] For Hall, the "rising crime rate equation" in Thatcher's Britain accomplishes a managerial function related to the enforcement of social control. In Hall's perspective, crime statistics are often skewed by the state for political and economic manipulation; moral panics create public support for law enforcement to "police the crisis."[35] For Negri, a "permanent revolution" is made when the ruling elite, "for its own self-preservation," asserts "its own class essence as a capitalist state, shunning the taint of populist or traditional progressive ideologies."[36] In the post–civil rights era, this moment of danger constitutes a racial crisis as a function of white anxiety, specifically among the top 10 percent of Americans who own 80 percent of the country's total wealth and who are committed to neoliberal principles of privatized accumulation and possessive individualism and de facto racial segregation enabled by the promise of multicultural inclusion.[37] Accordingly, the racialization of Asian and black bodies was crucial to maintaining the conditions of work and the property system, while stemming the tide of revolutionary currents seeking to upend the extant social order. Thus, racial crisis usually denotes a challenge to white supremacy linked to the cyclical crisis of capital. Its attendant formation is co-optation and redirection and denial, in essence resetting the table of discursive encounters through narrative crisis management.

In hospital emergency rooms, the "golden hour" is the critical time period for resuscitation and survival after a severe trauma such as a heart attack or stroke. It is the crucial moment when the risk of systemic failure, death in no uncertain terms, threatens to become irrevocable. The viability of market democracy became uncertain when a perfect storm of discontent collectively confronted the centers of decision-making power in the United States. Never before and never since has the United States experienced such multiple and varied assaults from a wide array of social participants and collective political mobilizations, both from within and from afar. The country secured its multiethnic future by eliminating immigration quotas from Asia and Latin America, and Fordist and Keynesian modes of production were discarded in favor of growing neoliberal orientations. The post–civil rights era subsequently became an important moment of national reconstruction, similar to the radical reconstruction that took place in the postbellum South a hundred years earlier. The time marker "post" marks an end to the Civil Rights Movement, culminating in the passage of federal legislation, but it also indicates a new tug-of-war between reformist and radical approaches to reshaping the social contract.

Consider a timeline of the "golden hour" of 1965: President Lyndon John-son's Great Society speech in January; the assassination of Malcolm X in Feb-ruary; in March, Operation Jackhammer in Vietnam, the first official deploy-ment of U.S. ground troops, and the publication of the Moynihan Report; the occupation of the Dominican Republic in April to depose President Juan Bosch; in August, the passage of the Voting Rights Act and the urban revolt in Watts, Los Angeles; and, ending the year, the passage of the Hart-Celler Act, which inaugurated America's multiethnic future with Asian and Latino immigration. All hallmark the watershed year of 1965, a decisive calendar year, shaping imperial, racial, and revolutionary transformations within and against the tenets of market democracy and racial domination. Much has been written about the New Left year of 1968, but resetting the radical dyna-mism of the 1960s back to 1965 pinpoints a specific and invented trajectory of crisis management that responded to the making of "history from below."[38] The restoration of class power intersected with comparative racialization, leading to significant consequences. The rise of militant black masculinity would be contained through "mass-based punishment and liquidation," what Ruth Gilmore calls post-Keynesian militarism.[39] A quickening was seemingly on the horizon of American ruling-class hegemony, causing a recalibration of America's political equilibrium and rejuvenated narratives to legitimize its renewal. In such temporal conjunction and dialectical encounters, the bio-politics of discursive power in institutions and culture played a pivotal role in shaping class warfare and racialized consent.

This aggressive form of comparative racialization signaled a new era of subtle, hidden, seemingly more progressive discursive formations about race. Here, I am theorizing about the scale, scope, and character of comparative racialization between Asians and blacks in the mid-1960s that established the narratives for neoliberal and colorblind justifications. Catherine Lutz ar-gues that militarization is "simultaneously a discursive process, involving a shift in general societal beliefs and values in ways necessary to legitimate the use of force."[40] Chandan Reddy suggests that market democracy is a social contract for the authorization of state violence through idealized notions of freedom.[41] Additionally, Negri has aptly connected the rise of the warfare state in neoliberal nation-states with the increased domestic militarization of urban space.[42] In this sense, I expand the definition of militarization to include not only military action abroad but also the aggression of class and racial formation projects that utilize comparative racialization as the prima-ry style of thought for a new multiethnic era. In this way, the militarization of comparative racialization during the "golden hour" defines the post–civil rights era of class and racial warfare in two ways: first, the movement toward

neoliberal austerity thrust upon the working class and poor, which has resulted in an unprecedented gap between rich and poor; and second, the narrative production of numbness, boredom, and fatigue as affective weapons to
promote cultures of cynicism, apathy, and hopelessness that render invisible
those human beings suffering from political abandonment.

While the United States was internally experiencing racial and class-based
conflict in the country's urban centers, its defeat externally at the hands of an
impoverished "third world" Vietnam placed powerful stressors on the viability of market democracy as a global hegemon. Addressing the link between
domestic and international forms of U.S. militarization and containment,
Los Angeles police chief William Parker stated about Watts: "This situation
is very much like fighting the Viet Cong," intimating that South Los Angeles was under paramilitary siege.[43] The Watts riots and U.S. aggression in
Southeast Asia illustrated an Afro-Asian point of crisis that organized societal beliefs for the production of militarization in various manifestations.
Horne argues that the summer of Watts had been a black male revolt against
the white power structure, which utilized paramilitary tactics, the National
Guard, and Bell helicopters, a high-tech militarization that had been transferred from Asian battlefields to U.S. urban zones. Ultimately, a black male
revolt against urban poverty, police brutality, and cultural dehumanization
had been achieved for the first time in U.S. history.

The militancy of black men incorporated guerrilla tactics, displayed concise organizational skills, and mobilized the collective will of subjugated citizens, which would energize later social movements. Subsequently, the thesis
of the Moynihan Report gained traction in popular journalism and became
the lingua franca of the neoconservative counterrevolution. The *Los Angeles
Times* declared in a page-one headline: "Racial Unrest Laid to Negro Family
Failure."[44] In this period, during which there had been more than 150 racial
conflagrations, popular journalism ascribed the cause of Black Power mobilizations squarely on the failures of the black family unit. Even though reports
by the McCone and Kerner Commissions lay responsibility exclusively on
systemic abandonment, we can understand how such powerful expressions
of masculine antisystemic sentiment and organized resistance might need
some form of domestic containment.

After the landmark civil rights legislation during 1964–1965, Daniel Patrick Moynihan and William Peterson, both sociologists, the former an ad-
viser in the LBJ administration and the latter a professor at the University of
California, Berkeley, set the table for a new racial conversation about urban
poverty, black revolution, and family values. These shapers of public discourse helped align social realities with public opinion, acting in their role as

traditional intellectuals to set the parameters of national debate about race relations. Both academics shaped national consent; they mediated a manifold of racial anxieties through prescriptions of racial comparison. To be sure, Moynihan and Peterson were acutely aware of black revolutionary activities in the United States and abroad, and these antisystemic currents became the main threats they sought to mollify. Their point of analysis was to explain the conditions of urban poverty, juvenile delinquency, systemic racism, and national security threats through neoliberal doctrines of less government intervention and more redirection emphasizing family values and middle-class consumption. In so doing, through Afro-Asian racialization, they changed the tone and focus of race relations at a moment of crisis and created a new episteme that maximized neoliberal principles for the continuation of class and racial power in the post–civil rights era.

In 1965, Moynihan diagnosed the historic moment in his "The Negro Family: The Case for National Action," writing: "The United States is approaching a new crisis in race relations."[45] Then serving as an assistant labor secretary, Moynihan maintained that cyclical poverty among black urban families was related to deficiencies in their family structure and their dependence on welfare. The black family structure is a "tangle of pathology," to cite chapter 4's title.[46] Matriarchal arrangements explain the feminized position of black men and the erosion of nuclear family units as the basic component of the capital imperative in black American society. Moynihan redirected the problem of race and poverty not through the lens of the "possessive investment in whiteness" or capitalism's systemic abandonment of the poor, but through cultural narratives of moral corruption and individual failure.[47] The timing between LBJ's War on Poverty and his policy prescriptions in the Labor Department is revealing about the ways in which whiteness, drained from collective fatigue, recalibrated itself against black demands for equality: "The fundamental problem here is that the Negro revolution, like the industrial upheaval of the 1930's, is a movement for equality as well as liberty."[48] Citing fellow sociologist Nathan Glazer, with whom he coauthored an earlier book about race and welfare, Moynihan states his position quite clearly: "The demand for economic equality is now not the demand for equal opportunities for the equally qualified: it is now the demand for economic results. . . . The demand for equality of education . . . has now become the demand for equality of results, of outcomes."[49] The repetitive "demand" that Glazer indicates represented the mounting pressure for introspection in white society and the need for self-preservation in the "golden hour" affected by weariness from black critique. As such, the Moynihan Report has represented the prima facie playbook for conservative and neoliberal counterassaults on working-class and poor black communities racialized as breeding grounds for welfare queens and gangster thugs through a white liberal discourse—the femininity of the Linda Taylors and Sister Souljahs, the masculinity of the Willie Hortons and Trayvon Martins. Throughout these developments, we witness the conflation of neoconservative and liberal sociology as a project to sustain white supremacy and neoliberal power in the post–civil rights era with 1980s trickle-down economics, the 1990s dismantling of the welfare state, and the Barack Obama administration as prime examples of the success of this project.

In his first chapter, "The Negro American Revolution," Moynihan writes about the "international implications" of the Civil Rights Movement, specifically calling attention to its political repercussions and militant upheaval of the existing social order:

> [That t]he nations of the world will divide along color lines seems suddenly not only possible, but even imminent. (Such racist views have made progress within the Negro American community itself—which can hardly be expected to be immune to a virus that is endemic in the white community.) The Black Muslim doctrines, based on total alienation from the white racist world, exert a powerful influence. On the far left, the attraction of Chinese Communism can no longer be ignored.[50]

For Moynihan, the specter of Black Islam and Chinese communism are double threats to the racial order of the nation-state and its global expansion. Moynihan's assertion that "the nations of the world will divide along color lines" reveals a long tradition of racial apocalypse in white identity, a tradition found in Lothrop Stoddard's *The Rising Tide of Color* and Samuel Huntington's *The Clash of Civilizations*. As Lois Parkinson Zamora states, "the apocalyptic is never nihilistic but rather is a dialectical tension between equilibrium of chaos and order."[51] The discourse of black pathology incorporated a global and domestic dimension of racial and revolutionary crises management that reflected the redoubled fears of a black non-Christian planet and a red communist order. For Moynihan and other leading policy makers, herein is the speed limit to reform: one may assert equal rights, but do not pass the limits of the Civil Rights Movement.

The Moynihan Report builds the parameters for acceptable forms of black masculinity, categorizing all forms of militancy as contrary to the requirements of the nuclear white family. As Rod Ferguson states: "The Moynihan Report enunciated liberal ideology through an identification with and conception of the African American male as castrated and therefore bereft of heteropatriarchal entitlements."[52] It is through such gendering and racial-izing the post–civil rights moment that the Moynihan Report carries such a powerful ideological sledgehammer. Much has been discussed about the accuracy of the Moynihan thesis, with William Ryan's *Blaming the Victim* the most impassioned response.[53] Yet, the debates formed from these conversations fail to mention the revolutionary context that underlines the motivations for these seminal arguments.

According to the state, the incommensurability of black men to the national project of post–civil rights domesticity is fixed and taken as a symbol of displacement. In such symbolic productions, there is a categorical understanding of black masculinity in its totality, as a homogeneous political construct. The latter shows the failures of "family," "values," and "race" that may infect and corrupt the smooth efficiency of U.S. market democracy. Sander Gilman explains the relationship between pathology and racial stereotype: "Our understanding of the pathological is rooted in an awareness of the human organism's fragility—not simply its mortality . . . but its susceptibility to disease, pollution, corruption, and alteration, things that we experience in our own bodies and observe in others."[54] In such a rendering, an affect of compassion with an understanding of how the past affects the present is rendered an unusable epistemology, and a new post–civil rights definition of individual failure becomes the necessary moral prescription to move toward neoliberal austerity and ideological assaults on the humanity of the poor. When we examine Moynihan and Peterson together—as Siamese twins of liberal sociology—we look through a window into the making of crisis narratives by the university, the state, and the media, devising a new common sense about poverty and race in the "golden hour," one that binds, in our contemporary moment, Asian American citizenship to the tenets of antiblackness.

Coined by William Peterson in his "Success Story: Japanese-American Style" in the *New York Times Magazine*, the term "model minority" conspicuously emerged into national prominence after the release of the Moynihan Report and the emergence of the Black Power movement. Peterson emphasizes that family structure and cultural values of hard work allowed Japanese Americans to overcome legacies of discrimination, "by their own totally unaided effort."[55] Peterson states: "By any criterion of good citizenship that we choose, the Japanese Americans are better than any other group in our society, including native-born whites."[56] Peterson can arrive at such an appraisal by providing comparisons to black Americans. Before he praises the Japanese American community, he discusses the dilemma of "slum life" and the "well-meaning programs and countless studies now focused on the Negro."[57]

Because of historical discrimination, Peterson contends that these conditions produce, "as we all know these days, what might be termed 'problem minorities.'"[58] Japanese Americans are not "problem minorities," nor do they indicate "social pathology" like their black Muslim, Japanese No-No Boy, Berkeley protester, or juvenile delinquent counterparts, whom he names later in his piece. Instead, model minorities exhibit, as he terms it, "good citizenship," which can only be ascertained in reference to the bad citizenship of protest and dissent during the "these days" of his writing. He characterizes Japanese American assimilation into the nation-state as successful and chosen without coercion, mainly due to middle-class consumption and the liberal value of pulling oneself up by one's bootstraps: "even in a country whose patron saint is Horatio Alger's hero, there is no parallel to this success story."[59] Thus, Peterson's conception of "good citizenship" unifies, in timely fashion, the fields of sociology and popular journalism with the neoliberal doctrines of individual uplift and consumer consumption. During the "golden hour" with respect to questions of race, protest, and market democracy, his exposition of racial comparison would be crucial for the consolidation of national consent, with Japanese Americans, still suffering from collective trauma and silence, as the vehicle to drive home neoliberal notions of self-reliance and compliant politics.

According to Peterson, Japanese Americans are "law-abiding," a characteristic that he is careful to mention three times during his exposition of their experience under "color prejudice." Informed by his Japanese American students at the University of California's Berkeley campus, Peterson profiles their undergraduate majors, social clubs, language skills, political tendencies, and even personal hygiene. As such, his sociological archive of Japanese American behavior, a gaze in the orientalist tradition, is complete and transparent. When he uses quotations to characterize urban life, for example in discussing the "causes of crime," instead of poverty or police profiling, his national audience is asked to consider cultural values through model minority figurations.[60] However, as Elaine Kim writes, "the 'model minority' Asian, by never challenging white society, at once vindicates that society from the charge of racism and points up the folly of those less obliging minorities who are ill-advised enough to protest against inequity or take themselves 'too seriously.'"[61]

In *Race and Resistance*, Viet Nguyen discusses what he terms "the model minority thesis," a popular analysis in Asian American studies that has somewhat succeeded in theorizing its historical and racial function:[62]

> Asian American intellectuals have generally come to a consensus regarding
> this historical function and its ideological support, what I will call here the

model minority thesis, to distinguish such a position from the one held by others who simply accept the Asian American as a model minority as face value. In the model minority thesis, the model minority works as a buffer between whites and blacks, who are separated by not only racial difference but a related class antagonism as well.[63]

Overall, the model minority thesis in Asian American studies validates the divisive function of the stereotype, as it serves to alienate Asian and black communities through predominately moral prescriptions. Yet, the model minority thesis has never fully addressed the revolutionary challenges to market democracy that are at the core of Peterson's article. Nor has it appreciated the convergence of the Moynihan Report and Peterson's article, paired up to engage in a form of crisis management. Subsequently, the model minority thesis becomes a watered-down discourse, diluted because it never critiques the legitimacy of the social contract and its inherent contradiction of the capital imperative. The model minority thesis seeks relief from comparative racialization but fails to address the constitutive link between race making and the suppression of revolutionary currents, between the existential crisis of market democracy and the shock of revolutionary social movements.

Peterson's article includes a cartoon of imprisoned Japanese American children, who are playing behind a barbed wire fence. Visually, the cartoon symbolizes the arguments Peterson expresses in popular journalism. It sanitizes mass incarceration and mass trauma inflicted by the nation-state, conditions that are seen through the eyes of happy, smiling children in captivity. The cartoon infantilizes brute state power and whitewashes trauma to the level of childish wish fulfillment in order to lessen national culpability and collective guilt, thus alleviating the revolutionary pressures that produce white fatigue. In the wake of the Civil Rights Movement, conformity, order, and individualism were necessary for the diffusion of market democracy, and the rule of law was needed to differentiate between good and bad citizens. Conversely, John Okada's novel *No-No Boy* explores the psychology of Japanese American oppression after military incarceration during World War II and beautifully paints a broad spectrum of Japanese American men, examining the masculinity of No-No Boys who question the benevolence of the nation-state and suffer from social isolation.

Peterson views the Berkeley student demonstrators and the Tule Lake prisoners as symbols of failed assimilation and conformity, as "problem minorities" who exhibit signs of social pathology because they deviate from the norms of national unity, which requires citizen-subjects to "disavow the existence of the American imperial project."[64] To question patriotic universality and American exceptionalism is to critique the bedrock of market democracy. He constructs an imaginary Asian American figuration that is, at once, a form of colonial paternalism (he's the professor; they, his charge). During the turmoil of student radicalism and opposition to U.S. imperialism in Asia, political activism or dissent in response to U.S. foreign policy was seen as antithetical to a "national moral character" that sociological knowledge, in tandem with the economic theories of modernization, must contain discursively. Peterson pinpoints law and order, economic frugality, and technocratic education as the most important cultural traits for minorities and even for white families. What becomes most important then is the law: a system of order performed by the juridical function of a militarized institution. In the end, this disciplinary force is self-sustaining, so that Asian American communities come to police political delinquency and criminal behavior themselves, actually expelling social pathology, as Peterson advocates, via "retribution [by] the whole [Asian American] community."[65]

Popular newsmagazines including *U.S. News and World Report* cited Peterson's claims, further disseminating the notion that cultural values, law and order, and political docility should be the civic duty of the citizen-subject. Subsequently, through popular journalism, Asian American culture became knowable and transparent, at the same time that Southeast Asians became openly transparent and visible as victims of chemical warfare. An article in *U.S. News* reads: "At a time when it is being proposed that hundreds of billions be spent on uplifting Negroes and other minorities, the nation's 300,000 Chinese Americans are moving ahead on their own with no help from anyone else."[66]

The same *U.S. News* article suggests that Chinatowns are "havens for law and order."[67] After earlier articles in magazines such as the *Wasp* and state health agencies had circulated representations of Chinatowns as spatial dens of vice and disease, *U.S. News* reconceptualized Chinatowns as law-abiding communities and examples of successful jurisprudence.[68] Chinatowns became racialized spaces of successful police surveillance in which the emergence of America's military domination of Asia was mediated by the presumed conformity of its diaspora. The article thus illustrates the construction of racial fantasies within the geographic borders of the American racial imaginary in which fears of Asian-black radicalisms in turn symbolized the moral force of U.S. imperialism in Asia. Representing Chinatowns as spaces of racial order internationalized the moral authority of neoliberal expansion as an inevitable progress of American hegemony.

Such panoptic surveillance proposed that Asia, Africa, and Latin America, the geopolitical arena of W. E. B. Du Bois's "darker races of the world," were part of a global assimilation process for the maintenance of Western neoimperial regimes. This formation of the global/domestic called on racial magnetism *within* the United States to create a necessary racial paradigm to deal with the increasing complexity and dynamism of *global* anticolonial race relations. As Ann Laura Stoler and Gauri Viswanathan demonstrate, the relationship between core empires and peripheral colonies is mutually constitutive. They show how the implementation of colonial policies is often enacted in the colonies first, and later instituted in the imperial center.[69] Commenting on core-periphery racial projects, Stefi San Buenaventura argues that the comparative racialization of racialized communities in the United States served as models for the export of U.S. imperialism. She says: "The Native Americans served as the prototype for American colonial policies and administrative strategy in the governing of the Filipino *indios* in the archipelago. Blacks represented the justification and model for extending 'second class citizenry' and Jim Crow segregationist behavior in the Philippines."[70] In this sense, this historical legacy that links domestic racial formations to imperial aspirations developed into a moment of critical mass in the post–civil rights era. Specifically, domestic racial containment through the design of racial magnetism established the stage for exporting this model of discipline to the Asian and African continents. Asia and Africa had been decolonizing as well as forming alliances through the 1955 Bandung Conference and other initiatives. In the 1980s, the four "Asian Tiger" economies of South Korea, Hong Kong, Singapore, and Taiwan were heralded as models by U.S. economists and media outlets. Moreover, the widespread inclusion of Asian Americans in mainstream discussions of race converged with the influx of Asian capital in the United States.

The Moynihan Report, popular journalism, academia (particularly the disciplines of sociology and economics), and the mainstream media had been successful in advancing two convergent post–civil rights projects: first, to establish a new dominant ideology through public policy and popular suasion (as James Lee writes, "to hasten death for urban communities of color deemed pathological and therefore expendable"); and second, to restructure race and class narratives to suture the citizen-subject to the project of neoliberal accumulation and white supremacy.[71] As David Palumbo-Liu states, "[the] Asian American serves both to prove the rightness of American democracy as a *worldwide* model and to remind Americans of the traditional values it had cast aside in its rush to modernization."[72] Thus, the comparative racialization of Asian and black masculinity into a post–civil rights narrative of revolutionary containment helped consolidate the codes of acceptable citizenship including individualism, meritocratic values, and political silence.

As we have seen, market democracy fears of Maoist China, nationalist

Vietnam, and black revolution served notice that an Asian-black alliance would be dangerous and antithetical to acceptable behaviors of citizenship. Subsequently, Asian collectives and individuals catalyzed an Afro-Asian sensibility, including I Wor Kuen, the Workers Viewpoint Organization, the Red Guard, the Ichibans, the Yellow Brotherhood, and the League of Revolutionary Struggle, as well as Yuri Kochiyama, Richard Aoki, Grace Lee and James Boggs, Pat Sumi, Steve Louie, Lee Lew-Lee, Guy Kurose, Fred Ho, and many others. Together, these formed the Asian American Left; they maintained important interfaces with black liberation and elucidated salient critiques of "the less visible deformation of human potentials into the hierarchies of race, class, gender, and sexuality, and to the shaping of national histories in ways that glorify and legitimate military action."[73]

In *Native Speaker*, the debut novel by Chang-rae Lee, rising politician John Kwang is on the fast track to become mayor of New York City and relays to protagonist Henry Park his immigrant experience when first arriving in the United States during the heyday of the Black Power movement. As a witness to black protest in public spaces, Kwang refuses to accept the assumptive process of antiblackness for Asian immigrant belonging when he recalls, "I thought *this* is America!" in reference to the energy and pulse of Black Power's well-organized and surging social movement.[74] Representing the future of multiethnic New York, Kwang sings, too, the praises of America. Yet he avows his rapture and identification with the nation-state through a process Lisa Lowe calls disidentification, "a space in which alienations, in the cultural, political, and economic sense can be rearticulated in oppositional forms."[75] For the immigrant Kwang, his affirmation of the nation-state is routed through a complex series of disidentifications that include wonderment, empathy, and unity with black radicalism: "I didn't speak English very well, and like anyone who doesn't I mostly listened. But back here, the black power on the streets. Their songs and chants . . . They were so young and awesome, so truly powerful, if only in themselves, no matter what anybody said."[76] Black Power, as the specter of urban protest and organized revolutionary practice, serves as an inspiration and a guide, a lodestar for racialized and working-class bodies, which forms Kwang's idealization linked to social movements that sought to reconceptualize the racial contract in America. In a rare instance of crossing the color line in Asian American literature, he marvels nostalgically about his rite of passage from foreign outsider to immigrant insider, a procession of *affect, movement,* and *embodiment* in which "a [black] man pulled me right out from the sidewalk and said I should join them. I did. I went along. I tried to feel what they were feeling."[77] From an earlier speech, we learn how Kwang compares white supremacy to Japanese colonialism; under those kinds of racial logics and historically layered oppression, black and Korean people have each struggled with the heel of self-hate.[78]

Kwang's consciousness exemplifies an awareness of racial and colonial power, an understanding of the vertical gap in power relationships from the minority periphery to the white power center, which allows for his horizontal validation of the black Other. This is the touchstone that activates his sense of social justice and political empathy with Black Power. Most Asian immigrants are attracted to the magnetic power of antiblack citizenship and white identification. Others, like Kwang, develop a critical consciousness and countervision that challenges the divisive racialization of Asians and blacks. Kwang and his unnamed, black counterpart form a powerful albeit ephemeral moment of male homosocial bonding based on physical intimacy that activates alternative dreams of freedom empowered by validating rather than cannibalizing the Other. Unlike Henry's father, who stereotypes blacks as lazy troublemakers, Kwang disidentifies with this kind of "racialized cannibalism" formed by whiteness, which partially accepts Asians but conditions its acceptance on the politics of antiblackness.

Furthermore, Kwang addresses Asians who consent to model minority stereotypes that punish black subjects, particularly Asian communities that are complicit with or accomplices of journalistic reports and sociological studies purporting masculine black women who dominate effeminate black men. Kwang iterates "the challenge for us Asians in America. How do you say no to what seems like a compliment? From the very start we don't wish to be rude or inconsiderate. So we stay silent in our guises."[79] Later in their conversation, Henry laments to him: "It's still a black-and-white world." However, Kwang gently rebukes Henry's schema of race relations by addressing Gary Okihiro's query, "Is Yellow Black or White?"[80] Relating Kwang's encounter with black radicalism with the implicit racism of the model minority compliment, *Native Speaker* allegorizes the trajectory of comparative racial, radical, and Afro-Asian formations in the post–civil rights era and how they shaped the rise of contemporary Asian America and its structure of feeling. As a national allegory of Afro-Asian political and cultural crossings, *Native Speaker* presents critical visions, the politics of empathy, and an epistemology of disidentification that resist the temptation of casting Asians as obedient subjects over and against black subversive subjects. Fictionalizing the Los Angeles riots of 1992, *Native Speaker* in 1995 connects the working-class and workless poor revolt in Los Angeles as the doppelgänger to the class and racial revolution that erupted in the Watts riots in 1965. In so doing, Kwang's disidentification with the imperative of antiblack identification fictionalizes the historic Afro-Asian sensibilities of the Asian American movement that challenged racial magnetism's oppositional prescriptions.

Historically, the Asian American Left emerged in congruence with the New Left and Third World Left political formations. Its mobilization of working-class consciousness, solidarity with oppressed nationalities, and production of revolutionary culture solidified its historical impact for conceptualizing, organizing, and empowering modern Asian America. Indeed, Asian American consciousness, organizations, and self-determined identity animated from revolutionary youth politics. The San Francisco student strikes in 1968 are memorialized in Asian American studies and ethnic studies as a lyric moment of identity-based and multiracial student organization, copying almost verbatim the platform of the Black Panther Party. Diane Fujino, Daryl Maeda, Laura Pulido, Fred Ho, and the anthology *Asian Americans: The Movement and the Moment* chronicle this era and the prominent participants and ideas that shaped its critical vision and social relations.[81]

Several groups espoused radical departures from the Civil Rights Movement, claiming the ethics of human dignity and freedom from global capitalism and institutional racism. As a global struggle encompassing four continents, these liberation politics valued an antiracist state, the elimination of capitalist class divisions, and democratic governance.[82] Their heroes were not Martin Luther King Jr. but Malcolm X, Mao Zedong, and Frantz Fanon. The various groups espoused several common issues: supporting community enrichment, ending police brutality, fostering racial pride, institutionalizing ethnic studies, and building alternative social relations.[83] As their moral compass, they fought for democratic freedom and the emancipation of human potential from market principles and private property relations.

Grace Lee and James Boggs had collaborated with C. L. R. James in Detroit on the Johnson-Forest Tendency. In his 1965 article "Black Power: A Scientific Concept Whose Time Has Come," James Boggs, referring to Maoism and the Chinese Communist victory as well as the Black revolution, discusses whether revolution could arise from an urban proletariat.[84] During this same period, Yuri Kochiyama supported the Revolutionary Action Movement, a liberation group working with the writings of Mao, Marx, Lenin, and Malcolm X. Diane Fujino recounts the important functions Kochiyama performed, including bailing out prisoners, hosting meetings, and inviting like-minded activists to gatherings in Harlem.[85] Further, Fred Aoki, before the Black Panther Party (BPP) was founded in 1966, hosted many wine-and-cheese conversations in his home with Bobby Seale and Huey Newton, discussed different forms of socialism, helped draft the famous Ten-Point Platform, and supplied the BPP's first armaments.

One of the historical roots of Afro-Asian radicalism was the crisis of the racial state, triggered by the Civil Rights Movement and the third world politics that ensued: a crisis that reshaped the careers and works of Asian American cultural producers. The group of activists, artists, and intellectuals whom I refer to as "radical ethnics" were only a part of the wave of revolutionary politics, but their cultural presence was vital. Mostly born during World War II and raised during liberation struggles that were occurring around the globe, these radical ethnics emerged in the decade following the Civil Rights Movement. Their cultural predecessors were the communist, socialist, and leftist artists from the 1930s to the 1970s; they allied themselves with third world liberation, including black struggles in the United States. The east and west coasts were their bases, clustering in New York and the San Francisco Bay area. There were several interconnected Asian-black groups. Writers and activists included Janice Mirikitani, Yuri Kochiyama, Al Robles, Francis Naohiko Oka, and Pat Sumi. Slogans such as "Power to the People," "Serve the People," and "Yellow Peril Supports Black Power" represented the alliances that were formed for the purpose of community enrichment and interracial coalitions.[86] Their domestic concerns included the fate of the Soledad Brothers, three members of the Panthers locked down at Soledad Prison in California, as well as the forced shutdown of the I-Hotel, a San Francisco housing project for the poor and elderly. Some of their global concerns were Hiroshima's nuclear fallout, third world decolonization, and U.S. military intervention in Asia. In an article in *Gidra*, a community newspaper published by activists and artists in Los Angeles, Alan Nishio writes:

> As the Black and Brown communities push for changes in our present system, the Oriental is set forth as an example to be followed—a minority group that has achieved success through adaptation rather than confrontation. . . . Orientals in America have become affluent through their hard work and silence.[87]

Nishio reveals the price of "hard work and silence" due to model minority racialization and an awareness of minority challenges to the social contract. Therefore, the evolution of American orientalism to an Asian American consciousness reflected the transformation of collective silence to political voice and empowerment through panethnicity, which in turn resisted the attraction of racial magnetism.[88] In many ways, it had been the awakening of an entire community to political consciousness; or, as Junot Díaz writes about this era, "the generation that despite the consensus that declared change impossible hankered for change all the same."[89]

Clearly, the emerging Asian American consciousness had solidified through an understanding of the oppression that people of color endured daily, an endurance that contributed to the mounting radicalization of grassroots politics. For example, Chris Iijima, a folksinger connected to the Asian American movement, expresses the influence of Malcolm X on Asian American radicalism:

> There were two groups that we worked with when we had the storefront called "Chickens Come Home to Roost." As Nobuko [Iijima's wife] tells young people these days, we wanted something militant sounding, so we took a phrase of Malcolm's for our name. Of course, we were known around the neighborhood as "The Chickens."[90]

Iijima recalls Malcolm X's subsequent invocation of social and poetic justice for black Americans. Yet Malcolm X spoke for aggrieved populations throughout the world, and his particular revolt activated the militancy of Asian Americans. Writers, activists, and intellectuals had formed an oppositional consciousness shaped by the radicalism of black masculinity. They easily borrowed from each other the platforms, members, organizing strategies, theories, and collective power of cross-racial politicization.

An important advocate of Afro-Asian revolutionary relations is the abovementioned Richard Aoki. A child prisoner held at the Topaz War Relocation Camp in Utah from 1942 to 1945, Aoki later joined the U.S. military and eventually attained the rank of field marshal in the Black Panther Party. He linked the Third World Liberation Front at Berkeley with various radical community groups in Oakland. In the book *Seize the Time*, Bobby Seale wrote about his relationship with the "Asian Panther":

> Richard Iokey [*sic*] came in—the Japanese brother who gave Huey and me the M-1 and 9mm—and he got talking about how he had a .357 Magnum. We got the .357 Magnum from him and a couple more pistols, and the brothers got to getting money together, and started buying weapons.[91]

The possibility of creating coalitions continually set the agenda of the Black Panthers, as evidenced by such Asian-black alliances that armed them for mutual self-defense. The Panthers also had close ties with Los Siete de la Raza, a group supporting the release of seven Latinos accused of killing a San Francisco policeman; the Young Lords, a Puerto Rican gang that turned political in Chicago and New York; and the Young Patriots, a group of poor whites who were vanguards for working-class communities. Seale wrote:

"We can relate well with them because they are in opposition to the power structure's oppression."[92] Stylized in leather jackets, military berets, and black gloves, Aoki and the Panthers embodied militant revolutionary politics, an image that radiated the cool pose and theoretical rigor of the times.

Afro-Asian radicalism generated organic movements against racially magnetized color lines orchestrated by the state, popular journalism, and the media. By identifying with black revolution, the Asian American Left distanced itself from the tenets of antiblackness and joined black freedom dreams that had been constrained by the militarization of economic and racial power. Seen through the optics of power and self-determination as a means for human liberation, Afro-Asian radicalism called into question the mapping of American society as organized by pitting Asian and black communities against each other. They introduced an Afro-Asian vision of interracial coalition building that disavowed the essentialist and flattening gaze of racial magnetism, and their innovations in political organizing, social consciousness raising, and cultural fusion still have a lasting legacy today. In short, the schema I present below offers a visual diagram of the analyses I have made:

crises of capital and race in the mid-1960s ➔ *caused by falling profit rates, recalibration of white supremacy, and the rise of race-based social movements (especially Black Power)* ➔ *market democracy needed to rearticulate and secure racial and economic legitimacy* ➔ *state, academic, and popular journalism discourses created legible narratives, using the figures of Asian and black masculinity* ➔ *model minority/ black pathology, good/bad, subversive/compliant, institutional failure to individual failure reinforced a politics of antiblackness (through moral prescriptions I call "racial magnetism")* ➔ *for common sense, which enabled a conservative counterrevolution heralding a neoliberal/colorblind era* ➔ *allowed for the erasure of social movement/revolutionary challenges.*

East Meets Black is a project at once academic and political: academic because it charts, through theoretical synthesis, the economic, cultural, and masculinized ways in which Asian and black men have been structured over and against each other; and political because racial divisions within minority relations create entrenched color lines that reinforce the interests of decision-making centers of power. This book addresses this manufactured divide as a disabler for cross-racial vision and solidarity and nudges all of us to think comparatively and compassionately about the world we live in and the world we want.

Theorizing how popular sport, cinema, literature, and performance arts are critical responses to state, academic, and media discourses of racial magnetism conceptualizes the limitations of discursive formations. The fixed, static, and oppositional framework of racial magnetism is destabilized by fluidity, mixture, and hybridity, which, with respect to Asian and black masculinity, the following chapters attest to. But this happens unevenly. For example, in popular sport and Hollywood cinema, these realms are dominant forms of culture, cash cows, and hegemonic culture industries; whereas Asian American literary anthologies, hip-hop, and spoken word are more unknown, underground, or avant-garde in expression. Walter Benjamin, Judith Butler, and Fredric Jameson offer methods to describe how cultural production is a site of both domination and resistance, often simultaneously. Benjamin discusses the culture industry, in which repetition and dissemination of representations are quite radical even in the "age of mechanical reproduction."[93] Critical consciousness can be forged from within the culture industry because capital can never totalize the human experience. In *The Psychic Life of Power*, Butler describes the simultaneity of subjection and resistance within the production of power upon the subject's body and the cultural body politic.[94] Yet, excess is omnipresent, power is never totalizing, and resistance is the surplus energy that is produced by both subjection and hegemonic reproduction. Moreover, in *The Political Unconscious*, Jameson evinces that the political horizon of literature is exculpable through a multivalent Marxist interpretation of the capital imperative.[95] Similarly, in *The Politics of Culture in the Shadow of Capital*, Lisa Lowe and David Lloyd suggest critical approaches to reading alternative cultures within "neocolonial capitalism." Disrupting the notion that capital homogenizes global culture, the authors sustain an understanding of the "sites of contradiction that are effects of its always uneven expansion" and therefore cannot be reduced to mere commodification.[96] Each of the chapters in this book follows the strands of thought from these leading theorists of cultural production within the capital imperative.

Afro-Asian bonds of literary masculinities, Asian athletes in predominately black global sports, Asian martial artists and black hip-hop buddies in cinema, and Afro-Asian fusions in spoken word and hip-hop music exemplify these "sites of contradiction" within neoliberal capital insofar as they showcase the heterogeneous and hybrid linking of Asian and black masculinities. Insofar as racial magnetism is the superstructural arrangement of Asian and black male bodies in the post–civil rights era, the various chapters in this book respond to and challenge such an essentializing and cannibalistic framework. In the literature chapter, Asian American and black American men are shown to have created alternative collaboration and publication networks, what may be called an Afro-Asian mode of cultural production, which bypassed the white liberal publishing houses in New York and in so doing launched the Asian American writing movement and the rise of multiethnic literature. In the global sports and film chapter, Ichiro Suzuki, Yao Ming, *Romeo Must Die*, and *Rush Hour* are located at the heart of neoliberal culture industries that include Major League Baseball, the National Basketball Association, and Hollywood. Yet, even at the epicenter of neoliberal profit making, these various Afro-Asian representations cannot be contained by mere political economy insofar as they disrupt white cultural domination and invoke an oppositional consciousness from spectatorship. Finally, by examining avant-garde and underground sites, the music and spoken word chapter attests to the future of more radical formations taking place outside the neoliberal epicenter and leaning more toward digital and youth cultures.

The archives in *East Meets Black* guide readers to emergent representations of race and masculinity that follow a sustained tradition of bonds between the Black Atlantic and the Asian Pacific, what Yuri Kochiyama suggested we learn in the epigraph to this introduction. As evidenced by her words and practice, she understood the primacy of apprehending the black condition under white capitalist power as a means to reaching an understanding about power in general for all people. What are some of the concepts, histories, and nomenclatures—an interwoven narrative of Afro-Asian America—that represent the economic connectedness, cultural fusions, lived intimacies, and fragmented silences between Asian and black Americans? This project is pocked with pitfalls to essentialize or romanticize such bonds. Currently, the color line that W. E. B. Du Bois spoke so eloquently about is fractured, multilinear, contingent, and situational. Moving through a range of entanglements and contradictions in literature and popular culture—inspiring moments of interracial solidarity and ruptures of racial apocalypse—this book offers the possibilities and limits of interracial coalitions in the post–civil rights era.

In this way, *East Meets Black* is a theoretical and cultural story in which Asian Americans fit into the discourse of ethnic assimilation and transnational class relations within and between U.S. racial minorities, and in which Asian American citizenship constitutes the disavowal of black freedom and humanity. In *Freedom Dreams*, Robin Kelley quotes at length the hope and love found in Martin Luther King Jr.'s vision by emphasizing that freedom for black people is freedom for all:

> We Negroes have long dreamed of freedom, but still we are confined in an
> oppressive prison of segregation and discrimination. . . . To guard our-
> selves from bitterness, we need the vision to see in this generation's ordeals
> the opportunity to transfigure both ourselves and American society. Our
> present suffering and our nonviolent struggle to be free may well offer to
> Western civilization the kind of spiritual dynamic so desperately needed
> for survival.[97]

Black freedom dreams as a critical mirror to market democracy have been a
consistent and persistent hope over the past few centuries, and the making
of modern Asian America during the post–civil rights era is structured by
this ongoing struggle for recognition and equality within the tenets of antiblackness. Thus, *East Meets Black* is an examination of how race, capital, and
culture have formed masculinized social relations, and a consideration of the
artistic expressions found in Afro-Asian cultures that direct us somewhere
else.

This book is divided into four chapters and an epilogue. Chapter 1, "The
Asian American Writing Movement and Blackness: Race and Gender Politics in Asian American Anthologies," reconsiders the genesis and formation
of Asian American literature by focusing less on the Chin-Kingston debate
and more on the impact of black radicalism. I explore *Aiiieeeee! An Anthology of Asian-American Writers* and *Yardbird Reader 3* and show how the
editors utilize the rhetoric of black radicalism to conceptualize the racial
emasculation of Asian American men from cultural manhood and thus route
citizenship and manhood claims through black masculinity and interracial
identifications. During the post–civil rights moment of racial realignment,
black radical thought is the counterpoint to forced Asian ethnic assimilation; this Asian-black sensibility challenges an uncritical complicity with racial magnetism that tries to negate black liberation politics. The editors of
Aiiieeeee! employ the vernacular languages, performance styles, and oppositional consciousness of black masculinity as a means to expose the contradictions of abstract citizenship during the formation of the Asian American
writing movement. In *Yardbird 3*, the personal and professional bonds between Frank Chin and Ishmael Reed advance the cause of Afro-Asian collaboration in alternative publishing, ushering in the birth of a multiethnic
sensibility. Both anthologies showcase the centrality of blackness as a conceptual and material basis for Asian American writing as it emerges in the
post–civil rights era.

Chapter 2, "Yellow Bodies, Black Sweat: Yao Ming, Ichiro Suzuki, and
Global Sport," focuses on the relationship between Asian and black athletes,

global multiculturalism, and sport internationalism. Ichiro Suzuki and Yao Ming represent in clear ways the figuration of the Asian male body as both cultural phenomena and transnational commodity. This chapter describes the marked turn from the Asian male body as an unattractive representative for marketing commodity exchanges to an imported spectacle capable of generating transnational capital for the National Basketball Association and Major League Baseball. However, it does not simply offer a conventional study of the political economy involved in the global expansion of popular sports. Rather, it attempts to illustrate how Asian men in U.S. sports presuppose and indeed attempt to produce Asian masculinity by inverting the bodily emasculation of Asian American men. Throughout this chapter, I detail the ways in which popular sports have been racialized as a "black" space of colonial fantasies and fears and how Asian male athletes break down the fixity of biological discourses that hinge on visual common sense.

Chapter 3, "'I'm Michael Jackson, You Tito': Kung-Fu Fighters and Hip-Hop Buddies in Martial Arts Buddy Films," argues that the rise of the martial arts genre in cinema has wide appeal for racialized communities and young audiences because it is the genre of the underdog. The martial arts film had its introduction in blaxploitation films and the cult hero Bruce Lee and quickly became a staple of Saturday matinees in urban areas. The genre that Lee catapulted into mainstream currency has recently been adapted to the standard buddy film format prevalent in Hollywood Westerns and 1980s action films. As a result, the coupling of a streetwise black American boasting hip-hop credentials with an ethical martial arts hero with humble bravado has served notice to mainstream audiences and cultural critics. As such, this chapter examines Asian-black spectatorship as an oppositional gaze in martial arts buddy films. For this reason, films such as *Rush Hour* and *Romeo Must Die* produce Afro-Asian bonds through interracial identification, a critique of white power structures, and hybridity in cinematic genres.

Chapter 4, "Afro-Asian Rhythms and Rhymes: The Hip-Hop and Spoken Word Lyricists of I Was Born with Two Tongues and the Mountain Brothers," addresses the conductive power of live performance by Asian American men in hip-hop music and spoken word and links the possibilities of Asian-black cultural fusions, using the Internet as their main medium of communication. It calls attention to the role of public intellectuals, such as Dennis Kim of I Was Born with Two Tongues, and the role of art, activism, and culture intertwined with Asian American cultural production and black musical expression. The Mountain Brothers offer a different perspective on Asian-black connections in hip-hop because they are an Asian American group signed by street-credible Ruff House Records. Significantly, this chapter focuses on little understood, yet highly significant cultural practices taking place in Asian American communities, especially among youth and Internet cultures. Altogether, it emphasizes the Asian-black interface of spoken word and hip-hop as a self-professed, avant-garde revolutionary undertaking, one that disrupts the constancy of racial magnetism in matters of social policy and public discourse.

Examining literature, popular sport, film, music, and spoken word, *East Meets Black* suggests the primacy and possibilities of Asian-black cultural crossings. It presents critical race, queer, feminist, Marxist, and cultural theories that offer a method of analyzing Asian American and black gender relations. It privileges the power of Afro-Asian cultural resistance to produce conceptions of present time, the material life of here and now, and culture as theory for imagining possible, the impossible. By exploring Afro-Asian culture in the post–civil rights era, this book attempts to break down the misconceptions and rivalries that divide Asian and black people from each other. To promote such an aspiration, *East Meets Black* brushes with a vibrant and exquisite stroke the bonds between Asian and black masculinities.

1. The Asian American Writing Movement and Blackness

Race and Gender Politics in Asian American Anthologies

The Asian American writing movement, a cultural movement that encouraged Afro-Asian collaboration and resulted in the publication of multiethnic literary anthologies, grew out of the "perfect storm" of antisystemic challenges discussed in the introduction. To challenge the tenets of antiblack citizenship, Asian American writers borrowed from black masculinities, and this union impacted U.S. national culture at large. This chapter places the concepts, masculinities, and institutions of blackness at the center of Asian American literary formation—what could be described as an Afro-Asian mode of literary production. As an innovative reaction to institutional exclusion, this Afro-Asian exchange, an alternative imagining and praxis vis-à-vis mainstream publishing, inaugurated the field of Asian American literature and helped forge the multiethnic contours of post–civil rights national culture. Two works of Asian American literature—*Yardbird Reader 3* and *Aiiieeeee! An Anthology of Asian-American Writers*, both published in 1974—illustrate the conceptual and material bases that blackness afforded through an Afro-Asian literary alliance. Yet this historic Afro-Asian alliance is not without negative ramifications; in shaping the field of multiethnic literature, a myriad of mistakes were made, power arrangements were reproduced, and theoretical assumptions were left unexamined.

In the November 1972 edition of *Changes* magazine, noted authors Ishmael Reed and Al Young discuss the relationship between literature and cultural revolution during the zenith of the Black Arts movement and third world liberation. Both affirm the central role of art and representation as a prerequisite for political transformation within broad social movements. Reed, who describes his own aesthetic practice as "Neo-HooDooism," places importance upon who controls the means of cultural production within U.S. culture. The Black Arts movement, which Larry Neal had pronounced "the aesthetic and spiritual sister of the Black Power concept," had influenced post–civil rights writers like Reed, Toni Morrison, Gwendolyn Brooks, and Shawn Wong.[1] By calling into question the prescriptions of racial magnetism, these literary pioneers challenged Eurocentric aesthetics, critique, mythology, and knowledge as the universal power center and standard in American life. Later, when Reed laments the obscurity of Chester Himes and Zora Neale Hurston, he addresses the conditions for the publication not only of black literature but also of other minòrity literatures, "all of us who were under the thumb," including Asian American, Chicano/a, and Puerto Rican works. In the middle of the magazine interview, friend and fellow writer Frank Chin walks into Reed's house and jokes, "all the people who don't publish us are in New York [laughter]."[2]

Through insider humor, Asian and black male writers mutually affirmed, during the birth of Asian American literature and the explosion of African American writing, a parallel experience of exclusion in attempting to publish their respective works. Chin's quip binds through synecdoche the "thumb" of white liberalism that burdens the publication of Asian American literature with the same institutional difficulties African American writers have faced. Because the American literary canon almost exclusively favored white writers, Asian and black writers would form their own multiethnic coalitions and fulminate their voices in U.S. national culture. Later, Reed called for a wholesale process of "decentralization" whereby minority writers would produce works outside the mainstream publishing industry. In discussing liberal whiteness in New York and the publication of multiethnic literature, he commented: "The liberals are afraid of our competition. Even more so, I think sometimes, than the Right Wing."[3] Despite the inroads made by black writers under the banner of Black Power, Reed envisioned a different axis of racial solidarity through horizontal rather than vertical camaraderie, with an important caveat about antiracist coalition building: "I mean, we all don't have to love each other; I don't have to love Frank [Chin]. . . . We may not even be able to work together on certain issues. . . . But we're on the right track in that we are trying to assert our independence, which is something new."[4] Reed's comment directs our attention to the promises of self-determination movements and the limitations of interracial cooperation. Although focused on an antiracist initiative, Reed's vision of coalition building is contingent and issues based, reflecting Kandice Chuh's assertion of a "subjectless discourse" in which common interests rather than identity are crucial for sustained counterhegemonic projects.[5]

This chapter begins with the inspired exchange between Reed and Chin in order to position the Asian American writing movement as a process of Afro-Asian collaboration, multiethnic vision, and remaking of Asian American masculinity. Asian and black men formed powerful literary bonds, a horizontal structure of identification, whereby black male writers and black presses recognized and validated the significance of Asian American literature. Despite the divisive imperative of racial magnetism, Asian and black masculinities crossed the color line, joining up on the intrepid journey for artistic recognition, public voice, and manly respect. And no bond of affiliation was more important than that between Reed and Chin, due to the groundbreaking publication of *Yardbird Reader 3* and *Aiiieeeee!*[6] While *Aiiieeeee!* has been recognized in Asian American literary circles, *Yardbird Reader 3* has received inadequate attention and is out of print. Analyzing both anthologies as extensions of each other, I examine more fully the Afro-Asian mode of cultural production that activates the genre of Asian American literature. I specify how both collections set the cornerstone for the emergence of Asian American literature by remaking the legal category "nonwhite" into a moniker of resistance, race, and remasculinization. Writers of color morphed the category of nonwhite, first designated in the 1790 Naturalization Act, to fit the necessities of multiethnic coalition building under the banner of third world liberation and cultural revolution. Formed in reaction to perpetual black exploitation by white supremacy, the Black Power movement affected Asian American consciousness and literary production. Blackness provided the inspiration for multiethnic coalitions and became a lodestar for oppressed people of color around the globe, and Asian Americans were no exception. This chapter examines Chin's unpublished letters, *Yardbird Reader 3*, and *Aiiieeeee!* to explain the "polycultural" bonds between Asian and black masculinities at the genesis of Asian American literature.

In the anthology *Afro Asia*, Reed chronicles his manifold collaborations with Chin through literary and homosocial bonding. At a book party in 1969 celebrating the publication of *19 Necromancers from Now*, the future editors of *Aiiieeeee!*, whom Reed lauds as the "Four Horsemen of Asian American literature"—Jeffrey Paul Chan, Frank Chin, Lawson Fusao Inada, and Shawn Wong—became acquainted for the first time. Reed helped publish Chin's "A Chinese Lady Dies" and *The Year of the Dragon* and Wong's *Homebase*, the first novel to be published by an American-born Chinese male; he made the important introduction between Charles Harris of Howard University Press and the *Aiiieeeee!* editors. Throughout the post–civil rights era, moreover, Reed has sponsored the literary careers of Asian American women writers including Jessica Hagedorn, Mei-mei Berssenbrugge, and Cyn Zarco.

Subsequently, numerous literary works, critical journals, writers' organizations, publishing houses, festivals, and regional theaters embodied the multiethnic coalition building that Reed exhibited, particularly expressing an Afro-Asian sensibility. The transition from racial essentialisms, supported by cultural nationalists such as Ron Karenga and Elijah Muhammad, to multiethnicity and interracial bonds is also reflected in the direction and substance of Young's interview with Reed. William Harris suggests that "by the mid-70s black writers such as Al Young and Ishmael Reed were beginning to envision literature as multiethnic instead of mono-ethnic."[7] Reed's racial positioning showcased the morphing of the Black Power concept to the contours of multiethnicity and multiculturalism, as initially an extension of racial and cultural revolution in the post–civil rights era. "[N]either . . . movement apologist[s] nor advocate[s]" (Reed wasn't invited to participate because he "was considered an integrationist"), Reed and Chin reference the theoretical diversity within broad social movements and the multiple, interlocking contestations along race, gender, class, and sexuality lines at this time.[8] Chin and Reed were not considered political radicals in the same sense as the Red Guard of San Francisco's Chinatown or Amiri Baraka's Black Arts Repertory Theatre/School, yet their respective works illuminate Antonio Gramsci's historic bloc, which, Michael Denning writes, "connotes both an alliance of social forces and a specific formation. The connection between the two lies in the concept of hegemony."[9] From the sanctuary of his prison, Gramsci expressed an important theory of alliances, which may be structured by similar goals and interests even though the participants may have different backgrounds. Through their belief in cultural revolution, Asian and black men challenged white supremacy, specifically East Coast liberal whiteness in the publishing industry and cultural assumptions about the creative inferiority of minority writers.

Understanding the important relationship between Reed and Chin as well as the impact of black radicalism on the rise of Asian American literature offers three points of consideration for scholars of comparative racialization and multiethnic literatures. First, for Asian American literary scholars, the Afro-Asian mode of cultural production may contribute to a more fully realized understanding of the material, social, and political realities that empowered the Asian American writing movement. Much of this work is just beginning and not yet fully conceptualized.[10] Daniel Kim, for one, has written a remarkable study tracing the homophobic and misogynistic tendencies in Chin's work, "to gain some sort of analytic purchase on how and why it is that the things most useful and even moving about Chin's writings are inextricably linked with what is most hateful."[11] Because many scholars have rightly charged male writers of this era as cultural nationalists, much of the scholarship about the literary formation of Asian American studies that occurred at this time seems to focus on the limitations of this anachronistic position, in the process leaving Chin to "the dustbin of literary history."[12] If cultural nationalism is defined as an ethnocentric, homophobic, and masculinist construction of an essentialist oppositional identity, then Asian and black masculinities collaborating across color and gender lines present a more complicated portrait of the contradictions and revolutionary aspirations embedded within it. This might seem surprising to those who associate Reed and Chin with the cultural nationalist project, but it is important to acknowledge that Reed's and Chin's involvement displayed expansive theoretical flexibility, including support of women of color writers. For example, to theorize the conditions of Asian American literary exclusion, the *Aiiieeeee!* editors gave prominence to the author Sui Sin Far, who published short stories "that [were] neither Asian nor white American. And interestingly enough, in her work, there is no cultural conflict between East and West."[13] That the editors would elevate Far to the first page of their introduction as an exemplar of Asian American writing about cultural hybridity—an assertion later made by poststructuralist and postcolonial theorists in Asian American scholarship—illustrates that their remasculinization project is neither a wholly male-dominated discourse nor without theoretical forethought. In fact, they also promote Monica Sone's *Nisei Daughter* as a prime example of how Asian American writing can explain the function of William Peterson's model minority stereotype and the role of silence as a pervasive condition of Asian American double consciousness, a dual-heritage model structured by the investment in national assimilation. Because of these paradoxes, the *Aiiieeeee!* editors' brand of cultural nationalism was inconsistent and had porous boundaries, often defining a racial essence for national inclusion through homophobic and patriarchal impulses while *simultaneously* envisioning a rebellious ethos of transgression that included the work of female writers of color and other racialized literatures in their anthologies.

This elastic back-and-forth between fixity and fluidity encompasses to some degree Robin Kelley's idea of polyculturalism, which Vijay Prashad expands upon in *Everybody Was Kung Fu Fighting*: "The framework of polyculturalism uncouples the notions of origins and authenticity from that of culture."[14] Prashad illustrates the Afro-Asian connections in the history and origins of Garveyism, showing how Lajpat Rai and Hucheshwar G. Mugdal aided Jamaican activist Marcus Garvey in the international struggle against racial and colonial domination. The concept of polyculturalism extinguishes all notions of purity and origins, contending that we are all infused with the cultures and histories of Asia, Africa, the Americas, and Europe. Nodal points emerge always, dependent only on the depth of our looking glass. The transracial and cross-gender formations found in anthologies of cultural nationalist literature gesture toward an incipient polycultural understanding of shared experiences and histories, a transgression that should be more widely acknowledged. Although not outside of reproducing power relations, the Afro-Asian mode of cultural production within Asian American cultural nationalism was the first theoretical writing to explore the mutuality of epistemological and ontological conditions connecting Asian American and black literature.

As the most prominent proponent of cultural nationalism in Asian American literature, Chin has been overshadowed by his jeremiad directed at Maxine Hong Kingston. Despite the existence of earlier Asian American anthologies, including Kai-yu Hsu's *Asian American Authors* and David Hsin-fu Wand's *Asian American Heritage*, the 1974 publication of *Aiiieeeee!* has been widely acknowledged as marking the successful emergence of Asian American literature from cultural obscurity. Yet, subsequent critical work on *Aiiieeeee!* emphasizes the feminism of Asian American women and the cultural nationalism of Asian American men. Hero worship meets the feminist revolution: this was the choice of Asian American critics analyzing the literary tree of Asian American writing, deeply entrenched, with roots formed from this opposition.[15] However, the famous and productive debate between Chin and Kingston focused little attention on how African American people helped shape the contours of this intraracial and gendered conversation.

The relative absence of Chin's work in Asian American literary criticism should be revisited, not to canonize his oeuvre but instead to complicate the easy binary opposition between hero worship and feminist critique. To this end, I theorize how his homosocial bonding with black masculinity is arbitrated by his failure of intimacy, both artistic and personal, with Asian American women. Chin wrote in an unpublished letter to Kingston, "I was rigged against going for yellow women cuz I was a hot yellow artistic type, and yellow women in the arts were rigged against going for me."[16] A nostalgic and somewhat bitter lament, we read from this correspondence that Chin initially sought more intimate and personal relationships with Asian American women writers. His hopes for artistic and romantic connections were dashed, as he did not get the validation and encouragement he needed, however much he may have contributed to his own alienation. Because of these failures, Chin's desire for mutual confirmation with Asian American femininity, a reciprocal gaze, was redirected elsewhere. Consequently, as I posit later, Chin found his artistic validation through black masculinity and masculine homosocial bonds, where the homosocial always has an economy of erotic desire.[17] Chin's letter connects the ways in which race, gender, and sexuality impacted the triangulation between Asian masculinity, black masculinity, and Asian femininity as a nuanced supplement to Claire Jean Kim's model of triangulation between whites, Asians, and blacks.[18]

A second point of consideration regarding the impact of black radicalism on the rise of Asian American literature is that the Afro-Asian mode of cultural production in Asian American literary anthologies was instrumental in the birth of Asian American literature in the post–civil rights era. It revived lost, forgotten work and built a foundation of prominent writers who would later become the literary voices of the Asian American writing movement. Themes were often about identity and national belonging, settlement communities and everyday life, the processes of assimilation, the conditions of immigrant work, relations between parents and children, the deployment of ethnic vernaculars, the role of humor and gossip, and the carrot-and-stick pursuit of the American Dream. *Yardbird Reader 3* and *Aiiieeeee!* fall under the category of general anthologies and include Afro-Asian content in their prefaces. In fundamental ways, the Afro-Asian mode of cultural production apparent in both prefaces inaugurates the discipline of Asian American literature and illustrates an early cultural formation that resists the rivalrous framework of racial magnetism.

In so many ways, literary anthologies with Afro-Asian sensibilities often excavate lost works rather than commemorate well-known writing. If traditional anthologies have been synonymous with nation building insofar as they render literature and nationalism synthetic, then Asian American anthologies with an Afro-Asian exchange established an entire field by contesting such homogeneous, modernist constructions of national identity. This event horizon, a point of no return, catapulted a whole booklist of Asian American literature into public discussion, university syllabi, and cultural prominence and generated later anthologies such as *Forbidden Stitch: An Anthology of Asian American Women's Writing*; *Charlie Chan Is Dead: An Anthology of Asian American Fiction*; and *The Big Aiiieeeee! An Anthology of Chinese American and Japanese American Literature*. As such, no anthology has had quite the impact of the original *Aiiieeeee!* on the study of Asian lives in America. And theorizing *Yardbird Reader 3* in relation to this event horizon more clearly defines the polycultural context of Asian American literature. Therefore, these anthologies contest rather than canonize; they validate racialized alienation rather than exclude through racial cannibalism; and they reveal context, movements, and power relations rather than aestheticize through internal and intertextual New Critical approaches that dominated the period.[19]

And, as for the third consideration, in my analysis of Asian and black masculinities in *Yardbird Reader 3* and *Aiiieeeee!* I specify how, as cultural historian Daryl Maeda theorizes, "performances of blackness catalyzed the formation of Asian American identity."[20] The editors of *Aiiieeeee!* and *Yardbird Reader 3* rejected the black-white framework of U.S. racial discourse. As a means to find a point of immanent critique, they mirrored black protest masculinity—an example of interracial identification and mimesis. The process of dissimulation, through the performance of interracial mimesis, countered the dominant discourse of Asian ethnic assimilation into an uncritical white identity or, as a *Newsweek* article celebrated, "outwhiting the whites."[21] During the post–civil rights moment of racial realignment, black radical thought was the counterpoint to forced Asian ethnic assimilation; this Asian-black sensibility challenged an uncritical complicity with white supremacy that had suppressed Black revolution. In *Aiiieeeee!*, the editors employed the vernacular languages, performance styles, and oppositional consciousness of black masculinity as a means to expose the contradictions of market democracy and the violence of racialization. Shirley Hune suggests that the black-white paradigm of race has bulldozed over "a multiplicity of simultaneous racial group dynamics that included horizontal subordinate-subordinate or minority-minority relations."[22] The Asian-black interface constructs the contours of cultural citizenship through the racialization of another-Other, and thus the editors complicated the fixed, closed identity of cultural nationalism. Despite the productive engagement between Asian American and black American voices in *Aiiieeeee!*, this chapter also explores those points in the work at which interracial alliance through mimesis becomes self-congratulatory and addresses the limitations of such maneuvers. I emphasize this idea to dissect the critical axis of race and gender and to point out where remasculinization and the tenets of antiblackness fall into this mapping.

The editorial collective of *Aiiieeeee! An Anthology of Asian-American Writers* consisted of Jeffrey Paul Chan, Frank Chin, Lawson Fusao Inada, and Shawn Wong. In 1974, for the first time in American literature, the editors centered Asian American masculinity as the subject of history and literary production in U.S. national culture.[23] Consisting of excerpts from novels, short stories, poetry, and drama, the *Aiiieeeee!* anthology chronicles the literary voices of ten men and four women from various Asian ethnicities (predominantly Chinese and Japanese American), literary genres, and historical periods. *Aiiieeeee!* introduced readers to the study of Asian American literature including Louis Chu, Hisaye Yamamoto, Monica Sone, Diana Chang, and John Okada. Authors Carlos Bulosan, Oscar Peñaranda, and Sam Tagatac are also in the collection, representing Filipino diasporic literature. Above all, by anthologizing these forgotten authors, the editors were literary pioneers, the first movers who detailed rigorously the heterogeneity of Asian American identity, articulated the unique blend of Asian American experiences, and deconstructed the engine of white supremacy in Asian American life.

These Asian American male writers performed a literary coup d'etat in the Bay Area to expose "America's dishonesty—its white racist supremacy passed off as love and acceptance—[that] has kept seven generations of Asian-American voices off the air, off the streets, and praised us for being Asiatically no show."[24] Frantz Fanon rebukes this kind of racist white love in his classic *The Wretched of the Earth*.[25] In her groundbreaking text *Asian American Literature*, Elaine Kim suggests that Chinese American male writers, Chin's "Chinatown Cowboys," needed to clarify "their uniquely American identity" after the legacy of Vietnam and civil rights politics.[26] As a centerpiece of Asian American letters, *Aiiieeeee!* launched the revolutionary birth of the Asian American writing movement in reaction to conditions in which "the first Asian-American writers worked alone within a sense of rejection and isolation to the extent that it encouraged Asian America to reject its own literature."[27]

Aiiieeeee! starts off with three introductions: "Preface," "Preface to the Mentor Edition," and "Fifty Years of Our Whole Voice." Using historical, theoretical, and literary analysis of the status of Asian American literature, the editors map the transition of Asian American writing from orientalized invisibility to a known Asian American sensibility with its own voices, vernaculars, and unique cultural blend. It was the first time Asian Americans were imputing their collective humanity in American literature. In *The Politics of Culture in the Shadow of Capital*, Lisa Lowe and David Lloyd write that culture "constitutes a site in which the reproduction of contemporary capitalist social relations may be continually contested" and where politics "must be grasped instead as always braided within 'culture' and cultural practices."[28] *Aiiieeeee!*'s editorial collective carved a literary space where discussions of assimilationist literature, minority relationships, Asian American manhood, and the force of comparative racial hierarchy are examined. In doing so, the editors, using black masculinity as a model of protest, embarked upon a project of remasculinization by underscoring the importance of cultural integrity for Asian America's identity, consciousness, and survival—the languages employed, point of view, writing topics, literary genealogies, and political viewpoint. However, since the anthology's publication and subsequent critical reflections, the Afro-Asian connections found in *Aiiieeeee!*—the influence of blackness—is never mentioned and should be more widely celebrated as a historic instance of building coalitions during cultural revolutions.

First, *Aiiieeeee!* was published by Howard University Press, a publishing house just starting up in one of America's historically black universities. Asian American writers had found difficulty getting published by mainstream U.S. publishers, and it was a black press that gave *Aiiieeeee!* and its authors literary breath. This step was unprecedented and extremely important. While mainstream presses ignored Asian American literature for most of its history, Howard University Press's reception and distribution of *Aiiieeeee!* established an Asian-black literary alliance that created a material foundation for the anthology's Afro-Asian content. In a succinct personal letter, Howard University Press editor Roberta Palm wrote to Chin: "Obviously, the introductions hit them where it hurts."[29] Palm's letter indicates her press's willingness to be an editorial accomplice to Chin's incendiary introduction in *Aiiieeeee!* Most writers realize the importance of editors who understand the purpose of their work and the impact of this appreciation in supporting their artistic vision. Because white critics and publishing houses rejected the initial manuscript of *Aiiieeeee!* as trivial and sophomoric, Chin archived his brief correspondence with Howard University Press as a reminder of this historic participation between black decision makers and Asian American writers.

Second, the important gesture by the editors of *Aiiieeeee!* to seek identification with black radical masculinities is a rare inscription of Asian-black content in Asian American literature. By identifying with blackness, the editors put forth representations of black masculinities as the political personalities that they aspired to be—vocal in electoral politics, shapers of U.S. national culture, and desirable as sexualized men. In one passage, the editors write:

> Thus, fourth-, fifth-, and sixth-generation Asian Americans are still looked upon as foreigners because of this dual heritage, or the concept of dual personality which suggests that the Asian American can be broken down into his American part and his Asian part. This view explains Asian American assimilation, adaptability, and lack of presence in American culture. This sustaining inner resource keeps the Asian American a stranger in the country in which he was born. He is supposed to feel better than the blacks, whose American achievement is the invention of their own American culture. American language, fashions, music, literature, cuisine, graphics, body language, morals, and politics have been strongly influenced by black culture. They have been cultural achievers, in spite of white supremacist culture, whereas Asian America's reputation is an achievement of that white culture—a work of racist art.[30]

Asian American racial formation hinges upon a dual-worlds model of identity and the tenets of antiblackness, "to feel better than the blacks." However, *Aiiieeeee!* challenges this condition of post–civil rights citizenship in which black culture becomes a sphere of cultural integrity and creative renewal, a nobility of survival. The editors disputed the racial classifications that defined Asian American identity as perpetually foreign to the U.S. nation-state. Sustained to reinforce the entitlements of whiteness, the dual-heritage model splits the Asian American body politic symmetrically between normative whiteness and inscrutable alien. In *The Possessive Investment in Whiteness*, George Lipsitz intimates that "as the unmarked category against which difference is constructed, whiteness never has to speak its name."[31] In contrast, race and resistance is a staple of black social consciousness and cultural practice, whereas the silence found in Asian American assimilation produces "a work of racist art." That the benchmark is "the amount and kind of noise of resistance generated by the race" indicates a diagnosis of Asian American self-determination as significantly more quiet than radical black expression.[32] Stephen Sumida relays that the editors attacked the dual-identity concept and its fundamental link to white assimilation, and this literary noise animated a new opening for other writers.[33]

Later, the editors connect Asian masculine physical stereotypes to literary production with language as the main trope for investigation. Theorizing the ontology of the Asian male body in problematic terms, they explain the emasculation of Asian American manhood from hegemonic masculinity:

> The white stereotype of the acceptable and unacceptable Asian is utterly
> without manhood. Good or bad, the stereotypical Asian is nothing as a
> man. At worst the Asian American is contemptible because he is womanly,
> effeminate, devoid of all the traditionally masculine qualities of originality,
> physical courage, and creativity.[34]

Chin, in an unpublished letter to Maxine Hong Kingston, wrote: "In my lifetime, white men have always favored yellow women over yellow men and yellow women have always put down yellow men for not being all them nice white things, from aggressive to original, to sexy . . . just like you."[35] The complicated relationship between Chin and Asian American female writers is illuminated by his experience of twofold rejection by both white masculinity and Asian American femininity.[36] Through the matrix of white manhood and the entitlements of heroism, Chin's letter to Kingston and *Aiiieeeee!*'s preface bind the experiential to the theoretical whereby racialized desire produces anxiety due to separation from both homoeroticism with white men and heterosexual union with Asian American women.

The editors conclude their discussion by echoing the famous New York City speech by Malcolm X, when they allegorize the Asian American cultural voice by raising the volatile distinction between field slaves and house slaves:

> The deprivation of language in a verbal society like this country's has contributed to the lack of a recognized Asian American cultural integrity (at most, native-born Asian-Americans are "Americanized" Chinese or Japanese) and the lack of a recognized style of Asian-American manhood. These two conditions have produced "the house nigger mentality," under which Chinese- and Japanese-Americans accept responsibility for, rather than authority over the language and accept dependency.[37]

Cultural integrity, the means to produce a recognizable Asian American cultural imprint, is equivalent to the language, tongue, speech, and writing of a people to activate their sense of uniqueness and cultural vitality. Depicting both public and private spheres of failed recognition, the triangulated relationship between Asian American men, Asian American women, and blackness sets the cornerstone that exemplifies *Aiiieeeee!*'s archival project as a treatise informed by conditions of manhood and representational control.

To be sure, this gesture was an Asian-black birth of a sensibility, and it was central to the success of *Aiiieeeee!* as an important work. Daniel Kim notes that Asian American literature is "a site where racial invisibility that reigns in the political order can be compensated by the kinds of representations to be attained in literary culture."[38] The editors had borrowed black rage and militancy and incorporated the audacity of Black Power, and thus situated Afro-Asian hermeneutics as a style of thought and vision in the formation of an Asian American consciousness:

> White racism has failed to convince the blacks that they are animals and failed to convince the Indians that they are living fossils. They did not destroy their impulse to cultural integrity, stamp out their literary sensibility, and produce races of people who would work to enforce white supremacy without having to be supervised or watch dogged.[39]

Novels such as Ronyoung Kim's *Clay Walls* and John Okada's *No-No Boy*, and Hisaye Yamamoto's short story "A Fire in Fontana," fictionalized scenes of Afro-Asian interaction in American life. Yet, it was not until the publication of *Aiiieeeee!*, specifically elucidated in the preface, that Asian American writers conceptualized the lived contours and theoretical implications of an Afro-Asian literary imaginary and movement. For the editors, Asian American manhood was literary recognition. Refusing the expected capitulation of Asian ethnic assimilation, this important identification allowed the editors an expressive form that could reveal their own sense of racialized alienation and displacement from national manhood.[40] In many ways, the editors realized the difficulties involved with Asian ethnic assimilation in the post–civil rights era, a period of racial magnetism that had positioned as rivals the social construction of Asian masculinity over and against black masculinity. In *Narrating Nationalisms*, Jinqi Ling argues that one should reread *Aiiieeeee!* from the point of view of the discursive moment in which it came forth, adding that the anthology's "ideological thrust" constituted for the first time in over a century "a public claim on rights."[41] In *States of Injury*, Wendy Brown posits that the emancipatory power of rights is always historically and culturally situated, whereby rights are "protean and irresolute signifiers, varying across time and culture, but across the other vectors of power whose crossing they are sometimes deployed to effect."[42] In this way, the editorial collective pinpointed the main locus of citizenship in the cultural sphere, through national inclusion, further commenting that a lack of such cultural legitimacy produced forms of ideological violence structured by masculinized inferiority and literary alienation. All this is persuasively performed by cross-racial desire and the mimicry of black radical masculinity. Who better to exemplify the violence and anguish of emasculation than the abject black male body?

In *Blackface, White Noise*, Michael Rogin argues that blackface is the performance of racial identity rooted in European imperialism, a material and psychological investment made by both colonizer and colonized in the world capitalist system. It inverted and assigned a system of racial classification by fixating blackness as an immutable and transparent category. Blackface formed ideologies of national belonging. It was performed on the stage, in vaudeville, in traveling shows, in Hollywood films, and on the radio. Racial cross-dressing helped produce an imagined community in which white anxieties concerning African American miscegenation, citizenship demands, and criminality were contained by rigid boundaries of racial difference that only whites could transgress.[43] Moreover, tales of racial passing have been historically tales of citizenship and modernization.[44] From novels such as James Weldon Johnson's *Autobiography of an Ex-Colored Man* to Nella Larsen's *Passing*, from films like *Old San Francisco* to *Gone with the Wind*, narratives of passing disrupt the certainty of fixed racial categories and reconceptualize the visual dependence of racial hierarchy in constituting the nation. Archetypal figures like the tragic mulatto and moral panics like the fear of miscegenation have revealed the deep anxiety of whiteness and its fear of mongrelization. But passing narratives have mostly centered the white, heterosexual male as the signifier of desire, the subject to pass for and thus to masquerade as. Yet, for the *Aiiieeeee!* editors, the horizontal crossing of the Asian-black color line complicated the vertical cross-dressing that Rogin addresses. Through cross-racial identifications, the editors mimicked the voice of African American trauma, national belonging, and public authority. Therefore, in many ways, this type of racial transgression is the moral and taxonomic opposite of the nation's previous representations of racial passing.

The narrative of racial passing rests in its theatrical approach to masculinization. Minstrelsy and blackface incorporated the use of makeup, costumes, dialogue, and staging. These stylistic, theatrical elements were transferred to Hollywood production codes in the Big Studio era and colored up white performers for the mass entertainment of white audiences. The stage or screen had been the mirror, a transgressive carte blanche showing racial narratives of passing that helped construct the American imagined community, which moved white settlers and ethnics into the melting pot by keeping minorities out. As for the editors of *Aiiieeeee!*, their theatricality rests in their performance of language: the style, tone, metaphors, and polemics that laid out their play on words. In the context of language and literary production, they state: "There is no conflict between East and West. That is a modern invention of whites and their yellow goons—writers who need white overseers to give them a license to use the English language."[45] They recreate a kind of textual theater in which "yellow goons" played assimilationist writers, "white overseers" represent mainstream publishers, and the "conflict" established the dramatic crisis. With characters in place and the plot in motion, not only did they call out performances of Asian American writers who had passed across the Asian color line but they also re-created the color line by reproducing the flattening and homogenizing gaze of whiteness.

Donning racialized accoutrements, the editors deployed a contradictory performance of black masculinity through the performance of cross-racial masquerade. First, this type of masquerade is the transitional, processional, and ongoing rearticulation of racial discourses and transformation by donning the mask of black radical masculinities. However, making these interracial identifications, the allusion to slavery as a prime example, comes with many contradictions. Slavery as an etched cultural memory in America's racial imaginary is the racial terror of de jure segregation, but linking that history to another aggrieved group ignores the ways in which the legal apparatus of the state enacts processes of racialization unevenly at different historical moments. This is the point at which the editors' Asian-black cultural connections break down into a paradoxical quagmire. The bold invocation of African American injury onto Asian American bodies conflates black and Asian difference as discursively homogeneous and reduces the institution of slavery and Asian ethnic assimilation as a Janus face of history.

Nevertheless, *Aiiieeeee!* shows that Asian American cultural politics can and should engage more critically with black liberation through Asian American literary production and interrogate what Gwendolyn Brooks has called "the politics of everyday oppression."[46] This critical approach is important to acknowledge, because how we remember and what we remember conceptualize our understanding of political injury and form our conceptions of nation and manhood. Stuart Hall has indicated that we have to think about identity in relation to others and difference.[47] In this sense, the Asian-black interface in the Asian American writing movement portrays how interracial expressions of radicalism and cross-racial identifications were crucial to the genesis and development of necessary cultural institutions that explored the workings of nation, masculinity, and racial difference.[48] Furthermore, during this pioneering era of coalition building and multiethnic vision, the *Aiiieeeee!* editors revolutionized Asian American consciousness, voice, and recognition, whereby Asian Americans represented themselves. Through incendiary language and remasculinized verve, the Four Horsemen of Asian American literature reshaped Asian America's social contract with whiteness: the terms of assimilation, the masculine dimensions to literary emasculation, and the decolonization of the mind from white supremacy's gaze of inferiority. No such Asian American literature exists today; or, in the words of poet Ishle Yi Park's performance piece "Sa-I-Gu," "Where are our Malcolms? Our Martins . . . no eloquent, rapid tongue."[49] *Aiiieeeee!*, in many ways, signaled the arrival of Asian American tongues through the manifold ways in which the radicalism of black masculinities helped forge its emergence.

A collective of ten people founded Yardbird Publishing Incorporated in 1971, with Wayne Daniels as chairman of the board and Ishmael Reed, Al Young, and William Lawson as editorial directors. As part of the third world effort to transform U.S. national culture, Yardbird Publishing circulated five volumes of literature and visual art, naming *Yardbird Reader 3* the "Asian American issue" due to the guest editorship of Frank Chin and Shawn Wong. If the preface of *Aiiieeeee!* showcased Afro-Asian performance in its content, *Yardbird Reader 3* explicitly detailed the material support from black publication houses, which initiated the Asian American writing movement. Significantly, *Yardbird Reader 3* cannot be simply labeled as an Asian American literary anthology because it also includes a collage of photographs, interviews, visual art, and literature by Native American and black writers. Perhaps this explains *Yardbird Reader 3*'s remarkable absence in Asian American literary scholarship, because ethnic studies has balkanized into monoracial analysis for most of its institutional history. Yet, in this section, I want to highlight the anthology's significant contribution to understanding the comparative racialized and cultural formations between the Asian American writing movement, Black Power writers, and third world liberation. Inspired by black writers and black self-determination in publishing, *Yardbird Reader 3* celebrates Afro-Asian collaboration more powerfully in scope than *Aiiieeeee!* On the dedication page, the editors salute John Okada, Louis Chu, Duke Ellington, and William Gardner Smith. Without a point of reference, this dedication seems incongruous and perplexing. However, Okada and Chu were unknown writers until the publication of *Aiiieeeee!* in 1974, and Ellington and Smith were, respectively, important musical and literary figures who both died in 1974. Coupled together, the placement of Asian and black men in the cycle of birth, death, and rebirth set the tone for *Yardbird Reader 3* as a milestone in Afro-Asian literary collaboration at such a historic convergence.

The front cover shows a childhood passport photograph of James Wong Howe, adorned with the shaved head and pigtails of the Qing Dynasty. He would later become a leading cinematographer in Hollywood, with ten Oscar nominations and a career spanning over six decades. On the back cover, the editors of *Aiiieeeee!* smile on a wooden front porch, a black-and-white shot capturing the Four Horsemen during a leisurely moment. In text printed underneath the photograph, Ishmael Reed relates the multicultural dimensions of Yardbird Publishing: "We proved them wrong and now this is our third issue, THE ASIAN AMERICAN ISSUE, edited by Frank Chin and Shawn Wong which includes leading contributors to the ASIAN-AMERICAN RENAISSANCE. American People. Our folks."[50] Reed validates Asians in America as political and cultural citizens of the nation-state, "[o]ur folks" in his vernacular. He defines Asian American writing as a "renaissance," reflecting his tutelage and affirmation of Asian American literature by bestowing an equal camaraderie. Later in the back-cover copy he writes: "Political revolution means nothing if hearts and minds are unchanged. Join in a real revolution by supporting YARDBIRD, the Reader of a New America!"[51] The political agenda of minority writers expresses a radical turn in the cultural trajectory of the United States, one inspired by reinventing the epistemology and ontology of cultural revolution. From front cover to back cover—the passport photo indicating Howe's immigration history, the Four Horsemen captured at rest, Reed's tribute to Asian American citizenship—*Yardbird Reader 3* is a special record of the progress of Asian American writing at a critical juncture for multicultural, multiethnic, and Afro-Asian collaboration.

Following the dedication page, Chin pens his most direct appraisal of Asian and black race relations in the United States. While *Aiiieeeee!*'s editors do not mention Howard University Press in their preface, *Yardbird Reader 3*'s preface establishes the special collaboration between a black press and Asian American literary production in the very first sentence: "*YARDBIRD PUBLISHING* is a black company."[52] Forward and concise, this statement establishes the explicit Afro-Asian connections for publication that *Aiiieeeee!* failed to explicate. Later, Chin documents the residential and classroom intimacies between Asians and blacks on the West Coast, incorporating the diction of hybridized Chinese English, *longtime Californ*, to chronicle the uniquely American temporal and spatial proximity between the two communities. Yet, what follows is a diagnosis of Asian American citizenship that pivots on the tenets of antiblackness and black American ridicule of Asian American assimilation into the category of honorary whiteness. As a condition of racial hierarchy, the architecture of racial magnetism in full measure, the racialization of the model minority versus black resistance is a prominent topic in the early pages of the reader. However, Chin makes an adept move in response to this contradictory condition of proximity and negation, intimacy and contempt, in suggesting that writers such as Young, Reed, Wong, and himself are not "attempting some kind of racial literary coup d'état with a mixed junta. This volume of *YARDBIRD READER* is no interracial treaty."[53] Setting the limitation for any interracial utopia, Chin simply says that he does not think there is much hate between the two communities. This revelation is extraordinary for acknowledging the vast differences between Asian and black communities while simultaneously revealing the possibility for something greater. Given that Asian and black people have lived together, attended the same schools, and even formed literary bonds, Chin suggests that race mongering generated by comparative racialization cannot supplant the experiences and intimacies that Asian Americans have shared with blackness.

According to Chin, the expression of hate toward black America is a condition of Asian American racial oppression and "racial self-esteem." He directs his attention internally at Asian America, an intraracial diagnosis of the state of Asian American consciousness, historical memory, and artistic practice. Many Asian Americans belittled the artistic pursuit by Chin and Wong as simply mimicking white culture, which is similar to how black Americans mocked the aspirations of Richard Wright in Mississippi. The exclusion of

Asian American three-dimensional representations in U.S. national culture and historiography produces legacies of internalized inferiority, what Kenneth Clark's doll test evinced in *Brown v. Board of Education* in 1954. Organizations like the Japanese American Citizens League, the only mainstream political mouthpiece allowed by the U.S. military, advocated literary critics like Allan Beekman and Bill Hosokawa, whom Chin chastises as the epitome of the white critical gaze setting out to critique Asian American literary merit and ultimately Asian American humanity. This diagnosis of Asian America in 1974—the interpellation of antiblackness for Asian American citizenship, the growth of intraracial self-contempt, and the influence of white literary criticism—offers the provenance to recognize the editorial intent that Chin and Wong invested in *Yardbird Reader 3*.

If *Aiiieeeee!* explores the literary contributions of Asian Americans through a genealogical record, then *Yardbird Reader 3* expands upon this strategy to include other multiethnic dimensions of culture and identity. The preface concludes with familiar names found in *Aiiieeeee!* including Louis Chu, John Okada, Sui Sin Far, Hisaye Yamamoto, Monica Sone, Lawson Fusao Inada, Toshio Mori, Bee Fee, and Sam Tagatac. Yet, the inclusion of Native Americans such as Simon Ortiz and Leslie Silko, and African Americans like Mbembe (Milton Smith) and Joe Johnson, showcases the dynamic and improvisational moment of *Yardbird Reader 3*'s multiethnic literary formation.

The second preface in *Yardbird Reader 3* is more personal and geohistorical. It begins with Chin and Wong narrating their relationship with David Ishii in Seattle, the home of John Okada, Monica Sone, and James Sakamoto. The reader senses, through more traditional storytelling, the practical friendships and serendipitous experiences among small-scale booksellers such as Ishii and others that nurtured the survival and growth of Asian American literature. At Ishii's bookstore, customers could purchase the first collection of Asian American essays, the *Bulletin of Concerned Asian Scholars*, edited by Victor and Brett DeBary Nee, Shawn Wong, and Connie Young Yu. Chin and Wong refer to Washington state as the center of Asian America, more so than California or New York, and *Yardbird Reader 3* testifies to its geographic and historical importance to the maintenance of Asian American identity. Thus, the second preface expands the locations of knowledge and showcases the regional diversity embedded in the Asian American writing movement. The editors proclaim: "The state of Washington has always been the capital of Asian American culture."[54] In comparison, San Francisco holds a special space in their geography of U.S. racialization, a "racist kennel," in their words, that withheld Asian American political participation for more than 140 years. To differentiate between space and place, Peter Taylor suggests that "spaces, therefore, are the outcome of top-down processes; places can be the site for bottom-up opposition."[55] *Yardbird Reader 3* designates San Francisco as a space of racial exclusion from civic participation and Seattle as a place of important everyday interactions among ordinary but committed people. Washington state, the editors assert, is a place where mobility and obstruction to citizenship coexist in contradictory fashion. They list prominent Asian Americans from Washington whom they designate as either wholly assimilationist, such as Bill Hosokawa, author of *Nisei: The Quiet Americans*, and Keye Luke, the "number one son" in the Charlie Chan movie series. Yet they also distinguish, quite problematically, Asian Americans who embody successful citizenship such as superior court judge Warren Chan, councilwoman Ruby Chow, rodeo champion Willie Wada, and the above-mentioned James Wong Howe. This second preface is the only place where the editors name Asian Americans outside the field of literature, and their binary distinction between what they would later identify as "real" and "fake" in *The Big Aiiieeeee!* suggests that they use the nation-state and depth of assimilation as benchmarks for their appraisals.

Returning to the question of publishing, Chin and Wong define the moment of recognition that would launch Asian American literature as a site of investigation, national acclaim, and literary merit. They write: "Yardbird Publishing is the first Berkeley–San Francisco based national publication to acknowledge the existence of an Asian American cultural tradition that is not mere mimicry or exotic artifact."[56] The construction of validation, for which judgment is a prerequisite, is an important communal process in the creation of multiethnic social movements: "validation is an enabling, confirming, and supportive process."[57] Validation's function is to subvert and question systemic invisibility; it is a moral judgment whose "development . . . articulation, and . . . progress to methodological status . . . is required by the community."[58] Thus, the preface continues, "the blacks were the first to take us seriously and sustained the spirit of many Asian American writers."[59] This, in short, is the core exchange at the heart of the Afro-Asian mode of cultural production: a tangible building of intellectual, emotional, and literary capacities that produces possibility when all around expound the impossible.

With Afro-Asian support, *Aiiieeeee!* and *Yardbird 3* together inaugurated the field of Asian American literature and helped establish the necessary institutions to make it flourish. Revisiting this moment of arrival in conjunction with antiracist social movements allows for an understanding of how multiracial coalitions form and gives us a blueprint for how future coalitions may come into existence. During the early period of racial magnetism, Asian and black male writers rejected cannibalistic gestures toward their respective racialized counterparts. This chapter has illuminated the personal, professional, and textual interconnections between Asian and black masculinities at the historical intersection between Black Power and the Asian American writing movement. By expressing interracial sensibilities, theorizing multiethnicity, and practicing constructs of validation, these writers built important literary futures for minority literatures, enabling them to gain institutional, mainstream, and national acclaim. Their legacy of mutuality and affirmation suggests the power of an Afro-Asian mode of cultural production to imagine alternative communities and social relations, a march toward human recognition and literary respect. Through what Russell Leong describes as "lived theory," readers learn about the vital literary visions and conditions of struggle that are required for any lasting social transformation.[60] Although many imperfections can be found in the texts, both *Aiiieeeee!* and *Yardbird 3* assumed the monumental task of being the first movers in a literary world being shaken by historic Afro-Asian pioneers. This is why we look toward cultural vanguards, for they show us a different path, a mirror to our own lived experience and a compass to another place.

2. Yellow Bodies, Black Sweat

Yao Ming, Ichiro Suzuki, and Global Sport

Afro-Asian connections were pivotal to the birth of Asian American literature, a cultural movement that contested the early enforcement of racial magnetism and showed the possibilities and limitations of interracial coalitions. The protest masculinity of blackness was grafted onto Asian American male bodies, a project of racial passing and remasculinization through the forging of cultural agency and a literary tradition. In this chapter, I telescope to a more mature period of racial magnetism's authority in American culture, an era of advanced neoliberal realignment and the consolidation of multicultural consent. One of the central precepts of racial magnetism is its reliance on biological prescriptions for racialized masculinities in the production of visual common sense. This chapter explores the culture industry of popular sport, a mainstream site where visual meanings of masculinity, race, and manhood are hegemonic and commoditized. I also explore the often hostile connections between Asian and black sports figures within the logic of nationalism, global multiculturalism, and the expansion of transnational sports.

Figuring the Asian male body in popular sport, Alexander Global Promotions has made bobblehead dolls of Ichiro Suzuki, Major League Baseball's Most Valuable Player in 2001 and currently star right fielder for the New York Yankees (although he established his considerable credentials in a twelve-year career with the Seattle Mariners). Called Ichibobs, the three-dimensional caricatures stand a mighty seven and a half inches tall and weigh 1.2 pounds; they are marketed as "stronger than ceramic" and in "mint condition." Officially licensed by MLB, the dolls are a product of the global commodity chain—made in China, distributed throughout the Pacific Rim, and sold for less than twenty dollars in the United States. News that Ichiro bobblehead dolls would be given away for free to the first twenty thousand fans at a game between the Seattle Mariners and the Minnesota Twins in July 2001 nearly caused a human stampede, in which "the appeal for the new [dolls] is strictly p-r-o-f-i-t."[1] Anticipating some commotion as a result of the promotion, the Mariners had prepared for the event by implementing extra secu-

55

rity, setting up portable toilets, and bringing in additional garbage cans; the bobblehead craze had met the sports world, and it was Ichiro who seemed to be head and shoulders (wobbly though they may be) above the competition. Ichibobs are diminutive replicas of Ichiro's body: at once, a miniature representation of his racial identity, his masculine physicality, and, on a global level, his cult status as an Asian superstar along the Pacific Rim. They are simulacrums of his masculinity, made of plastic and paint, and representations of his body and his prowess on baseball's field of dreams.

Ichiro represents in clear ways the figuration of the Asian male body as both cultural phenomenon and transnational commodity. This chapter describes the marked change from viewing the Asian male body as an unattractive vehicle for marketing commodity exchanges to an imported spectacle generating transnational capital for the NBA and MLB.[2] Yet, I do not intend simply to offer a conventional study of the political economy involved in the global expansion of popular sport. Rather, I will illustrate how Asian men in popular sport presuppose and indeed attempt to produce Asian masculinity by inverting the bodily emasculation of Asian American men. The fact that race and masculinity are profoundly difficult to separate from stereotypes of the body is a fundamental aspect of biological racism. In *Society Must Be Defended*, Michel Foucault traces the binary structure of biological racism, a permanent war for centralizing power in state apparatuses, as "a race that is portrayed as the one true race, the race that holds power and is entitled to define the norm, and against those who deviate from that norm, against those who pose a threat to the biological heritage."[3] This "race struggle," as he characterizes it, is inherent in Western epistemologies of the body, which evolved from the eschatological myths of the Middle Ages, seventeenth-century radical English thought, French aristocratic insurgencies against Louis XIV, the early-nineteenth-century postrevolutionary project to compile a people's history, and, later, the classification of colonial "subraces."[4] Thus, it is difficult to separate the body from racial hierarchy because of the penetration of nineteenth-century "race struggle" discourses based on pseudoscience. Even today, this biological trajectory acts as a specter that haunts our racial imaginary even as culture has superseded, but not erased, biology as an explanation for racial difference.

Spectacular athletes like Kobe Bryant and LeBron James seem to be public illustrations of black individual accomplishments after civil rights, who simultaneously distract us from the persisting impediments that most black men face in other spheres like education and the criminal justice system. Rising Asian American sports stars such as Jeremy Lin represent the changing face of popular sport, which predecessors such as Ichiro and Yao Ming first challenged with respect to biology, the Asian male body, and athletic achievement. However, even "Linsanity" cannot stave off charges that Lin's hard work and intelligence have been the primary reasons for his success rather than physical speed and quickness, which his NBA combine results attest to. As such, this chapter details the ways in which popular sport has been racialized as a black space of colonial fantasies and fears, and how Asian male athletes have broken down the fixity of racialized spaces that hinge upon bodies, essentialism, and visual common sense. Because popular sport harbors this biological trace, the fetishization of the black male body saturates our commonsense understanding of black male racialization in the post–civil rights era. Therefore, the ways in which Asian male bodies inhabit black cultural spaces illustrate the complex process of Asian ethnic assimilation into national culture, a process that depends on mechanisms of black racialization already in motion. By inhabiting the realm of bodily agency, an arena that has been denied to Asian male bodies in the popular mind, the racial logic that positions black men as only the body and Asian men as bodiless displaces visual commonsense understandings of racial difference. Yet these representations of Asian sports stars within the context of global multiculturalism depoliticize forms of black radicalism in earlier breakthroughs of the color line in popular sport.

Other analyses of Asian American masculinity have looked at literature and film, considering characters or personalities such as Charlie Chan, Fu Manchu, Frank Chin, and Bruce Lee.[5] Yet, little investigation has been undertaken concerning Asian American men in other cultural productions. Addressing this lack, I analyze the cultural phenomena of Ichiro Suzuki and Yao Ming, both of whom are icons of heroic masculinity on sports' grandest stages. From a postnationalist perspective of our revered pastimes, popular sport not only reveals the impact and importance of less analyzed cultural institutions, but it does so by exploring the important relations between men of color both ideologically and materially. In this sense, the relations between minority masculinities in popular sport play a powerful ideological role and carry a material force in defining manhood, public authority, and national culture. The mediation of how these axes intersect and confirm each other centers the theoretical and historical concerns of this chapter.

Scholarly scrutiny of men and sport has attempted to explain the construction of masculinity. Contemporary discussions of Asian and black masculinity have concerned themselves with the relationship between racial hierarchy and the male body. Many claims about manhood have been associated with citizenship claims embodied in political, economic, and social voices, from Frederick Douglass to W. E. B. Du Bois to the editors of *Aiiieeeee!* In directing our attention to popular sport, I ask, where else are manhood claims so personified yet maintained? But another, more basic question may arise: what is masculinity and why does popular sport play a pivotal role in its definition and influence? Judith Halberstam defines it this way:

> Masculinity in this society inevitably conjures up notions of power and legitimacy and privilege; it often symbolically refers to the power of the state and to uneven distributions of wealth. Masculinity seems to extend outward into patriarchy and inward into the family; masculinity represents the power of inheritance, the consequences of the traffic in women, and the promise of social privilege.[6]

I utilize Halberstam's important idea of linking gender identifications to state formations, kinship networks, material life, and power relations. A brilliant analysis in gender studies, her project questions the persistent tendency in gender and queer studies to subordinate alternative masculinities, including female and minority masculinities, and focus exclusively on white, middle-class masculinity.[7]

In addition, Gail Bederman helps us understand masculinity this way: "Manhood—or masculinity, as it is commonly termed today—is a continual, dynamic process." Through that process, "men claim certain kinds of authority, based upon their particular type of bodies."[8] Bederman identifies the shifting, historical definitions of masculinity linked to the body and race. She uses the example of boxer Jack Johnson to analyze men's bodies to specific class (Victorian) and racial (white) formations. She relates an incident in which Johnson wore extra gauze over his genital area to instill fear and awe in his white opponents and the white boxing public, thereby performing the stereotype of black masculinity. Bederman's analysis allows us to consider the impact of "particular type[s] of bodies" and the "kinds of authority" these men can claim as well as "the promise of social privilege" that arises. Using popular sport's influence on manhood, she asks what ideological productions are occurring in "the process which creates men by linking male genital anatomy to male identity, and linking both anatomy and identity to particular arrangements of authority and power."[9]

Conventional studies of popular sport have used the lens of gender to explicate the reproduction of hegemonic masculinities in sport as well as the subordination of women.[10] Michael Messner and Donald Sabo incorporate feminist perspectives that have analyzed the gender order of sport, and the ways in which masculinity is constructed in relation to femininity.[11] A critical intervention, Messner and Sabo's collection, *Sport, Men, and the Gender*

Order: Critical Feminist Perspectives, demonstrated the fundamental intellectual importance of feminist theory in the emerging field of men's studies in the 1980s and 1990s.

Other texts acknowledge the growing immersion of gender analysis in popular sports, with sociologists doing the majority of the research. This critical perspective emphasizes the negative outcomes of men's experiences in sport, such as physical injury, patriarchy, homophobia, and misogyny.[12] Yet relying on a methodology that privileges gender consequently does not pay adequate attention to race and class. Although sociologists such as Harry Edwards have described the linkages between sport and class inequalities as well as structural racial discrimination, I find the literature on sport and men's studies focused heavily on the construction of nationalism and the commodification of popular sport as part and parcel of globalization. Without giving adequate attention to race and masculinity, many authors consequently fail to challenge prevailing conceptions of sport, aside from its mere political economy.[13] In all, this chapter challenges such assumptions and concurrently addresses the importance of comparative race analysis in rethinking the role of popular sport in global society.

Popular sport seems to have exemplified, since the late nineteenth century, dominant definitions of manhood and manliness formed around notions of power, strength, aggressiveness, heteronormativity, patriarchy, competitiveness, and domination. Its genesis as the dominant cultural site of masculinizing the male body emerged in response to the emasculating effects of industrial capitalism. During the proletarianization of the American economy, a crisis of masculinity emerged from the loss of personal economic autonomy, including control over one's labor and ownership of the means of production. Alfred Chandler has elucidated in *Scale and Scope* the impact of managerial capitalism on industrialization and the scientific rationality employed to increase productivity and profits.[14] Working bodies were routinized in a system of production that managed their time and disciplined their physical actions in a highly developed business imperative to maximize labor power. Displaced from agrarian and artisan social life and relegated to the confining enclosures of factories, working-class bodies became the objects of labor exploitation through low pay, dangerous health conditions, and lack of work protections. This labor-intensive process had a detrimental effect on working men's bodies, which incarnated the contradictions between capital and labor. Marx eloquently described the process: "The more the worker produces, the less he has to consume; the more values he creates, the more valueless, the more unworthy he becomes; the better formed his product, the more deformed becomes the worker."[15] Marx expresses the "alienation" workers feel not only from the commodities they produce but also from themselves. In this sense, nineteenth-century laborers had lost the means to control their daily work and the fruits of their labor, and their manhood was intricately tied to their lost sense of independence, ownership, and freedom.

Manhood symbolized the American Way, to use Sacvan Bercovitch's phrase—an ethic of open-ended freedom through entrepreneurship and property ownership. The West and the frontier, patriarchy and heteronormativity, and imperialism and genocide—these were the outward expressions of masculine mobility.[16] At the end of the nineteenth century, white men felt an acute loss of their own bodies, although simultaneously they had excluded women, immigrants, and minority men from their own sold sense of American belonging in the nation's body politic. Popular sport offered white men a means by which they could emphasize the male body as a locus for remasculinization. Many leading thinkers and moralists of the day espoused that the feminization of American manhood went hand in hand with the growth of modern capitalism.[17] This sense of feminized manhood revealed the deep anxieties and fears of a generation living in a tumultuous era of economic, political, and social transformation.

Middle-class white bodies were not immune to a sense of lost manhood. Indeed, popular discourses of men's health suggested that Victorian culture created men who were oversophisticated and effete. Hundreds of books and pamphlets detailed a contemporary condition—nervousness, or neurasthenia—that reputedly stemmed from overcivilization. George Beard's *American Nervousness* and S. Weir Mitchell's *Sexual Neurasthenia* document the psychological and somatic effects that resulted from the Victorian ideal of manly restraint, including such symptoms as loss of vital fluids, brain collapse, nervous exhaustion, and hysteria. Many psychologists, intellectuals, and moralists also felt that Victorian domesticity, with its emphasis on conformity and sexual repression, enervated the development of rugged, physically powerful men. Responding to these fears of feminization, gymnasiums, baseball diamonds, and boxing rings became popular venues during the late nineteenth and early twentieth centuries.[18] Remasculinizing America was a powerful leitmotif for the problems citizens perceived with American modernity. The modernist sensibility that sought to make sense of steam power, industrial factories, telegraph communication, technocratic sciences, and increasing urbanization relied upon first understanding the role of masculinity, sport, and the body.

Working and middle-class men viewed popular sport as the antidote to the feminizing effects of industrial capital and the ideology of Victorian culture. Sport epitomized the rugged individualism of a Jacksonian usable past whereby the display of physicality and manhood was routed through the body. Michael Kimmel writes:

> This preoccupation with the physical body facilitated the transition from inner directed men, who expressed their inner selves in the workplace and at home—that is, in their "real" lives—to other directed men, concerned with acquiring the culturally defined trappings that denoted manhood. The increasing importance of the body, of physicality, meant that men's bodies carried a different sort of weight than expressing the man within. The body did not contain the man; it was the man.[19]

Indeed, the male body was the repository of capitalist contradiction. For example, according to Elliott Gorn in *The Manly Art*, boxers resisted proletarianization. Sports such as boxing and baseball reinvented masculinity. Working-class men resurrected the lexicon of skilled artisans when describing their matches as "a profession," "went to work," "made good work," "art," "science," and "craft." Boxers controlled their own bodies in a physical sense, but symbolically they negotiated the exchange of their labor for remuneration in the open market of the ring and canvas; they were free from authoritarian management and discipline as well as from routinized wage labor.[20] Here was a sport constitutive of bodily adeptness and mobility, for it allowed the formation of working-class masculinities in contrast to bourgeois gentility.[21]

Evolving definitions of manhood and the male body transformed masculinity at the turn of the twentieth century from inert, effete stereotypes to meanings tied to the physicality of sports. Along with the growing popularity of popular sport came a consumer culture that commodified sport leisure activity for a mass audience. The transition of popular sport from an emergent social practice to a mass cultural institution developed through complex negotiations with America's consumer society and racial apartheid. Baseball especially captured the imagination of the nation and quickly reinforced capitalist characteristics such as obedience, self-sacrifice, and discipline as well as de jure segregation, whiteness as ownership, and sport icons as proper national men. While African American ballplayers were relegated to the Negro leagues, white masculinity flourished both ideologically and materially as the filter through which consumerism established the standard of national manhood. As Thorstein Veblen writes in *The Theory of the Leisure Class*, the formation of a leisure culture followed the emerging capitalist order: "The end of acquisition and accumulation is conventionally held to be the consumption of the goods accumulated—whether it is consumption directly by the owner of the goods or by the household attached to him and for this purpose identified with him in theory."[22] Nowhere was this more apparent than in baseball as a participatory and spectator sport.

Sport masculinity saturated U.S. national culture with live games, cartoons, moving pictures, newspapers, dime novels, radio broadcasts, and, most importantly, health commodities that structured antimiscegenation codes between white and nonwhite men. Consuming manhood meant buying vast quantities of manly concoctions that white masculinity in popular sport epitomized such as Sylvester Graham's crackers, C. W. Post's Grape-Nuts, and John Harvey Kellogg's rolled flakes. Men bought various advice manuals and guidebooks to read about ways to maintain manly vigor and health that baseball players like Ty Cobb and Shoeless Joe Jackson symbolized. Books such as William Blaikie's *How to Get Strong and How to Stay So* and Bernarr Macfadden's *The Virile Powers of Superb Manhood* were best sellers of the new century. Terms such as "sissy" entered popular discourses to classify men who did not partake in baseball. Perhaps Zane Grey best summed up the sentiment of the times: "All boys love baseball. If they don't they're not real boys." What all these remedies reconceptualized was the regulation of the male body through racialized discourses centered on white masculinity as the epitome of health, physicality, and manliness. The reinvention of turn-of-the-century masculinity reflected the transformation of the consumer culture that baseball actively incorporated in its rules, play, and values.

From the inception of popular sport as both a leisure activity and a mass cultural institution, race played a crucial role in its cultural and material formation in U.S. society. The contested political landscape of popular sport reflected the twentieth century's turbulent crisis over the color line and, in this milieu, created new cultural agents of social transformation. African American men, as racialized subjects excluded from citizenship, made significant strides in popular sport. Their desire and exuberance for engaging in popular sport differed from that of white men. When schools did not educate their minds, when employers refused to give them jobs, and when vigilante mobs lynched their bodies, African American men wholeheartedly made use of other opportunities wherever they came. One such opportunity was using their bodies in popular sport symbolically to claim a stake against institutional and cultural racism.

C. L. R. James, an avid player and critic of West Indies cricket, understands better than most the power of playing sport in the face of racial exclusion. He eloquently describes in *Beyond a Boundary* the significance of race, class, and popular sport by analyzing local West Indies culture within the hierarchy of colonialism. James's extraordinary analysis interrogates the ways in which marginal men remasculinized their sense of lost humanity, essentially their lost manhood, through playing cricket. He writes about the formation of self-determination and freedom, once-forgotten ideas in a culture of skewed rules and dehumanization: "The class and racial rivalries were too intense. They could be fought out without violence or much lost except pride and honor. Thus the cricket field was a stage on which selected individuals played representative roles which were charged with social significance."[23] The cricket field contested British hegemony by creating a cultural space of respect and dignity, using the bodily ritual of physical performance. Thus, C. L. R. James and his teammates demanded with their bodies and minds a politicized and racialized sense of dignity and respect by playing games, a way to hold their heads high. The remasculinization of black bodies for James illustrated the defeat of their colonial masters at their own game, where the rules applied equally to all. Likewise, popular sport in the twentieth-century United States was a critical cultural practice to examine the ways in which minority men used their bodies to confront institutional and cultural barriers to full citizenship. It offered them an alternative means to conceptualize being human, of being a man, mainly in response to the processes of racialization and exclusion from political, economic, and cultural life. Legacies of genetic or cultural inferiority, long the workings of irrational systems of colonialism, were widely held beliefs, maintained to propagate the intellectual, physical, and spiritual inferiority of racialized men.

A survey of black masculinity in popular sport provides a rich, varied history of black radicalism as it contested and overturned these prevailing myths. Indeed, the impact of black radicalism in motion has formed alternative narratives of citizenship and national belonging for men of color. This demand for recognition cannot be underestimated. When Jesse Owens imploded Hitler's propaganda regarding superior Aryan stock in the 1936 Berlin Olympics, his triumph was a watershed for African American men excluded from membership in other spheres of American life due to de facto segregation. Likewise, Joe Louis, the great black heavyweight champion who followed Jack Johnson, created immense racial pride for the African American community when he defeated the white boxer Max Baer. Richard Wright wrote in "Joe Louis Uncovers Dynamite" that Louis's victory refuted "the theory that Negroes are inferiors who inevitably fail when they match skill or knowledge with whites."[24]

No one more than Jackie Robinson embodied the wholesale rejection of black inferiority when he shattered the color line in Major League Baseball on April 18, 1946. His groundbreaking entry into the big leagues spawned intense media publicity by television shows, nonfiction books, and newspaper articles. After Robinson's grand debut, a writer for the *New York Amsterdam News* wrote:

> Thus the most significant sports story of the century was written into the record books as baseball took up the cudgel for democracy and an unassuming Negro boy ascended the heights of excellence to prove the rightness of the experiment. And prove it in the only correct crucible for such an experiment—the crucible of white hot competition.[25]

Clearly, to participate in popular sport for black men was to participate in American democracy. Manhood became symbolized by base hits, slam dunks, and knockout punches, on level playing fields. Additionally, Muhammad Ali relished his newfound opportunity in the 1960s not only to perform arias of physicality in the boxing ring but also to stand up for political issues. Ali exemplified the fullest expression of popular sports' promise as a cultural institution of social change when he used his mass platform to fight for political causes including the plight of poor blacks in America, anti-imperialism in Vietnam, and interracial solidarity during the Black Power movement.

The Civil Rights Movement and identity-based social movements fundamentally changed the tenor of race. In the post–civil rights era, black men have completely displaced the white male body, once the icon of physical and mental superiority, as the exclusive ideological signifier of athletic superiority. Popular sport is a mass cultural institution that embodies the new racial formation in America in which whiteness has reconstituted itself by being less reliant on ocular displays of power. Michael Omi says: "The prospect that whites may not constitute a clear majority or exercise unquestioned racial domination in particular institutional settings has led to a *crisis of white identity*. In this respect, whites have been racialized in the post–civil rights era."[26] Babe Ruth, Mickey Mantle, and Joe DiMaggio, as icons of white masculinity, personified the rugged, working-class ethic that the nation's eyes turned to for heroes and for paragons of proper national masculinity. Today, Michael Vick, LeBron James, and Derek Jeter are among the many examples of black men who have supplanted white men as objects of hero worship. The transformation of popular sport from white, working-class heroes to black sports icons reminds us that cultural critics must retheorize the trajectories and circuits of national culture, citizenship, and power.[27]

From the 1970s to present day, the conflation of black men and athletic performance has become common currency in our representational and material life. It conjures up notions of physicality and blackness, often stereotypically embodying wealth, glamour, and the fashionably hip. Yet Harry Edwards reminds us that "the disproportionately high number of black athletes in sports at all levels, and their domination of these endeavors is due to white racism in the general society."[28] Because of this circumstance, black men "often utilize sports as one means of masculine self-expression within an otherwise limited structure of opportunity."[29] Popular sport offered a way out for black bodies from police surveillance, urban ghettos, and economic destitution. The black body signified ambivalence over the meanings attached to success and poverty, freedom and confinement. But it definitely conjured up in the national imaginary powerful conceptions of what kinds of activities black men excelled in (and what they did not). Racializing popular sport as a black space of hope erased the contradictions of wealth distribution, class antagonism, and the property system. Yet, it was also a space of desire in which white boys now wanted to be black. The black male body came to dominate celebrity and hero worship, an identificatory process creating what Norman Mailer once coined "the white negro"; or, to use a famous slogan from a popular sports drink, everyone wants to "Be Like Mike." But in that process of idolization, reducing black men as only the body revealed the problems inherited from raciological thinking. Paul Gilroy writes in *Against Race*: "As actively de-politicized consumer culture has taken hold, the world of racialized appearances has become invested with another magic . . . that [has] added a conspicuous premium to today's planetary traffic in the imagery of blackness."[30] Gilroy explains that the "planetary traffic in the imagery of blackness" depends upon race and bodily difference. Shaquille O'Neal, Lennox Lewis, Kobe Bryant, and Barry Bonds each generate at least ten million dollars annually in earnings from appearances and product endorsements, appear in hundreds of newspaper stories, and brandish their faces on global magazine covers. As such, Gilroy's postmodern aesthetic reveals the traffic of blackness to be firmly within global capital, whereby "the old hierarchy is being erased," presumably the structure of capitalist culture reliant on white male bodies for its perpetuation.[31] Nevertheless, the "old hierarchy" seems to have a resilient life, constantly reappearing in different guises and shapes. Cultural ideologies of masculinity and race persistently tied racialized bodies to colonial discourses that had created racial hierarchies tied to sexuality and the male body. Of course, these taxonomies of the body have their legacies in slave empires, colonial conquest, and imperialism. Meanwhile, residual stereotypes of male bodies remain as residual cultural formations that keep racial hierarchy persistently intact. Moreover, the reliance on black masculinity for the sustenance of transnational sport has moored the key concept of racial fetishism in stereotypes of the black male body.

In *Welcome to the Jungle*, Kobena Mercer describes the fetishization of the black male body and its reliance on stereotypes of the body and sexuality. Mercer explains that "blacks 'fit' into this terrain by being confined to a narrow repertoire of 'types'—the supersexual stud and sexual 'savage' on the one hand, or the delicate, fragile and exotic 'oriental' on the other."[32] Mercer allows us to understand, by looking at Robert Mapplethorpe's photography, the reduction of the black male body as sexual object, as a reified body that effaces the material process involved in the production of the image.[33] Indeed, the overdetermination of the black male body as the embodiment of colonial sexual fantasies reveals the idolization of Otherness. During the 1990s, some evolutionary discourses utilized "Mongoloid," "Caucasoid," and "Negroid" categories, first employed by eugenicist scientists a century earlier looking for the Holy Grail of racial taxonomy to schematize physicality, mentality, and behavior. As social service programs contracted during Bill Clinton's presidency, intelligence and race as well as academic performance and sexual behavior became controversial topics in popular books such as *The Bell Curve*; *Race, Evolution, and Behavior: A Life History Perspective*; and *Taboo: Why Black Athletes Dominate Sports and Why We're Afraid to Talk About It*.

According to these arguments, genes rather than social conditions explained the racial divide and class divisions in society. This was a modern-day rehashing of colonial-era scientific racism. Erasing institutional culpability, ranging from affirmative action to school vouchers to welfare safety nets, the redux of gene discourses ignored contextualizing poverty, cultural depravity, and other societal ailments as factors in deindustrialization and the crisis state. Furthermore, think tanks and neo-eugenicists created a well-funded backlash that was a fundamental part of neoconservative attacks on multiculturalism and its dividends: affirmative action policies, declining white male privilege, panethnic solidarity, and racial diversity in culture.[34] Robyn Wiegman has called this development the "politics of visibility," a term that describes viewing diverse representations as multiculturalism's end game.

In *Taboo: Why Black Athletes Dominate Sports and Why We're Afraid to Talk About It*, journalist Jon Entine tries to prove the myth of black physicality. He invokes whites, blacks, and Asians in making a general observation about athletic demographics. His specious argument displays the remarkable staying power of racial hierarchy and the biological trace, and the ways in which visual culture plays a dominant role in its reproduction. Entine remarks:

Asians, who constitute 57 percent of the world's population, are virtually invisible in the most democratic of world sports, running, soccer, and

basketball. . . . In the mid-1960s the racial breakdown in the National Basketball Association (NBA) was 80 percent white, 20 percent black; today
it's almost exactly reversed. . . . White running backs, cornerbacks, or wide
receivers in the NFL? Count them on one hand.[35]

Entine's comment "virtually invisible" tells us that visual evidence, what the
eye can see and discriminate, the *representational effect* of racial thinking,
is the litmus test for hard science. But that visual evidence correlates with
common sense, what everyone supposedly thinks but no one talks about.
This type of commentary represents the traces of colonial taxonomies, the
ever-present legacy of biological explanations of race. As Wiegman says, the
symbolic value given to the power of looking had been the superficial gaze
upon which white supremacy connotes a whole host of racial meanings in
which pigmentation of the skin unlocks the racial objects' innermost development. Visual culture and its attendant human taxonomy supposedly have
revealed such inner developments of human bodies.[36]

Offering a more graphic example, in *Race, Evolution, and Behavior: A Life
History Perspective*, J. Philippe Rushton sets out an ambitious project to map
the complex associations among intelligence, brain size, and physical endow-
ments.[37] Schematizing the male body by quantifying individual traits such as
aggressiveness, strength of sex drive, anxiety, and rule following, he tries to
legitimate the relative characteristics of Asians (he uses the term "Oriental"),
whites, and blacks. A racial hierarchy that scaffolds into a triangle emerges
where Asians are classified as having the largest brains and smallest genitalia, whites ranked in the middle, and blacks last in intelligence and largest in
genitalia. Thus, to speak of the physicality of black men is to speak of their
superiority as brutes, separating the skin and body from the intellect, or, as
Eldridge Cleaver calls it, the embodiment of "Brute Power" where "society
is deaf, dumb, and blind to his mind."[38] To speak of the physicality of Asian
American men is to speak of their invisibility, distinguishing the mind from
(body) matter in a negative dialectic of absence, or what Richard Fung identifies as "Looking for My Penis."[39]

Invisibility can exist in minority masculinities, perhaps similar to Ralph
Ellison's scene of the "Battle Royal" in *Invisible Man* where racialized physicality is put on display, but it is made transparent by the gaze of those watching and those blinded. Stuart Hall has described the splitting of the imperial
eye that manufactures stereotypes as dependent on dual representations of
sexual and bodily difference.[40] He describes these dual representations as
"both a nostalgia for an innocence lost forever to the civilized, and the threat
of civilization being over-run or undermined by the recurrence of savagery,
which is always lurking just below the surface; or by an untutored sexuality

threatening to break out."[41] Not only have colonial discourses produced dialectical representations of race within racial groups, for example the savage beast and the impotent house slave, but they have also relied upon the politics of antiblackness for the maintenance of racial hierarchy. Popular sport then can be a crucial site from which to interrogate the logic and fixity of this raciological system.

This context is important in order to understand the significance of the entry of Asian sports stars into a predominately black, racialized cultural space. The symmetry of racial stereotypes of the body is quite appealing, because the logical structure is seemingly supported by visual evidence. To be sure, my key interest in mapping this hierarchy is to illustrate its tectonic fragility, the tenuous ground that relies upon ocular common sense to maintain its coherence. In this way, Yao Ming and Ichiro Suzuki have entered the world of popular sport in which the meanings associated with the male body and physicality are firmly moored to the way the black male body has been racialized as a figure of colonial phantasmagoria. Yet, the Asian male body reveals the contingency of hierarchical ideology, the main circulatory agent of stereotypes. Homi Bhabha has suggested: "An important feature of colonial discourse is its dependence on the concept of fixity in the ideological construction of otherness."[42] Otherness in popular sport relies upon visual culture, the television broadcast, the print ad, the bedroom poster, the images seared in our collective mind.

If Yao and Ichiro were merely ordinary players or even all-star caliber, then their presence to the skeptic may seem trite or even analogous to tokenism. However, their prominence as the leading faces of marketing in basketball and baseball, respectively, and their popularity as legitimate cultural icons suggest that we should not underestimate their value. Neither their revenue-generating capabilities nor their immense physical skills fully illustrate their impact on the study of postnational racial formations. If we are to believe Maurice Merleau-Ponty and later R. W. Connell's assertions that who we are and how we relate to the world centers on our bodies, then representations of Yao and Ichiro break down the fixity of racial bodily classifications.[43] The concept of articulation enables us to understand the arbitrary closure of assigned meanings that link the male body to racialized stereotypes. Articulation in Stuart Hall's definition has a pragmatic double denotation. On the one hand, to articulate means to utter, to speak forth, to organically express. On the other hand, in Hall's Great Britain, local dialect speaks of an articulated lorry (semitrailer): a truck for which the front (cab) and back (trailer) can be linked but not indispensably; the two parts are connected to each other at a specific juncture that can be broken.

The theory of articulation allows both a way of interpreting how ideological elements organically manifest under particular conditions, to link together within a discourse, and a means of asking how they do or do not become articulated, at certain junctures, to distinct political subjects.[44] There is no necessary belongingness to racial stereotypes because they are purely ideological, established in the service of power and hegemony. The connection that binds racial hierarchy to minority masculinities is arbitrary, the signification of which transforms through cultural practice. As both cultural and political subjects, pioneers such as Ichiro and Yao have great impact on the cultural legitimacy of Asian Americans and, in particular, Asian American masculinity. In so doing, they undermine not only the racialization of Asian American men but also the racialization of Asian Americans in general as alien outsiders unable to appeal to mainstream America.

The 2001 Major League Baseball All-Star Game illustrates the reworking of masculinity and transnational capital on baseball's grand stage. The All-Star Game is an event that allows MLB to represent itself as a national event, to display its stars, and to promote meritocracy where baseball's stars shine. While athletes like Cal Ripken Jr. and Wade Boggs represent a throwback to baseball's past, with its white, male, and blue-collar ethic, international stars like Ichiro represent baseball's future of internationalization and global multiculturalism. This is not to claim that baseball has progressed beyond an often dehistoricized and depoliticized imagination. Safeco Field in Seattle, the site of the 2001 All-Star game, is a "throwback" stadium, built in the style of old ballparks with the addition of luxury boxes, which cities continue to build as "new-old" ballparks.

As Ichiro made his All-Star debut at the new nostalgic ballpark, his relatively short (five feet nine) and relatively small (160 pounds) body is a marker of his Asianness, a racial trope of physical size situated in racialized bodies. His body performs a particular masculinity in the national imaginary, in part praised by mainstream media for cultural values embedded in tropes of Asian American racialization including his quiet, unassuming persona as well as his work ethic, determination, and physical talents. Yet, Ichiro capitalized his talent, his batting title, his arm strength, and his revered eye-hand coordination that made people stop in their tracks and watch his performance as an eye-riveting spectacle. In *Subculture: The Meaning of Style*, Dick Hebdige argues that subcultures are "pregnant with significance."[45] Reading the gestures, movements, signs, styles, and speech of Asian sport icons shows us how the physical links with the symbolic and the ways in which this articulation impacts the political and social formation of proper national manhood.

Ichiro plays the game at his own tempo, which forces the opposition to make serious adjustments. His speed on the bases, velocity with the bat, arm strength, defense and amazing hitting ability all shift the opposition out of their comfort zone and put them firmly on the defensive. Pitchers must change up their "out" pitch because Ichiro hits anything, anywhere. Infielders must rush and hurry their throws. Defensively, Ichiro's arm gets respect—base runners are stuck with singles, and if they attempt to stretch out a double, they end up in an Ichiro highlight reel. Each at-bat is a singular experience, a discrete time capsule that reveals Ichiro's perceptive powers of seeing the moving baseball. His style of play produces alternative conceptions of baseball physicality apart from that of the stereotypical baseball player who bulks up and tries to blast the ball for a home run. Indeed, his style is his alterity, relying less on home runs (although he has surprising power) and more on the nuances of the game, the steals, throwing assists, and on-base percentage. Thus, his lead-off batting position, arguably the most important hitting position in baseball, establishes the scoring opportunities a team may have. Ichiro won the American League batting title in his rookie year, astonishing even his most ardent critics, because, in short, it is not supposed to happen that way.

For the Seattle Mariners, Ichiro represented a $27 million dollar bargain, a phenomenal hitter with a sprinter's speed and a rock star's allure. His masculinity appeals to a diverse set of people that cuts across nationality and race. His popularity specifies for Asian American communities a sense of belonging as redemptive insiders and not forever foreigners. Japanese Americans carry the collective sin of Pearl Harbor. When Ichiro hits the baseball better than anyone else, he has the redemptive power to make an entire community feel better about itself. Stephen Sumida amusingly said: "A few weeks ago, the minister asked, who is it we turn to for all our hopes and blessings? And the congregation answered with about maybe 75 percent saying Jesus, and the 25 percent saying Ichiro."[46] His cultural impact reveals the ways in which the particularity of Japanese American racialization works off the transpacific migration of a diasporic son that ironically tethers the racial formation of Japanese Americans to Japanese nationals. Asian American men have cultural heroes such as Bruce Lee or Jackie Chan, but that type of masculinity carries the veneer of exoticism and foreignness. Moreover, the physicality of martial arts, though considered masculine for its violence, does not carry the weight of popular sports' mass appeal.

Despite coming from Japan, Ichiro has dominated in America's quintessential game, his superb skills making him the most popular player in the 2001 All-Star balloting. Albert G. Spalding said it best when he proclaimed the appeal of baseball as the cultural institution of nation building and capitalist modernity: "American Courage. Confidence. Combativeness; American Dash. Discipline, Determination; American Energy. Eagerness, Enthusiasm; American Pluck, Persistence, Performance; American Spirit, Sagacity. Success; American Vim, Vigor, Virility."[47] Baseball not only allegorizes the U.S. nation-state, it also encompasses the redemptive space the nation-state turned to for collective cultural solace after the trauma of September 11, 2001. Indeed, Ichiro has created a unique form of hero worship in a quintessentially American popular sport, usually set aside for other megastars known only by their first names, because baseball symbolizes the progress of American modernity.

Safeco Field is a social space entangled with meanings over Americana, today's multiculturalism, and transnational sport. In a city and region embedded with the history of Japanese internment, Ichiro's masculinity references not only African American segregation in baseball but also anti-Asian violence in Seattle. Earlier on, I detailed Japanese American internment during World War II and the racial prejudices that followed it in the Pacific Northwest. More recently, Seattle's Asian community felt a backlash when Japanese-owned Nintendo bought the Seattle Mariners in 1992. In a marked turn celebrating Seattle's vanguard role in developing multiculturalism, Ichiro walked out of the dugout at the beginning of the 2001 All-Star Game, embraced as Seattle's own, to a standing ovation while introduced with a hip-hop soundtrack. The game was Ichiro's coronation as sport internationalism's key player, but also as the first legitimate Asian male superstar accepted by white America.

It was only fitting that hip-hop, the music that was once the voice of urban black youth filled the ears of well-to-do Seattle yuppies as Ichiro tipped his cap in appreciation of their adulation and cheers.[48] Hip-hop has blown up, traversing geographies of time and space on a global level. Likewise, Ichiro's iconography, framed as the poster child for the internationalization of baseball, is the reified body co-opted to promote baseball as a twenty-first-century game. Asian and white kids cried out "I-CHI-RO" while Fox Television's white broadcasters explained his impact on baseball with his MVP statistics, his .350 batting average and fifty-six steals, the hard Enlightenment science of aficionados.[49] The chalked lines on the playing field, the fence that separates players from fans, those who work in concessions and those who own teams, represent the racial geography of Safeco Field. It is a liminal space where consumer culture meets masculine performance and perhaps illustrates Marx's idea of epiphenomena, the synthesis of material and ideological structures. In this way, the ballpark is a boundary that regulates class and race, a space of work, leisure, desire, and profits.

The All-Star Game is the culmination of MLB's quest to put its stars on center stage for a world audience, where the game embodies the national project of meritocracy (individualism), belonging (patriotism), and civilization (sportsmanship) as well as internationalizing broadcasting, licensing, and sponsorship. In the opening inning, Ichiro blasted a one-hundred-foot single in his first at bat, then demonstrated his speed to first base, which is often compared to that of fleet-footed black ballplayers. His masculinity before his arrival had been questioned, but, by the time of the 2001 All-Star Game, "already his success has killed, once and for all, the long-held conceit that a small Japanese player . . . would be overwhelmed in the major leagues."[50] There seems to have been questions concerning Ichiro's power and size, the kind of imperial masculinity popular sport embodies during the Pax Americana of today. Yet, his ability to dominate without excessive displays of strength and brute force has endeared him to a public desiring physical performances that differ from those of home run specialists. In a sport dominated by power, overdosed on steroids and muscle-bound hulks, Ichiro is a contact hitter who happens to be the game's most popular player with the most hits and a plethora of endorsement deals.

Clearly, it seems that Ichiro's performance and appeal embody Asian American racialization and at once transition baseball from the days of segregation to global multiculturalism, thus consolidating the Pacific Rim markets tied to MLB sports internationalism. Replacing Seattle's revered baseball sons Ken Griffey Jr. and Alex Rodriguez, Ichiro expanded the Mariners' franchise, enabling Seattle to be one major point along the Pacific Rim circuit. Connecting the local and global, Ichiro signed endorsement deals with Cutter & Buck, a Seattle-based golf sportswear company, and the Mizuno Corporation, Japan's largest sporting-goods company.[51] However, Ichiro's ascent has drawn criticism from the league he left, the Japanese leagues that hinged upon national affiliations and racial homogeneity. Drawing comparisons to Jackie Robinson's departure from the Negro leagues, Ichiro leaving his old team, the Orix Blue Wave of Japan's Pacific League, has raised alarm about Japanese baseball.[52] This development, however, seems to have recodified the league and not the product. Ichiro and his Mariners were broadcast daily: all eighty-one home games and package deals were available to Japanese and Japanese American fans, and the club inaugurated a worldwide farm system. What I call the "Ichiro Effect" has reverberated, in large measure, to how globalizing popular sport promotes greater profits as well as how national affiliations are reworked in multiple and complex ways. As the All-Star balloting became global, making its way through all parts of the planet, MLB International's broadcasting, sponsorship, and licensing agreements require, in effect, that global multiculturalism capitalize on racialized men. However, this process plays off profound contradictions including the deepening gap in global wealth as well as the entrenchment of raciological thinking, including the entrenchment of the ever-present biological trace.

Ichiro's entry into MLB, both his record-breaking performance on the field and global marketing off of it, knows no limits to time, geography, or media. Highlighting the merits of multiculturalism, the Seattle Mariners boasted players from around the world, including a starting pitcher from Venezuela, a designated hitter from Puerto Rico, and a closing pitcher and (until 2012) MVP right fielder from Japan. Four out of ten players on Major League teams were born outside the United States, and the Seattle Mariners have signed their first Russian and Chinese prospects. Total viewership of MLB's World Series has reached more than one hundred million spectators, including almost one million U.S. armed forces personnel stationed in 175 international territories and on naval ships. Included in this global extravaganza is the planning of "multicultural celebrations" including Fiesta de Primavera in Mexico City, Choques de Estrellas in Venezuela, and the Radio Shack Opening Day in San Juan, Puerto Rico. Global multiculturalism binds Asians and blacks into a coherent narrative of the U.S. racial state's progress and veils the deep class contradictions of big-league baseball. It signals an important shift that ties the post–civil rights racialization of black athletes to the legacy of the color line in sports. In this concluding section, I look at a particular genealogy that baseball narratives establish, one that ties racial discrimination and segregation in baseball to the promise of global multiculturalism and diversity.

Major League Baseball International formed in 1989 to promote the internationalism of America's pastime, focused "on the worldwide growth of baseball through game development, broadcasting, special events, sponsorship, and licensing."[53] Boasting forty corporate sponsors—household names such as Anheuser-Busch, American Airlines, MasterCard, and Pepsi—MLB International also has broadcasting agreements in 224 countries and territories and all seven continents, including Antarctica. In the organization's 2001 Annual Report, Ichiro was the key figure promoting MLB global multiculturalism. He is the face of a multicultural future that moves away from the past segregation of African Americans. MLB International promotes baseball as the cultural institution that exemplifies the progression of race relations in the post–civil rights era while at the same moment glorifying the imperial reach of U.S. popular culture. Ichiro's image is the model representative of baseball's internationalization, but the move from America's pastime to the world's multicultural leisure activity represents two separate and wholly unequal breakthroughs in race relations. The narrative of racial pioneering in discrete historical contexts conflates Ichiro Suzuki's internationalization and Jackie Robinson's desegregation. Ichiro's racial transcendence seemingly answers Robinson's call for racial equality within the construct of a global multiculturalism that privileges racelessness rather than race consciousness, all the while making the once political—black radicalism in popular sport—actively long forgotten.

In a 2001 advertising campaign by MLB International entitled "Connect with It," one thirty-second television spot features a variety of images and traditional themes cut together, linking baseball's past, present, and future.[54] Showcasing a collage of visual representations and texts, "Connect with It" associates an image of Jackie Robinson with the phrase "with your heritage," adding "with history" in quick cuts, and equating "heaven" to a black-and-white newsreel of Yankee Stadium dubbed with scratchy radio commentary. Spliced after the image of Jackie Robinson in his Brooklyn Dodgers uniform, the text "with the world" cuts to an image of a little boy in a shantytown, shirtless and shorts tattered, hitting a baseball with a stick. His racial identity is ambiguous (Is he Latin? Is he of African descent?), and the message seems to suggest that poverty is made bearable if the boy plays baseball well; baseball makes whole and complete, erasing neoliberal policies that displace children into the streets. In the closing frames, shots of pitcher Pedro Martínez and a slight Asian female fan consummate the advertisement's racial multiculturalism and geographic diversity, harmonizing the transcendence of race with the transcendence of space. In fact, the movement in historical time and geographic space, illustrated by Yankees nostalgia and Jackie Robinson's breakthrough career, parallels the global internationalism that Asian male athletes promote. Global multiculturalism measures progress not in terms of social equality but, rather, in terms of the penetration of global capitalism.

By connecting Jackie Robinson and Ichiro Suzuki, the advertisement suggests that abolishing racial segregation in baseball mirrors the expansion of sport internationalism. The advertisement seems to evince that baseball's racialization weighs equally to internationalizing markets. This promotes MLB International's conflation of difference, promoting "Connect with It." As one executive suggests: "People mark time by baseball. . . . We want to celebrate those deep connections to get fans in seats, fans buying products, corporate sponsors and more viewing of our television programs. . . . This game is all about bringing people together in many forms through personal connections, through statistics, through stories, through purchasing apparel."[55] What "deep connections" are and what "it" connotes leaves much ambiguity. Nevertheless, it may be surmised that Ichiro's breakthrough, showcased by physicality and spectacle, illumines the complex ways in which Asian American masculinity works, earmarking the genealogy of baseball time from black protest to sports internationalism. Moreover, it may be apparent then, discerned from the linkage connecting Asian bodies, global marketing, and black radicalism, that Ichiro embodies and sutures these separate elements nicely together.

When Yao Ming emigrated from Shanghai, his transmigration was reminiscent of the panda bear Wei Wei. Wei Wei was the first goodwill ambassador from Communist China before that country's open embrace of capitalism under Deng Xiaoping. With that un-Maoist turn, Yao Ming bargained with and worked out for NBA scouts and general managers. This remarkable concession by Beijing allowed for the selection of Yao Ming as the Houston Rockets' first pick in the 2001 NBA Draft Lottery. The Houston Rockets hit the proverbial jackpot, and they quickly assembled a campaign strategy, bunkered down in their corporate war room and coming up with slogans such as "Remember the last time the Rockets picked No. 1?" Good question: the answer, of course, is Hakeem Olajuwon—the Nigerian-born superstar who delivered two championships in 1994–1995 and opened the African continent to NBA internationalism. Celebrated as the Rockets' top pick in 2001, Yao seemed to have captured the collective imagination of Houstonians when they exclaimed his arrival as the second coming of Olajuwon. Houston had lacked a successful professional football or baseball franchise in recent memory, and the redux of Olajuwon in the personification of Yao, along with his immigration into the NBA and the ensuing citywide fever that soon followed, developed a special name—Yaomania. Presently, the NBA has expected Yao Ming, even in retirement, to open the Asian continent to basketball and thus Western consumerism, fulfilling the dream of former NBA commissioner David Stern: "Yao Ming is attuned to the globalization of our sport."[56]

In an October 2002 issue of *Sports Illustrated*, an ESPN advertisement presents Yao to the American public. Marketing ABC/ESPN's 2.4 billion dollar television contract with the NBA, Yao was made the spokesperson for the globalization of professional basketball in the post–Michael Jordan era. In the ad, he sleeps in a child's bunk bed, hands nestled under a pillow, eyes closed shut, and soft comforter keeping him warm. Yet, something is awry in the picture. His body, all seven feet five inches, 296 pounds, extends beyond the bed frame, causing his size-twenty-two feet to dangle like miniature tugboats over the edge.[57] This humorous representation, as part of the marketing circuits of visual sport culture, depicts the Asian male body as half-man and half-spectacle. It juxtaposes Yao's body in an infantilized space and produces an affective and visual force centered on a contradiction framed within post–civil rights racialization; the representation of his body challenges stereotypes of Asian male bodies as physically diminutive and athletically unrepresented. Significantly, memorabilia of black masculinity—Kareem Abdul-Jabbar's trading card, "Iceman" George Gervin's poster, and Dr. J's pennant—mark the walls. Clearly, their prominence references the ideological dominance of black players in the NBA and, generally speaking, the cult of black male hero worship in popular culture. They signify the NBA as racially black, sexually heteronormative, and nationally American. Thus, the advertisement, in its frozen depiction of Asian and black masculinity, constitutively links the black and Asian body. In this sense, the racialization of the black male body produces conceptions of heroic, athletic masculinity and mediates the meanings associated with the Asian male body.[58]

Yao played the center position in basketball, the premier point in the NBA, known as the "one slot" because it is the prime focus in team play. Historically, black centers occupy a special place in our collective memory: Bill Russell, Wilt Chamberlain, and Shaquille O'Neal, to name a few, inspire sublime images of blackness because of their enormous size and championship heroics. Black centers reveal, by way of their extremity, that notions of excess—their height, weight, and black skin—equate to physical domination of others. Unlike other professional sports, basketball is a game suited to represent images of the black body with its emphasis on visual intimacy. There is a clear identification with players' faces, expressions, muscles, and skin color. Lacking football's and baseball's helmets and full uniforms, basketball's shorts and tank tops emphasize the visual realm, in particular the skin, and thus the sport is "perfectly suited to define American culture because of the ease with which it is represented through the media."[59] Moreover, basketball is the game associated with the street and hip-hop music, where Sundays at New York's Rucker Park and Public Enemy lyrics like "throwing it down like Barkley" are common crossover moves in popular culture. Approximately 80 percent of its practitioners being black men, basketball has been at the center of formative discourses of race and masculinity. Think for example of two commonly known stereotypes centered on basketball, race, and the body: all black men can play basketball, and white men can't jump. For Yao to enter this cultural milieu, his Brobdingnagian body and athletic performance seem to complicate the easy reduction of racial hierarchy that erases the Asian male body and fetishizes blackness.

Celebrating the dawn of Yaomania, a Houston Rockets poster contains a photograph of Hakeem Olajuwon dunking a basketball. Above him reads the aforementioned slogan, "Remember the last time the Rockets picked No. 1?"

Yao is the heir apparent to Olajuwon, and this employment follows the desire of the city of Houston to place itself as a world city. Boasting a multicultural population akin to Los Angeles and in particular a large Asian American population, Houston as the urban center of Yaomania makes perfect sense. For one thing, the transition from a black male center to an Asian male center represents the increase of foreign players in the NBA, while some media has cast black players as frontline troops protecting an American cultural institution. The discourse of race in professional basketball revolves around its urban roots, its street credibility that produces conceptions of masculinity linked to urban decay and police surveillance. On the other hand, Olajuwon's unorthodox style, his soccer-inspired footwork and multiple post moves, is indicative of Yao's original style of play.

Like Ichiro, Yao personifies a new cultural formation in Asian America because he is a pioneer. Yet, more than Ichiro, his status as a dominant center in the league hinged on the way in which his body came across under so much media exposure and scrutiny. Apple Computers placed him in an advertisement with Verne Troyer, the actor who played the sidekick Mini-Me in the Austin Powers movies. Visa, the credit card company, paid one million dollars for a thirty-second spot during the Super Bowl that featured Yao with an African American woman dressed in hip-hop clothes. Both representations of his likeness use humor to signify his size and his foreignness—his otherness. Yet, it is his body and race that prefigure prominently in discourses of Asian masculinity, China as the next superpower, and the globalization of the NBA.

Yao's figuration of the Asian male body touches on several key issues and implications involving both the international geopolitics of global capitalism and the domestic arrangement of Afro-Asian racial hierarchy. First, Yao exemplifies the emergence of China in the world capitalist economy, mainly relying on export models of industrialization and production. Second, for Asian Americans, and like Ichiro, he ties the diasporic imaginary of Asian Americans back to their Asian origins but simultaneously inaugurates the cultural legitimacy of Asian American cultural visibility and pride. And finally, his promise as a cultural ambassador for global multiculturalism in the service of NBA sport internationalism hinged on his representational force vis-à-vis black masculinity in the NBA. In a sport always hungry for seven-footers, Yao has tree trunks for legs and that all-important (read: Jordanesque) smile. He played defense as a shot blocker, which, in basketball parlance, means that he played above the rim, swatting away shots by the likes of Allen Iverson. His skill level is not on par with, say, a Tim Duncan, or comparable to Ichiro in his sport, but it is his size that is significant, that height that goes against the commonsense logic of racial hierarchy. Nowhere is this disparity more apparent than in the media publicity that surrounded Yao and Shaq. The controversy surrounding their feud exhibits the intersections of race, multiculturalism, and the cultural implications of Afro-Asian racialization.

Shaquille O'Neal's unwise taunt toward Yao in 2001 created intense media scrutiny by focusing on political correctness and multicultural tolerance. The question posed by the media and activists was: when is an ethnic joke a joke and when is it not? O'Neal appeared in a television interview in June 2001, and his Superman tattoo could not protect him from the media scrutiny that followed after he uttered what he later called a prank statement. O'Neal said: "Tell Yao Ming, 'Ching chong yang wah ah soh,'"[60] while mimicking martial arts moves in front of the camera. Six months later on Fox Sports Radio, O'Neal's comments were replayed on the *Tony Bruno Morning Extravaganza*, initiating a response from the Asian American community. O'Neal's comment had referenced American orientalism in the NBA, drawing upon Chinese racialization as coolie labor and emasculation as feminized immigrants. However, beyond that, his remarks in the national media were defined as a linguistically insensitive play on the Chinese "sound." Aside from the construction of Chinese as verbally incoherent to an American audience, O'Neal's comment had represented Asian American masculinity as the "Ching Chong Chinaman." From Bret Harte to Fu Manchu to playground taunts, Asian American racialization framed the ways in which the NBA[61] racialized Yao. In this sense, racializing the labor of Asian male immigrants had been the logical structure that constructed the legibility of black masculinity.

O'Neal sneered at the fanfare devoted to Yaomania, claiming that he himself was "a working-class hero. That's all I am. Guys are trying to make a superstar out of a guy from the Shanghai Sharks, make a phenomenon out of him already."[62] O'Neal later remarked that his labor was similar to that of "the construction workers, the police officer, the firefighters." In staking out the terrain of the NBA as working class, O'Neal constructed that space not only as a conflation of Asian American racialization (domestic) and Yellow Peril orientalism (foreign) but also as a blue-collar ethic that relied on a construction of masculinity as power over finesse, blackness over Asian feminization. O'Neal's antipathy for the publicity machine that produced "Yaomania" had centered on claiming himself as the common American person, someone embodying the rugged individualism that has traditionally been the role of white men. By breaking the genealogy of America's tradition of heroic masculinity, from John Wayne to Mark McGwire, O'Neal's inscription of himself in that discursive space comes through "policing" the foreign Other. By claiming a working-class identity, O'Neal relied upon sports celebrities as representative of an American masculinity—hard working, humble, and physically endowed—that elided questions of racial difference.

In addition to the proletarianization of the NBA, O'Neal had staked out the league as quintessentially American, an identification that privileged national belonging by demarcating a racial and linguistic border. O'Neal said: "Don't give me nothing. Just give me my fair share in America, because I'm American." Yao's teammate Steve Francis has remarked about Yao that "[h]e's not like an American player," marking Yao's foreigner status.[63] Foreign players' exodus from other countries, especially from European countries such as the former Yugoslavia and Germany, produces an African American response that acts as the border patrol of "American" values, credibility, authenticity, and nationalism. Thus, the opening of the Western border to the Asian continent has engendered a form of "black patriotism" that equates Americanism to urban masculinity in the NBA.[64] O'Neal had prepared a welcome for Yao, stating: "Street, playing in a gym, shooting jumpers and all that . . . that's fine. But I'm street. I'm how to take a 'bow to your nose and (make you) think about what I'm going to do next time down."[65]

O'Neal's invocation of "street ball" encodes Yao's assimilation into the Americanized NBA, and violence is the marked difference of physicality between foreign and homegrown players. Street masculinity maintains the racial contours and establishes African American men in the NBA as "authentic" and "credible." It not only foregrounds African American men as thugs and enforcers but it also is the convention, basketball ethics that cannot be learned in the gym. Toughness then becomes the language to legitimate those players who can "take it" (an elbow to the face) and those players who cannot (wimps). What exactly "it" implies can be read as a rite of passage for foreign players, a sadomasochistic initiation that instills nationalism in the giver rather than the receiver, in which a "welcome to the league [is] a welcome to our country."[66] Power equates to African American masculinity, and their physicality maintains the legitimacy of national culture as xenophobic.

The Asian American community questioned O'Neal's racist comments but relied on the same racial hierarchy used by O'Neal. The mobilized Asian American community called for the NAACP to revoke O'Neal's Young Leaders Award and demanded a public apology from O'Neal. Petition letters sent to NBA commissioner David Stern, Asian American listservs, and various publications drew attention to the situation. The most noted commentary came from Irwin Tang, a guest columnist for *AsianWeek* magazine and research fellow at University of Texas at Austin. Tang's article "APA Community Should Tell Shaquille O'Neal to 'Come Down to Chinatown'" illustrated the frustration and anger felt by Asian Americans, particularly males, who had long been the objects of racist scorn and violence.[67] The article was the primary reason media interest had been sparked to what was, by then, an already forgotten comment by O'Neal. Tang writes:

> This comment, combined with Shaq's racist taunts are particularly disturbing, as Asian Pacific Americans often suffer racial taunts while being assaulted or physically intimidated. Nevertheless, Shaquille O'Neal is not a stupid brute. That is, he may be a brute, but he's not a stupid one.[68]

However, the framing of O'Neal's blackness, in particular as a "brute," racializes him by representations that rely on Asian America's racial and sexual anxieties about African American masculinity, vocality, and politics. This is not to suggest that criticism of O'Neal had not been warranted, but reproducing white racism and colonial discourses seems to suggest white supremacy's staying power.

In this case, black bodies are threatening, aggressive, and loud, depicting a version of black monstrosity as attacking the weak "silent minority." For this reason, it is necessary for Tang to remasculinize Asian America, and more specifically Chinatown, as a discursive space that can contain black aggression: "But I am calling Shaq out. Come on down to Chinatown, Shaq. You disrespect Asian America, and we will break you down."[69] Yet, Tang's Asian American political response frames around collectivizing space (Chinatown) and race (the Asian Pacific American community) and expresses an identity politics that defines political response, partly in terms of domination, violence, and submission. Reinscribing manhood, to "break" someone down, follows a patriarchal and reactionary path on which "space" will domestically contain "race." Chinatown, then, can be read as a rhetorical location to subdue the black brute, and the journalist's role is not to establish new rules of performing and discussing masculinity but rather to play by the old ones. The result is that Tang does not challenge the racist and sexist representations of Asian and black men. Rather, he relies on both in order to achieve his point.

Calling O'Neal's comments an offensive slur, various Asian American political and community groups mobilized to seek an official apology. National organizations such as the National Association of Asian Professionals (NAAAP), National Asian American Student Conference, Asian American Journalists Association, Organization of Chinese Americans, and Chinese American Political Association (CAPA) joined the list of groups seeking redress. But it was Internet mobilization across various websites including Asian-Nation.com, Goldsea.com, Yolk.com, AngryAsianMan.com, and many others that pressed the issue into a national forum. Although I cannot explore it fully here, I find it significant that several media and communicative outlets solidified the powerful response to black racism toward Asians, at the same time drawing attention to the ways in which the media constructs interest in a particular topic, and what they consider newsworthy and what they do not. Asian American mobilization called attention to why white racism toward blacks receives heavy press coverage and why Asian American injury from racism does not. This idea translates into constructing black masculinity as a politicized identity that Asian Americans both feared and desired.

Asian American organizations viewed O'Neal's racist humor and the media's lackluster coverage of it as a crisis in Asian American political and cultural voice.[70] Framing cultural voice around power and masculinity, visibility for Asian American interests had circumscribed the desire to remasculinize Asian American spatial and discursive space. For Yao to do well in a predominately "black men's game," which O'Neal equated to the "street," meant that Asian American mobilization framed its response by remasculinizing Chinatown (spatial) and media coverage (discursive). In many ways, inscribing Asian American masculinity in black cultural spaces had conceptualized an emasculated Asian American political voice that depended on hypermasculinized notions of strength, aggression, and political struggle.

O'Neal's and Yao's responses to each other both verbally—in the media— and physically—on the playing court—show how corporate multiculturalism facilitated the conciliation between the two. O'Neal's halfhearted apology to Yao, calling himself a "prankster," centered on the discourse of ethnic humor in the age of politically correct speech. Stating, "I think it was a 70–30 joke. 70 percent funny, 30 percent not funny. And this guy [Irwin Tang] is one of the 30 percent who thought it wasn't funny," O'Neal's refusal to acknowledge his racist taunt only reinforced the perception by Asian Americans that they could be the topic of racist jokes without media scrutiny. This mounted pressure created some national exposure. Television and radio shows such as *Talk Back Live* on CNN and *The Tavis Smiley Show* on National Public Radio debated the controversy within the frameworks of multiculturalism and political correctness.[71] The Yao-Shaq showdown on the basketball court on January 17, 2003, in Houston culminated the political controversy over O'Neal's racial taunts and the mobilized response by Asian American political groups. Not since Bird and Magic had a duel between two players drawn so much media coverage, impressively telecast to hundreds of millions of spectators worldwide.

Before the tip-off, David Stern stated in an interview that O'Neal's comments were "insensitive, although not intentionally mean spirited." Mediating the controversy before any irreparable harm had occurred, the NBA knew that the race question would obfuscate NBA transnationalism's color-blind rhetoric. Clearly, expanding the NBA internationally hinged on Yao Ming, but it also relied (and continues to rely) on foreign players' perceptions of equal treatment and nondiscrimination. The NBA has opened offices around the world, facilitated recognition of its elite clubs (e.g., the Chicago Bulls) and personal logos (Magic Johnson and Michael Jordan), and placed what Eric Hobsbawm calls "the global triumph of the United States and its way of life."[72]

Capitalists of Western consumerism salivate when thinking about penetrating China's market of 1.3 billion people—a largely untapped market with an already established sports infrastructure. For this reason, Yao has been the spokesperson for global NBA and key marketing strategies that make brands identifiable for multinational corporations including Nike, Gatorade, Adidas, Coca-Cola, Visa, and Apple Computers. Combining existing international and national broadcasts, global NBA contracted with regional television networks worldwide to telecast 150 NBA games. Thirty of these games showed Yao and the Houston Rockets, with his estimated debut viewership numbering around five hundred million basketball-happy fans.[73] To be sure, licensing, broadcasting, and corporate sponsorship, as with MLB International, have wide-eyed possibilities when initiated in China. In many respects, the journey of Yao to the NBA has been a journey of China's self-promotion to transnational corporate business, of the country's willingness to accept open borders and open markets. As one of the last but spectacularly most important markets in which multinational companies can find new revenue streams, China continued its program of liberalization to coincide with the 2008 Olympic Games in Beijing.[74]

In conclusion, I call attention to the showdown between Shaq and Yao in Houston as representing the on-court and off-court convergence between racial hierarchy, sports internationalism, and the masculinity of Asian and black men. Outside Houston's Compaq Center, Chinese American protesters demanded that O'Neal acknowledge his racist comments. Inside the sold-out arena, the rivalry continued between Shaq and Yao, who had established NBA basketball as the premier imported sport in Asia and on U.S. cable television. The performance on the playing court was frantic and furious, especially when Yao blocked Shaq's first three shots. In later media accounts, headlines such as "Yao set tone early," "Surviving Shaq makes Yao's night a success," and "Yao wins showdown with Shaq" highlighted the news stories about the game. By all measure, O'Neal was still the most dominant player in the league, but Yao gained respect because he had withstood the "American" style of play. Afterward, O'Neal said of Yao, "He's a classy guy. I look forward to playing him. He's a great player. It's another challenge for me."[75] Strange words from O'Neal, especially after the controversy, but one might assume that racial animosity among NBA players hinders the business of basketball. Now the jabs and jousting were not verbal but strictly left to the court. C. L. R. James said it best: "The American civilization is identified in the consciousness of the world with two phases of the development of world history. The first is the Declaration of Independence. The second is mass production."[76] In this sense, U.S.-based sports internationalism, under the specter of Chinese capitalism and mass factory production in Guangzhou and elsewhere, needs to meet the consumer base of Chinese spectators eager for Yaomania and its successors, yet without stirring up feelings of foreignization among patriotic African American basketball players. Global multiculturalism and transnational sport are the winners, but the losers are yet to be determined.

3. "I'm Michael Jackson, You Tito"

Kung-Fu Fighters and Hip-Hop Buddies in Martial Arts Buddy Films

In the cultural sphere of popular sports, the athletic bodies of Asian and black masculinity were scanned and commoditized, as colonial bodies had been before, for the expansion of global multiculturalism, at the same time that oppositional racialization from the discourse of genes became blurred. In this chapter, I turn to another dominant sphere of race, masculinity, and manhood—Hollywood studio productions—and concentrate on how urban culture becomes pop culture in national culture. In the post–civil rights era, urban culture, namely hip-hop, emerges from neoliberal abandonment and youth alienation, whereas the martial arts action genre evolved from Hong Kong film studios and anti-imperialist dramas. In this way, this chapter theorizes the transpacific cultural fusions between Asian martial artists and black hip-hop buddies, an Afro-Asian pairing that sutures the lead heroes to multiethnic audiences and creates an "oppositional gaze," a direct disavowal of racial magnetism. This chapter theorizes the relationship between Asian-black spectatorship and screen image, cinematic representation and social movement politics, and the function of racialized suture and the visual reception of martial arts buddy films.

On May 16, 1973, the martial arts films *Fists of Fury, Deep Thrust: The Hand of Death,* and *Five Fingers of Death* were ranked one, two, and three, respectively, in gross box office receipts.[1] This was the first time in U.S. popular cinema that foreign films dominated box office receipts and garnered mass audience appeal. Although discriminatory production codes existed in Hollywood, Saturday matinees and drive-in theaters across the country capitalized on kung-fu fever; blaxploitation and martial arts films were advertised together on theater billboards and played back-to-back. Such commercial and aesthetic articulations had been nonexistent in U.S. visual culture, especially representations of racialized men captivating the moviegoing imaginations of multiethnic audiences with a newly cultivated social movement consciousness. In the wake of the Black Power social movement, blaxploitation films such as *Black Belt Jones, Cleopatra Jones,* and *Super Fly* incorporated martial arts, showcasing the physical and mental powers of Afro-wearing superheroes who achieved racial equality or even social revolution. Cinematic representations impacted urban reception when famous black martial artists such as Moses Powell, Sōke Little John Davis, and Sabumnim David Herbert were inspired to train in several disciplines, eventually becoming masters of jiujitsu, kumite karate, tae kwon do, and hapkido.

In the martial arts cinema genre, the *Rush Hour* series and *Romeo Must Die* have wide appeal among minority communities and young audiences because they champion the underdog. First produced and marketed from its anti-colonialist heritage in Hong Kong, martial arts films still pack a punch today because of the figure of the lone hero, who in most stories has an ethical motive for his violent escapades. Yet, the genre also requires the hero to punish other racialized men, who in the filmic narrative must be represented as the real threat, committing violence and off-limits transgressions in front of the camera. Subsequently, the sinister work of white supremacy is then depicted as an apparition in the filmic narrative, spectral, mostly invisible, and forgotten. In the early days of kung-fu fever, the martial arts genre made its initial entry into U.S. markets through blaxploitation films and the cult icon Bruce Lee.[2] Despite orientalist fears and fantasies over caricatures including the wildly popular Fu Manchu and Charlie Chan, the charisma and physicality of Lee in kung-fu choreography immortalized him as a global star and sparked the commercial viability of the martial arts action flick. The genre that Lee catapulted into mainstream currency has recently been adapted to the standard buddy film format prevalent in Hollywood Westerns and 1980s action films. Martial arts buddy films have emerged as an important medium expressing cross-racial solidarity for possible subversive politics by crossing the prescriptions of racial magnetism. The coupling of a streetwise African American buddy with hip-hop credentials with an ethical martial arts hero with humble bravado has served notice to mainstream audiences and cultural critics alike that this genre, using the critical lens of race and masculinity, can also be a vehicle for wide-ranging antiracist and anti-imperialist critiques. Subsequently, in present-day mainstream Hollywood and independent cinema, the popularity of Chinese and Hong Kong directors, actors, productions, and aesthetics has brought to light traditions that are reshaping the cultural politics of race and masculinity in U.S. visual culture. Indeed, Jamaican recording artist Carl Douglas sang in 1974 that "everybody was kung-fu fighting," and this fascination with martial arts refracts not only through the global popularity of hip-hop consumerism and aesthetics but also, historically, through the relationship between visual culture, social movements, and alternative spectatorship.

Not surprisingly, the martial arts genre still packs a multi-million-dollar punch today because it mixes the cultural juggernaut of urban hip-hop with the physical spectacle of martial arts. Released in 2000, *Romeo Must Die* was distributed by Warner Brothers and grossed over $55 million in the U.S. market. Historically, Warner Brothers has been the premier studio and distributor of martial arts action films, with such noteworthy productions as *Enter the Dragon*. More than twice the latter's production costs, *Romeo Must Die* created a cottage industry of Jet Li movies that mixed his wushu talents with supporting casts of black "whipping boys." Previously, in 1998, *Rush Hour* had redefined the action and comedy genres with box office sales of over $140 million in U.S. gross receipts and over $240 million in total worldwide gross. In 2001, *Rush Hour 2* grossed $347 million, making it the most profitable installment in the series, and in 2007 *Rush Hour 3* amassed $257 million worldwide. *Rush Hour*'s distributor, New Line Cinema, created a franchise that would position Jackie Chan as the first Asian action hero in the lucrative Hollywood action/adventure film industry.

Call it then a merger where East meets Black, or, as W. E. B. Du Bois writes, "men who know want and hunger, men who have crawled." In present-day society, we see in popular film, music, and literature numerous cultural representations depicting Asian and black masculinity together. Insofar as culture mediates the process within which the individual in the private sphere becomes a citizen in the public sphere, films incorporating the buddy pair and martial arts genre such as the *Rush Hour* films and *Romeo Must Die*, musicians melding hip-hop and kung-fu iconography such as the Wu-Tang Clan and Fu-Schnickens, and television shows such as *Martial Law* and *Lost* have coalesced into the national culture by entering mainstream popular consumption and aesthetic appreciation.[3] The past invisibility of Asian film culture in the United States has now been replaced by a blossoming industry due to the fertile influence of a "Yellow Pacific," a phrasal play around Paul Gilroy's famous notion of the "Black Atlantic."[4] Never before has the international traffic of bodies, in this case "alien" imports, and the movement of free-flowing Pacific Rim capital produced such a dynamic proliferation in daily leisure practices and representations. In addition, professional sports has reinforced this diasporic fusion of hip-hop culture and kung-fu symbology, especially in basketball, where stars such as Allen Iverson regularly sport tattoos with Chinese calligraphy. Moreover, the Japanese phenom affectionately called Ichiro received the Most Valuable Player award in our national pastime, baseball, which has historically acted as a careful measure of the color bar in national politics. Indeed, *something* curious is in the air. By redefining Asian American masculinity, race, and citizenship, these social transformations have reconfigured and recoded the relations of force—the movement of cultural transformations in social and political terms.

Theorizations of the body, the woman of color, the invert, the octoroon, the transgender subject, to name a few, have forcefully critiqued dualistic thinking and exposed its fallacy, thereby allowing for human agency through the disidentification of normative common sense.[5] This chapter follows through with this important work and places it within that tradition. Yet also, this chapter reorients the discussion toward an evaluation of how martial arts buddy films as a critical space in culture mediate state formations and citizenship within transnational circuits and flows. Whereas previous invocations of the kung-fu fighter had borrowed the mythic figure in order to proclaim an Asian America cultural nationalism predicated on a patriarchal and heterosexual identity, this chapter directs our attention toward what Antonio Gramsci calls the point of condensation, a collapsed moment in history from which the knot of a particular time and place emerges from cultural expressions and political conditions.[6] This chapter theorizes this convergence in film analysis, in which state imperatives of rivalrous opposition and multiethnic citizenship claims merge and in which transnationalism and masculinity intersect. These Asian-black cultural formations derived from global movements have created a new structure in relation to masculinity and race in our increasingly interconnected world. Asian American masculinity is undergoing a transitory period in which it cannot be conceptualized without investigating its relation to other masculinities as well as global culture industries. Hong Kong martial arts productions and black urban culture are the narrative modalities in which these cultural formations have evolved in the wake of transformations in state-sponsored market democracy and the restructuring of neoliberal capitalism.

After the social movements of the 1960s and 1970s and the fall of the Berlin Wall in 1989, this relationship between historical context and these emergent cultural expressions can be understood in terms of the transition from the Cold War era of ethnic liberalism to the post–civil rights era of multicultural market democracy. The former is based on "melting pot" assimilation and domestic containment of certain perceived menaces including blacks, homosexuals, and communists whereas the latter is predicated on pluralism and difference.[7] In promoting the ideals of assimilation to the American creed either in ethnic or multicultural paradigms, citizen formation has been a process of racial formation through the supposed shedding of old skin: those cultural, linguistic, and racial markers that cannot be assimilated into the liberal paradigm without violence and exploitation.[8] The various radical social movements of the 1960s and 1970s had called into question the contradictions found in market democracy, with its incessant crises of racism, homophobia, and patriarchy. The processes that are involved in market democracy and its expansion include its attendant ideology of possessive individualism and the market economy.[9] Market democracy as an entrenched political ideology works in tandem with global capitalism, which has undergone a sea change in its capacity to expand to greater markets in both absolute and relative terms. The contradictions upholding market democracy differentiate between public and private life, civil society and the state, and the "natural rights of man" and the market economy.[10]

In exchange for security of self and property, individuals enter into a social contract with the nation-state in order to establish rules regarding sociality and economic life in civil society.[11] The nation-state is best described through its role in constructing categories of variegated citizenship. In Marx's "On the Jewish Question," the ruse of power of the bourgeois institution of the modern state, in promoting the doctrine of the "rights of man" into a category of universal abstract citizenship, has masked the division of labor and assumptions of private property within capitalist modes of production in civil society. This mechanism of repression in civil life, which occludes real human emancipation or what Marx terms "species-being" (the manifold human capacities for mental and physical life-sustaining energies), is artificially transcended in bourgeois terms as "political emancipation" through abstract citizenship granted by the state. In specific historical terms, the regulatory function of the state in constructing modern subjectivity is necessarily grounded upon both its form and its mutual dependence with civil society, where the two work inseparably reproducing social-economic divisions of labor, exchange value, commodity fetishism, and the extraction of surplus value from wage labor.[12] From the representational visibility of racialized men in national culture, does this relative acceptance mean that liberal society is gradually progressing toward a racial promised land, or do the plenitude of representations occlude the growing disparity in material wealth and access to resources in the post–civil rights era? In order for narrative modes of market democracy to succeed, its promises of equal opportunities and inclusion in the political and economic process must seem to be fulfilled in order for its legitimacy to be secured.

The growing cultural acceptance and profitability of Asian-black representations, spurred on by transformations in market democracy and capital, are a relational matter involving a continual process of formation and superseding "unstable equilibria," a condition in which the relations of forces are favorable or unfavorable on the terrain of struggle.[13] Cultural expressions are immediately connected to political representation and ideology, a complex formation in an arena of different social contestations and social formations. In *Prison Notebooks*, Antonio Gramsci reminds us that in particular historical periodization, after the settlement of hegemonic blocs, *crisis* marks the beginning of their disintegration. His notion of crisis encapsulates the indeterminacy between the "popular" and the "economic" in which national culture, in constructing categories of citizenship, produces the consent-upholding hegemony as well as the locales for resistant cultural expressions.[14] The chronology of crisis, how it operates in the linear framework of time, is not explicit in Gramsci's work, but one surmises that crises may operate in two forms: one as rupture and the second as process. Therefore, in describing cultural expressions in signifiers of time and aesthetic content and the compounding effect of various social and cultural formations in a particular era, his idea of crisis can be applied to both historical and filmic analysis in which we see emergent articulations between Asian and black masculinity.

In order to see the importance of these Afro-Asian cultural expressions and how they are linked to the processes of racial formation in the United States, let us turn to how the history of Asian American masculinity is intricately tied to the racial formation of African American men. Much of *The Souls of Black Folk* by W. E. B. Du Bois is conceptualized in terms of citizenship rights equating to "this longing to attain self-conscious manhood."[15] If we understand the relational aspects of U.S. racial formation and claims of citizenship, then the intersecting histories of African American and Asian American masculinities tell the story of American dreams deferred and the promises of market democracy unfulfilled. Initially, during the process of rapid industrialization and Taylorist capitalism in the mid- to late nineteenth century, African American slaves and Chinese coolie workers were used as cheap, exploitable labor. Each racial group was pitted against the other in order to reduce wage levels through the "divide and conquer" rationalization of industrial capitalism. The expansion of the western frontier scripted from the doctrine of Manifest Destiny invoked the collective mythology of the United States as a white settler nation that needed to fulfill its imperialist development into a "shining city on the hill." Racialized men functioned to build the nation—the roads, railways, textiles, manufactured wares, agrarian economy—while simultaneously being excluded from political modes of representation in favor of white working-class rights called Free Labor Ideology.[16] In fact, the rise of industrial capitalism gave rise to modern forms of racism including raciology, eugenics, and sexology, which made "common sense" by delineating a stratified citizenship based on superficial skin differences. What eventually manifested in the euphoria of rationalism and science became the steely racial discourses that legitimated the domination of one group of men over another by invoking a superior culture and biological makeup.

The politics of skin emerged in the early part of the twentieth century as an entrenched ideology that consolidated white identity as an unmarked category of social privilege and economic advantage in colonial and imperial centers and peripheries. A prevailing hysteria among these so-called elites at this time called for the preservation and purity of the white races from degeneration by miscegenation between "superior" and "inferior" cultures of the world. Culture then became the dividing line, stratified by racial and economic hierarchy. Black and Asian people suffered daily humiliations from the racist discourses, along with violent retribution for transgressing social taboos even while living segregated in the social geography of urban slums, ethnic ghettoes, and shantytowns. Beneath this societal weight, racialized men consistently endured indignities through state policies and legal institutions. Specifically in the United States, the Supreme Court decisions *Dred Scott v. Sandford* (1857), *Plessy v. Ferguson* (1896), *Ozawa v. United States* (1922), and *United States v. Bhagat Singh Thind* (1923) all establish a legal record in not-so-uncertain terms that citizenship claims were based upon race. Jim Crow segregation; immigration exclusion in 1882, 1917, 1924, and 1934; and the alien land laws in 1913, 1920, and 1923 bespeak a systematic pattern to disenfranchise racialized men from property ownership and political involvement.[17] Indeed, the politics of skin has scarred the body politic in the United States with deep wounds that have yet to heal because the processes of market democracy have concealed the material exploitations and expropriations still taking place today in civil society.

By reading the martial arts hero as the subject who disrupts state-sanctioned property relations in *Romeo Must Die* and modes of cultural imperialism in *Rush Hour*, both the telos of U.S. exceptionalism, his deployment as a point of enunciation in national culture is a catalyst for social formations with potential cross-racial alliances.[18] The martial arts hero, as the bodily site of contradictions and open-ended negotiation in the dialectic between assimilation (the model minority) and racial difference (the Yellow Peril), identifies and characterizes a significant shift in U.S. cultural, racial, and sexual politics. This transition actively reflects Gramsci's notion of crisis. Constructed, educated, and disciplined by state power, the martial arts citizen-subject in aesthetic composition and content-oriented narratives in recent martial arts films has been conceived in a developmental narrative, inevitably for a symbolic ordering of the nation-state. The hyphenated term ties together the people and the state, which in turn represents the collective consciousness and will of private individuals, who are abstracted into stereotypes sustaining the racial state. Film culture documents the manner in which state narratives, including the logic of racial magnetism, get inscribed into the cinematic apparatus, but it also disrupts and defamiliarizes the coherency and consistency of the "equilibria" that sustain barriers to political embodiment and realized citizenship.

In *The Subject of Semiotics*, Kaja Silverman insightfully explains that suture is the process by which cinematic texts bestow subjectivity upon the viewer.[19] The operation of suture covers up the camerawork through the process of identification with the object. Concealing the regulation of what I term "cinematic citizenship," modalities of power are evinced through the "constructedness" by which we think of ourselves as unique. Cinematic citizenship designates the identifications made with screen images by both racialized and white spectators based upon suture in terms of who has subjectivity and who does not as well as how the cinematic apparatus enjoins subversive identifications with the racialized buddies against dominant state narratives. Thus, I want to borrow from bell hooks's idea of a critical spectatorship in which experiencing visual pleasure is also an oppositional gaze about contestation and confrontation, "to see if images were seen as complicit with dominant cinematic practices."[20] Film construction, then, can be an allegory of the mechanisms of market democracy and its incessant project to individualize communal sociality, to reduce structural considerations of power to unlinked individuals, and to mask whiteness as a noncategory that accrues actual and symbolic capital. However, state legitimation and hegemonic reproduction are in constant negotiation with the countervailing influences of marginal forces, and counterhegemony is a tactic that can be used in emancipatory politics. In this sense, the martial arts buddy genre reveals through cinematic citizenship the fissures and gaps in market assumptions of property relations, possessive individualism, and racial distinctions based on the politics of skin. In this configuration, the mapping of suture in martial arts buddy films creates interracial identifications. When racial difference is interrogated and deconstructed, racialized spectatorship interprets visually the markers of race and racialization by seeing their subjectivity within racialized images and in a manner that addresses scenes of interracial conflict, coalitions, and romance.

In this way, cinematic citizenship addresses what Manthia Diawara calls "resisting spectatorship." Concerning the intersection of race and spectatorship, he says: "Every narration places the spectator in a position of agency; and race, class, and sexual relations influence the way in which this subjecthood is filled by the spectator."[21] Returning to bell hooks, she reminds us that "within the Southern, Black, working-class home of my growing up, in a racially segregated neighborhood, watching television was one way to develop critical spectatorship."[22] Further, Stuart Hall describes critical practices that maintain that identity is "constituted 'not outside but within representation.'"[23] This chapter seeks to address the types of critical identities constituted in Asian-black representations in martial arts buddy films. Insofar as film culture produces sets of ideas and representations based on race and masculinity, I ask these questions: Do racialized men have subjectivity and agency within an Asian-black spectatorship? Is the audience allowed to have identification with them through the cinematic apparatus and with critical, oppositional gazes?

Reviews of *Rush Hour* and *Romeo Must Die* reflected the history of critical dismissal and racialized reception of the martial arts genre. For *Rush Hour*, the critical responses were mixed yet similar in theme, often referring to language, race, and nation. Most reviews coded comparative racialization using the language of interracial oddity, including such text clips as "mismatched duo," "wacky double-team scenario," and "truly opposites."[24] Specifically, many reviews focused on Chris Tucker's penchant for words and Chan's poor English. Newspaper reviews such as in the *New York Times* quipped, "Mr. Chan's own struggle with the language barrier has made him not only the current author least likely to have written his own English autobiography ('I am Jackie Chan') but also a silent partner in the film."[25] The *San Francisco Examiner* was noticeably less racist in its construction of Chinese accents, yet its reviewer still remarked about Asian and black language stereotypes: "A lot of good fun is made of the contrast between Chinese and Black stereotypes, and between Tucker's motor mouth . . . and Chan's reticence."[26] Thus, initial critical reviews dialogically racialized Tucker and Chan, establishing the markers of race and nation through the performance of the English language, and subsequently set the early parameters of spectator expectations and genre pleasure.

For *Romeo Must Die*, the overall sentiment of movie critics was unanimous in that race and sexuality were the primary categories of commentary. Most reviewers lambasted the method acting of Jet Li and focused their complaints on his supposed lack of screen charisma and sexuality. *TV Guide* lamented the "utter lack of chemistry between Li and Aaliyah."[27] Other critics reinforced Hollywood production codes by calling into question Li's sexuality and genre expectations of Asian masculinity: "Let's face it, no one's coming to a Jet Li movie for sex."[28] Yet another progressive review periodical commented on Hollywood production codes that denied Asian and black audiences' desire for interracial romance. An Asian American male movie critic, Dennis Lim of the *Village Voice*, remarked: "Race is the movie's gimmick. . . .

Meanwhile, the romantic angle promised by the title is barely acknowledged. Some Romeo—by the final scene, Han and Trish have barely worked their way up to holding hands."[29] Such discrepancies among various film critics suggest the comparatively racialized dynamic to spectatorship and critical reception. In this way, the expectations of reviewers were mediated through categories of sexuality, language, nation, and race encoded in the discourse of racial magnetism.

In many 1980s action films such as the *Rambo* films, *The Terminator*, and the *Die Hard* series, the white action hero is damaged grotesquely in some physical and psychological manner.[30] Likewise, the martial arts hero keeps on his journey for ethical revenge as well as reconciliation through bodily agency. In the process, he highlights the tension between individualism and communitarian principles, albeit in a postcolonial and transpacific context. Whereas the Greek tragic hero is central to locations of power, typically being an aristocratic or royal persona, the martial arts hero is a personage on the margins, delegitimated from power and mainstream society in some way, gliding through the rigid boundaries of society, a hero situated on the borders.[31] Before we turn to a history of the martial arts hero, some comments explaining major characteristics of the ethical/border identity of the martial arts hero would seem necessary.

As an activist for the community, the martial arts hero has much in common with the border ballad hero. In *With His Pistol in His Hand* by Américo Paredes, we learn about the border ballad hero in the "Corrido of Gregorio Cortez." The border hero confronts the dominant folklore of the Texas Rangers and the mythology of a homogeneous national identity. Ever the ethical and common man, the border hero must wear many hats, performing as a superhero, an everyday laborer, a warrior, and a trickster. The ballad in its many variants has a leitmotif that is useful in pointing out the tensions between the individual and the community:

Decia Gregorio Cortez	Then said Gregorio Cortez
con su pistola en la mano:	With his pistol in his hand,
—¡Ah, cuanto rinche cobarde	"Ah, how many cowardly rangers,
para un solo mexicano!	Against one lone Mexican!"[32]

Like the martial arts hero, he must fight against antimiscegenation taboos and corrupt state officials. Moreover, he fights against multiple interpellations from the church, law, family, and media, but his armor is limited and he carries a lone pistol in his hand. Trying to resist such forces, the border hero does not act impulsively, but when he moves, he moves decisively and courageously, defending his rights in a border region that was once part of Mexico but was artificially Anglicized following the Treaty of Guadalupe Hidalgo in 1848. Following this inquiry, the martial arts hero is racially marked as outside, an inauthentic subject who is in opposition to the mythology of imperial masculinities. Both heroes challenge the collective myth of origin in how the nation imagines itself.[33] The borders of the nation-state have been the liminal space for signification, especially in terms of how the citizenry is modulated by state apparatuses and cultural mythologies. As Roberto Alejandro reminds us:

> Citizenship, in short, belongs to the realm of the symbolic; that is, a space of symbols that previous generations constructed as well as a domain which is always in a process of reconstitution, and whose meaning the state seeks to define. The citizen, by contrast, is not a member of the symbolic. He inhabits everyday life, which is full of symbols, but which cannot be reduced to a sphere of symbols.[34]

A move for a symbolic collective memory, the corrido's intervention reinscribes a history that the racial state has erased. Underlining the role of folklore, the corrido repositions the man on the border in the national mythology. Similarly, the martial arts hero has an ethical category for identification, a border identity that shows the power of individual action without community resources, and the centrality of the body as the means for social transformation.

The physicality and fight choreography of the martial arts genre has its genesis in Peking opera, an aesthetic art form dating to the Song Dynasty (960–1280).[35] Through rigorous bodily gymnastics and craft apprenticeship, Peking opera forged actors, performers, and singers who could master several disciplines in theatricality. Elaborate face painting, costumes, and modest staging set the environment where "stylized celluloid fighting scenes" were the precursor to modern rapid-fire kung-fu scenes.[36] The stories derived from folklore, historical events, popular novels, and mythology. Stars such as Jackie Chan and Sammo Hung trained from an early age to take the mantle as future performers, whether on the stage or the silver screen.

From these grand origins, the modern martial arts hero came filmically embodied as a lone figure from Chinese history. His history is not unlike that of Gregorio Cortez. Wong Fei-hung, born in Guangdong province during the late Qing Dynasty, was a defender of the weak as well as a proponent of justice.[37] A Chinese nationalist and champion of Confucian values, Wong was also an herbal doctor and martial arts instructor specializing in the tiger-crane style with a fighting technique known as the nine special fists.[38] Much like the power of the corrido, his mythology spread like cultural wildfire, eventually inspiring a series of ninety-nine black-and-white films during 1949–1970 that were based on his life, with various actors playing the role of Wong.[39]

Action films such as *Drunken Master* and *Once Upon a Time in China*, which coincidentally launched the careers of Jackie Chan and Jet Li, respectively, dramatize the mythology of Wong Fei-hung in modern Hong Kong cinema. Before his arrival in Hollywood, the fictionalized Hong Kong action hero revived many of the real-life Wong's attributed qualities including a proud Chinese cultural identity and humanistic ideals such as defending the weak, promoting justice, and redressing past wrongs. In Hong Kong, perceptions of Westernization and modernization are ambivalent at best. In a Wong-inspired movie starring Jet Li, the martial arts hero wants to preserve those traditions that galvanize a sense of Chineseness within the community, but on the other hand he wants to help the nation equalize itself to the perceived level of the Western imperialists. The hero's efforts to reconcile these cross-purposes create a dual anxiety on his part. For example, it is lamentable that guns and dynamite have displaced kung fu as the predominant form of self-defense in China, but this loss contrasts with the nationalist doctrine seeking world parity through adopting Western science and war technologies. Therefore, British colonialism and its effects on the sociopolitical landscape of China established the hallmark of pre-Hollywood martial arts films.

Developed from Wong Fei-hung films, Hong Kong martial arts cinema incorporated Bruce Lee's kung-fu style, Jeet Kune Do, into kung-fu classics such as *The Big Boss, Fists of Fury*, and *The Way of the Dragon*.[40] In "The Kung Fu Craze," David Desser illustrates the wide impact of the martial arts genre as a top box office draw. At the forefront of the wave of kung-fu films coming into U.S. markets was Warner Brothers Pictures. Documenting the role of Warner Brothers in producing *Enter the Dragon*, Desser describes the tension between producing films to capitalize on an emergent bankable product and negotiating the complex web of consumer identity politics in order to appeal to several racial demographics. Thus, John Saxon was added to the project in hopes of securing white mainstream crossover appeal, and also Jim Kelly, now a legend as an African American action hero.[41] These films were popular in urban and working-class neighborhoods, where on Saturday afternoons, "kung-fu theater" enabled urban youths without bankrolls or fancy gadgetry to gain empowerment through cultural fantasy. Not having access to the Terminator's robotics or *Mission: Impossible* technology, audiences knew that the martial arts hero relied only on his body to kick or punch his way out of a cornered situation. As part of its central appeal, this self-sufficiency approach was a staple theme from which audiences received pleasure and temporary empowerment through racial fantasy. In one way, the construction of racial fantasy by communities of color was an indirect form of opposition to Daniel Patrick Moynihan's frantic production of racial apocalypse. According to recent scholarship on black cultural appropriation of orientalia, sometimes bodies are the only things that really matter.[42] Because these populations were experientially and literally beaten by institutional racism, material poverty, and surveillance by the police state, audience members gravitated toward "virtue lost and found, individual determination, righteous vengeance, and community struggle against all odds."[43] Thus, as Amy Ongiri puts it, "African American attraction to Asian culture via martial arts films provides a telling moment of slippage and indeterminacy in which notions of totalitarian nature of power and western notions of aesthetics, culture, and dominance are undone."[44] The oppositional gaze of communities of color often represented a negation of whiteness "by any means necessary," which meant forming Asian-black spectatorship that refused Hollywood's hegemonic pressure to assimilate into white spectatorship.

Through his epic and farcical improvisations, Lee has wide appeal for communities of color; as Dead Prez raps, "karate meant empty hands, so that it was then perfect for the poor man." Youths of color identified with Lee's iconography of class empowerment, making interracial identifications that simply ignored the dominant imperatives of film culture through the visual fetishism of white bodies. Often after watching a matinee, youths of color would go to the streets to mimic what they had just seen on the movie screen. Symbolizing the power of a lone hero able to fight for the needs of the community, youths of color felt empowered and free for a fleeting moment when dropping flying dragon kicks or making exaggerated "kung-fu" sounds. Interracial mimicking in the public sphere of urban streets opened up their imaginations and produced emergent conceptions of cross-cultural exchange that linked the politics of social movements with kung-fu matinee leisure practices. Despite these early formations of kung-fu subcultures, today's martial arts buddy films are still responding to the contradictions of market democracy's diverse symptoms: the Watts riots, the Los Angeles riots of 1992, the dismantling of affirmative action programs, the Gulf War, the men's movement of the early 1990s, and the War on Terror. Finally, they reveal a certain anxiety over how white masculinity imagines itself in the global context of managing empire, and they address the ways in which white racial superiority, predicated within the logic of multiculturalism, is located not only in visual hegemony but also in institutional and military power tout court.

Set in the waterfront district of Oakland, California, Andrzej Bartkowiak's *Romeo Must Die* is a martial arts action film centered around a territorial turf war between Asian American and African American crime families, both vying for control of a four-square-mile low-rent district. From the opening shot, the cityscape of San Francisco juxtaposed with large Chinese ideograms and dubbed with the hypnotic beats of a hip-hop soundtrack establishes from the very get-go the key markers of race. Showcasing the martial arts of Hong Kong hero Jet Li and the acting debut of the late hip-hop diva Aaliyah, this modern-day interpretation of Shakespeare's love tragedy makes an interesting departure from the original by incorporating the admixture of race and romance (or the lack thereof).

In contrast, *Rush Hour*, directed by Brett Ratner (known for his buddy film bonanzas in the *Lethal Weapon* series), opens in a more dissonant manner than does *Romeo Must Die*. A helicopter shot zooms from a skyline that could be Everycity to a seaport dock bustling with workers, commerce, and trade, a location where departures and arrivals from destinations unknown load and unload capital goods. It is at this precise moment that the audience deciphers the visual and aural markers of race—the orientalized music of tympani and gongs, Chinese ideograms scripted on shops signs, and the harbor boats with large unfolding sails worked by a nameless and faceless mass. The location is signified as Hong Kong, and the spectator is placed in an exotic and mysterious land awaiting the handover from British colonialism to mainland Chinese control. Not before the cultural artifacts of the Chinese nation-state, its collective historical and cultural memory, are looted and commodified, however. *Rush Hour* then is premised on this theft of Chinese cultural heirlooms, its Ming vases, Tang artwork, and Qing bronze statues, by an old British diplomat, who, prior to the handover, conscripts an Asian gang to transport the rare items from their indigenous resting place. Enter Jackie Chan and Chris Tucker, playing Inspector Lee and Detective Carter, respectively, two police officers from opposite sides of the cultural globe who team up to solve a murder-kidnapping caper involving Counsel Han's daughter in Los Angeles, a crucial racial and capitalist epicenter for the Hong Kong film circuit.

Whereas *Rush Hour* follows a generic formula with a male/male buddy pair, *Romeo Must Die* uniquely teams a male/female partnership. As an intersection of gender and race, the Asian-black interface of *Romeo Must Die* lends a crucial and important corrective to the homosocial world of the standard buddy format and allows audiences to grapple with Asian-black visual images that set and subvert representational boundaries of prescribed Hollywood production codes. In "Visual Pleasure and Narrative," Laura Mulvey sees the construction of gender relations in classic Hollywood cinema through binaries of male/female, active/passive, subject/object.[45] I would like to use this framework of dialectical oppositions to situate the racialized gaze in martial arts buddy cinema as Asian male/black female, Asian male/black male, and racial insider/racial outsider. Yet the dialectical oppositions of active/passive and subject/object are not coherently tied to one identity at the exclusion of another. It is this fluidity and blurred distinction of power relations that differentiates this genre from the usual suspects of white hero/black buddy films. Also, through the operations of the cinematic apparatus and racialized suture, the regulation of race and sexuality in these buddy films instantiates a language of violence and humor that marks the Asian-black male body as distinct from its martial arts and blaxploitation predecessors.

In *Rush Hour* and *Romeo Must Die*, the function of Asian-black buddies is different from the traditional Hollywood team of a white hero and black sidekick. Representations of Asian-black buddies break down master-slave power differentials because of their shared history of racialization under white supremacy. The black buddy, as in the *Lethal Weapon* series (also directed by Ratner), embodies the traits of the white female—the "comforter, nurturer, and partner," what I playfully term the Danny Glover syndrome.[46] In order to reestablish the ethos of a white male savior protecting white femininity and the nuclear family from racial or national evil—for instance, the evil, butt-kicking Jet Li in *Lethal Weapon 4*—the racialized buddy functions to support white manhood, which ultimately negates the subjectivity of women of color.[47] In contrast, the Asian-black buddy team parallels equal partnerships between Asians and blacks who have historically formed alliances to produce more powerful political blocs, including coalitions like the Non-Aligned Movement and Black/Yellow Power. But more than this, certain issues and ideas concerning Asian immigration, U.S. military intervention in Asia, and the power of black cultural resistance enters the narrative structure of these films, forming a politics of cultural engagement and mutual respect for each other's specific racialization. The disjuncture of immigration and the violence of war displaces the body of the Asian male hero from U.S. national culture, whereas in *Rush Hour* and *Romeo Must Die* the black buddy reinscripts the palimpsest body of the Asian male hero with an understanding of African American male racialization. Certain narrative devices are used to accomplish this reinscription through the binoculars of an Asian-black perspective that specifies the differentiation of the Asian/Asian

American dichotomy. One such example is found in *Romeo Must Die* when Han's brother is lynched by hanging from a tree, which does not need explanation to connect to the history of black men hanging as "strange fruit" in the Jim Crow South. This scene replays visually the history of violence and lynching directed at black men by the most popular voluntary organization in U.S. history, the Ku Klux Klan. That history is coded through the Asian male body. Graphically enjoining the Asian male body with U.S. racial terrorism, this scene frames the process of assimilation as injury onto foreign bodies outside the body politic of the U.S. nation-state.

In the scenes of first contact between Lee and Carter in *Rush Hour* and Han and Trish in *Romeo Must Die*, misrecognition by the black buddy occurs because the body of the martial arts hero performs class and gender mimesis of Asian American men's racialization and stereotypes. This type of racial/gender mimesis engenders questioning the axis of assimilation/racial difference within the architecture of U.S. racial hierarchy and Asian-black competition for economic, cultural, and political entitlements. The performance of racial and class mimesis by the martial arts hero situates him on the border between social categories, exposing how the cinematic apparatus inscribes variegated citizenship.[48] There is an exhibition value for unraveling the messiness tied to citizen formation in the performance of racial and class mimesis in the martial arts genre. Racial and class mimesis performs the function of assimilation gone awry. Insofar as the nation-state regulates racial assimilation through national culture, racial and class mimesis allows for political mobility. Because of his physicality and ingenuity, the figure of the martial arts hero is boundless, mobile, and fluid across rigid distinctions. As such, the martial arts hero documents the immigrant experience of Asian American representability and subjectivity.[49] In *Rush Hour*, the entire comedic performance is premised upon the clash of cultures between African Americans and Asian foreigners. The latter are marked in Asian American communities as broken-English-speaking, fashion-challenged immigrants who remind those Asians in the United States of their "Asianness" by connecting the traumatic history of U.S. imperialism in Asia to the present. The construction then of "Asianness" illustrates a displacement of historical time for present time. "Asianness" sets up clearly the assimilationist/nativist binary, illustrating those loyal subjects who assimilate into the national citizenry and those suspect individuals who cannot. Detective Carter functions as a hip, highly sexualized, streetwise buddy who makes the audience laugh by misrecognizing, presupposing, and translating U.S. mainstream culture as detrimental and African American culture as resistance to Lee. As such, interracial communication and dialogic racialization produces Asian-black buddies unwilling to conform to masculinities of intercultural war, contestation, and militarism.

Although the camera zooms to Lee at the door of the newly arrived airplane from Hong Kong, the angle from the tarmac represents Carter's perspective. Subsequently, the spectator hears the sound of an orientalizing gong, supposedly a commonsense aural marker of Lee's outside status in terms of race, nationality, and sexuality. The foreign status of Inspector Lee represents the hypersexualized yet nonheteronormative Asian multitude, what cultural critic Robert Lee terms a "third sex location" referencing the dominant threat of Yellow Peril hysteria. Therefore, in the role that Angel Island served previously, the airport represents a social space of entry and transgression, a space that is a locus of cultural, racial, and sexual definitions of insider and outsider, and this is where most of the humor derives initially. But instead of the gaze of the immigration state, via the eyes and medical instruments of white officials, Detective Carter establishes the gaze of black manhood and culture, which has encoded American orientalism onto the Asian male body.

When Inspector Lee meets Carter, the former does not say a word, thus seemingly reproducing Asian American racialization as the silent minority. Responding to the silent space, Carter constitutes onto the Asian male body stereotypes of Asian accents through a black performance of yellowface. Carter misrecognizes Lee as such (this is significant) and proceeds to produce his comic effect by performing black mimesis of yellowface, asking in exaggerated and obnoxious terms: "Do you speakuh English . . . Do you understand the words coming outta my mouth?" Positioning the spectator in the vantage point of an objective eye, the camera zooms to Lee just smiling, and the two-shot records Detective Carter physically turning his back on Lee. This refusal represents the negation of interracial identification or even an acknowledgment of Lee's humanity and mirrors the kind of liberal discourse used to explain such interracial cultural misrecognition between Koreans and blacks in Los Angeles. Carter clearly stakes out the subjectivity of the insider, and his interracial mimesis of yellowface establishes the boundaries of comedic performance, affect culture, and national belonging.[50] As situated in opposition to newly arrived immigrants, he operates as a racialized policeman of U.S. national identity and culture, much like Shaquille O'Neal in the Shaq–Yao Ming media battle. In this manner, the camera does not ask the spectator, through a classic shot–reverse shot, to identify with the two men of color, and thus an oppositional gaze is nonexistent. Therefore, the camerawork, dialogue, and comedic performance produce a form of racialized suture that creates interracial difference as flippant and hyperreal through black excess and patriotic policing.

In *Romeo Must Die*, the entertainment value found in the engine of the plot and dialogue centers primarily on the sublimated sexual tension between Han and Trish in the kung-fu action scenes. However, along with imitating a stereotypical South Asian taxi driver named Achebar, Han performs instances of interracial mimesis including mimicking a foreign Chinese delivery boy. Trish functions marginally as a support buddy, performing this role similarly to Detective Carter, although her sexuality and good looks act as an object for the scopophilic male gaze. This function is demonstrated when Trish gets into a cab driven by Han: the camera frames a full shot of her, then cuts to the rearview mirror showing Han looking at her. The spectator is in the scene, looking at Han gazing at Trish through the rearview mirror, so that Han's gaze is the active center of this scene by the visual representations. Adding a unique, gendered dimension to the buddy picture format, Trish performs the function of the classic fetish.[51] By negating Trish's gaze, the scene marginalizes the black female body as merely an object, and the racialized gazes from Han to Trish secure this reading initially. Cinematic citizenship in this particular scene designates a political, class, and sexual subjectivity found in Asian-black spectatorship. Maintained by the political gaze regulating cinematic citizenship, the romantic subjectivity given to most action hero leads is cut off in this scene by the operation of the racialized and sexualized suture.

In *Rush Hour* and *Romeo Must Die*, the martial arts hero is a palimpsest figure in the kung-fu buddy picture because he is expunged of the typical leading man's sexuality, even being denied a romantic kiss, a standard reward for the white male action hero. Beneath the overt visual economy of sexuality, the martial arts hero is reinscribed with violence par excellence. As Chris Straayer states in "Redressing the 'Natural,'" the classic kiss in Hollywood cinema represents sexuality. The symbolic power of the kiss "derives from its dual metaphoric and metonymic function. It both stands in for sexual activity and begins it."[52] Similar to the erasure of the homosexual kiss in classic cinema, the disavowal of a romantic subjectivity for the martial arts hero renders him, in Judith Halberstam's words, a sanitized subjectivity. Underlining this erasure, this process is a sexual bleaching and signals the anxiety of producers about the overdetermined sexuality of the hero.

The genre sanitizes all connotations of libido in the figure of the martial arts hero except as expressed through racialized violence. We see this exemplified in *Romeo Must Die*, in which the only physical contact that simulates intimacy of touch is in a fight scene. The fight scene that teams Han and

Trish against an Asian female reinscribes violence and sexual miscegenation for the reproduction of Hollywood production codes in kung-fu cinema. Thus, this fight scene maps the parameters not only of Asian American male sexual regulation but also of Asian-black antimiscegenation, and routes this taboo through choreographed violence. In *Rush Hour*, most of the explicit sexual energy is exhibited by Detective Carter, who manages to perform a stereotypical representation of black heterosexuality consisting of an over-determined status and masculine bravado. However, in contrast with Bruce Lee, whose humor was inadvertent or minimalist at best, Jackie Chan uses his bodily violence for comic affect, often narrowly escaping mortal wounds through last minute heroics that do not illustrate his invincibility but rather his vulnerability. In "The Construction of Black Sexuality," Jacquie Jones offers the idea that buddy pictures, films that portray a white male hero and a black sidekick, represent black male sexuality in the form of violence. She evinces the idea that "violent differentiation" is a substitute for black hetero-sexuality.[53] Her idea suggests that violence and race represent coded sexual-ity. As such, violence and gender mimesis produces black male subjectivity in the diegetic, or narrative structure of film texts.

In *Romeo Must Die*, Trish teases Han with sexual innuendo—"I like the yellow one"; "Is it true what they say about Asian men?"—as a measured barometer for the incessant antimiscegenation rule dictating the racial ro-mance in the film. She functions as a black female, delegitimizing black male heterosexuality in that her refusal of the romantic advances of black male characters (Maurice and Mac) represents the denial of black male sexuality. In both cases, racial differentiation engenders a masculine homosocial world that mostly negates racialized femininity, because in the end, critical repre-sentations should have not only functionality but also creativity and agency. If market democracy "entails the gradual emergence of civil society and the citizen-subject of the state out of the barbaric prehistory of human society," then the martial arts genre, much like the developmental narrative found in liberal assumptions of freedom and individual agency, reworks the standard-ized tropes of the more whitewashed buddy pictures but still relegates other "forms of opposition or sociality" to the margins of the diegetic.[54]

In her article "Avenging Women in Indian Cinema," Lalitha Gopalan pro-vides a useful mapping of how genre functions in order for the spectator to identify with the visceral images. This act then provides an opportunity for a critical understanding of why certain genres reproduce themselves repeat-edly. It penetrates to the heart of consumer desire and material anticipation. Gopalan writes: "Only genre simultaneously addresses the industry's invest-ment in standardized narratives for commercial success on the one hand, and the spectator's pleasure in genre films with their stock narratives structured around repetition and difference on the other."[55] She links the ideological and production investments in the workings of genres, but her definition omits how genres transform over time and mutate into different forms through processes in constant renegotiation with the political and economic circumstances of cultural productions. We see this process in motion by locating Jackie Chan and Jet Li as two distinct martial arts heroes; the former invokes a different kind of kung fu, namely complex fight scenes using set pieces and slapstick humor as a means to produce desire and affect in Asian-black spectatorship, whereas the latter follows the tradition established by Bruce Lee in using his body as a narcissistic vehicle for spectatorial identification.[56]

The mortal combat between Han and his black counterparts and the suppression of a romantic relationship between Han and Trish is a measured critique of the economy of masculinity and femininity circulating in the film. Interracial fighting and interracial sanitization unveils the white-black-Asian triangulation including Han's unnamed relationship with the white developers. Establishing citizenship as property ownership, this triangulation reveals the set of property relations narrated by the film, which exposes the contradictions of urban blight and white financial capital. The critical evaluation of the masculinist investment in private property is the film's attempt to conceal the contradictions of liberal individualism, its possessive assumptions concerning land accumulation versus communal ownership.

Early in *Romeo Must Die*, Mr. Roth, who represents elite white developers, meets Isaac O'Day, head of a black crime organization. They negotiate their plans to secure property deeds over a round of golf at a neatly manicured golf course. Responding to Roth's pressure to complete the transfer of low-rent property to secure land for building a multimillion-dollar sports stadium for an NFL football team, O'Day states that he "knows" the streets and thus will be able to convince the remaining holdouts who have so far refused to sell their property. We see a full shot framing all the men together in the same homosocial space, arguing over limited land issues. O'Day then takes his golf shot, his ball landing in a sand trap. In a two-shot with O'Day, the camera centers on Roth. Now his knowledge and not his body is on display, telling O'Day that golf is a "game of finesse and not power." Later, Roth breaks down the intricacies of the golf swing including the alignment of the wrists and hips, the most effective stance, and the balance of the feet. As Roth swings a fluid golf stroke, with a quick cut to his golf ball landing close to the hole, knowledge and power are sutured to the white male body.

Although Roth represents the stereotype of the unscrupulous Jew, the film does not focus on this dynamic as much as it does on the Asian-black racial battle for limited property rights. Throughout the golf course scene, many convergent layers of meaning circulate in the discourse about private property including Social Darwinism, nineteenth-century raciology, and Jewish incorporation into the category of whiteness.[57] Moreover, the editing of the scene ties the spectator to the accuracy of Roth's explanations describing masculinity in coded language, in which white men ultimately have the knowledge and power to maneuver around street "thugs" like O'Day. Legal scholar Cheryl Harris explains that the capacity for ownership of private property in the United States has always been constitutive of a social, economic, and cultural construction of a white identity. That is, a person has subjectivity, agency, and ultimately citizenship only when the equation "whiteness equals property" is realized.[58] When the camera closes in on O'Day's demoralized face after his failure, the shot accentuates that the "game" is based on rules over which he has little control.

As this golf game is an allegory for the "game" of propertied masculinity, Roth has the intricate knowledge needed to mastermind, like a puppet master, crime bosses and corporate financial scams. Not only does he condescendingly teach O'Day the mental aspects of the game, the word "finesse" connotes the ability of white national manhood to master the bourgeois game of golf through sports knowledge gained from the application of Enlightenment scientific rationality. Yet also, the regime of knowledge Roth commands enables him to feel a sense of security and modern personhood, a self-assuredness in property ownership and Western epistemologies of cognition that registers little threat from O'Day, condemned by colonial discourse to biological inferiority, the trace of his all-brawn-no-brains masculinity. As Eve Kosofsky Sedgwick illustrates in her *Epistemology of the Closet*, for any modern questioning of homosocial and homoerotic spaces, "knowledge/ignorance is more than merely one in a metonymic chain of such binarisms . . . knowledge meaning in the first place sexual knowledge; ignorance, sexual ignorance."[59]

Thus, O'Day can be read as legitimating and reproducing this hierarchy of white knowledge. His position as an outsider to bourgeois leisure activities leaves no choice but to evaluate his masculinity in the terms set forth by Roth. That is, the homosocial quid pro quo exchange between Roth and O'Day reinstitutes the logic of how masculinity is prefigured upon the movement from structural considerations of power to the biologistic-cultural paradigm. O'Day can be seen as both refusing the uneven relations of power between himself and Roth by asserting his "excessive" masculinity in terms of a "powerful unknowing as unknowing," and consenting to the hegemonic and reproductive framework established by Roth in rearticulating an essentialist binary of finesse/power.[60] Even later in the film, when O'Day tries to become "legit" by aspiring to the "owner's box" of the stadium development plan, he is shot and thus disciplined by his lieutenant, Mac, for his ambitions. Black-on-black crime becomes the dominant policing mechanism to admonish "uppity" black men who, in popular sport, perform entertainment, head coaching, and broadcasting labor while being denied access to ownership positions. While deploying a familiar trope in a familiar genre as a vehicle for circumscribing the plethora of maleness seen in the film (notice the lack of women such as mothers, wives, and romantic partners), the system upheld by the film justifies this occupational barrier for black assertions for propertied inclusion and decision-making power.

Resituating white masculinity in relation to cinematic citizenship, the narrative of whiteness in martial arts buddy films has to reimagine a universal, modern subject that is still white, but also on the criminal margins. In this sense, whiteness in mainstream film culture seems to need a white misfit who can be discounted. Much of the martial arts genre then uses the match-up between white criminals and racialized men as cops. White corporate crime represents whiteness as anachronistic, out-of-step with modern liberal progress based on law and order. This portrayal includes white men such as Roth, the pseudoaristocratic land developer in *Romeo Must Die*, and even the British ex–colonial official in *Rush Hour*. As such, they do not represent the benevolent, enlightened, heterosexual white male liberal. What we see in recent mainstream productions with racialized men is a troubled dualism constitutive of identification and disidentification. The genre requires the martial arts hero to punish other racialized men, who in the filmic narrative must be represented as the real threat, in front of the camera, committing the violence and off-limits transgressions. In this way, the sinister work of white supremacy is then hidden in the films, like a negative photographic imprint that is mostly invisible and forgotten.

As many critics of multiculturalism have stated, the new multicultural era has instituted more representations of people of color, but at the same time conceals the lack of actual political and economic power engendered to those groups. Conveying political correctness without real motivation for social transformation, the politics of racial visibility hides the culpability of white power in both cinematic form and narrative.[61] In particular, one function of film culture sets up points of identification for the audience in staking out divisions between citizen and outsider based on race and thus those to whom the cinematic apparatus sutures the audience, and those to whom it does not.

Nevertheless, audience identification or disidentification is also predicated upon the spectator's position in relation to social categories of differentiation. Due to the rhetoric of meritocracy and equal opportunity through standardized testing, multicultural market democracy must conceal the material privileges hidden within the category of whiteness; it must also sublimate and assuage, by the mediation of national culture, the guilt, anxieties, and hostilities of "angry white men" who, in the post–civil rights era, have been named as injured subjects of the reconstitution of white supremacy. Displacing culpability and responsibility onto other racialized men or white corporate crime, the visual culture of popular film regulates the dialogic racialization of Asian and black communities in cultural revolutions and counterrevolutions. When the Asian-black interface goes astray from presumed liberal goals of equal opportunity and self-sustained achievement, the buddies as racial cops help secure the promise of the U.S. nation-state by subduing white criminals. Yet racialized men as cops are violent, stereotyped caricatures, nullifying any incisive critique of white supremacy until the end, through interracial solidarity. These cops stand for law and order, but they somehow always remain outside modern society. In this sense, they enforce the law, but they are not self-disciplining citizen-subjects.

In *Rush Hour*, the clash of national cultures and the deployment of black culture as a site for critiquing U.S. imperialism abroad and the police state at home are worked through the buddy team. Establishing the role of the police state and the status of foreigners, Counsel Han tells the FBI, "I am not an American. My daughter is not an American." In not-so-subtle terms, this statement sets the stage for Chinese nationals and U.S. police powers to engage in the political field of national belonging and transpacific migration. In a scene depicting Inspector Lee coming to the United States to help Counsel Han, the FBI's Agent Russ says to Agent Whiting: "That's all I need is a foreign national getting his head blown off and turning this into an international incident." As a sexual connotation in literary and filmic analysis, the reference to decapitation in the dialogue presages the romantic castration of the martial arts hero. Equating violence with sexuality, the FBI, as a representative of the racial state, foreshadows the regulation of cinematic citizenship through the specter of symbolic castration. In the ensuing dialogue between the agents, a classic shot–reverse shot sutures the spectator to the point of view of the FBI. The FBI has a history of undertaking counterinsurgency measures, including its infamous COINTEL (Counterintelligence) program, as a means to disunite social and racial classes. More specifically, the spectator is sutured to the nation-state's police powers, which disparage, in their words, "Chung King" cops and instead recruit LAPD keystone cops.

In one scene, Detective Carter wants to show Mann's Chinese Theater to Inspector Lee. In the car ride to the tourist site, the camera moves side to side in the two-shot frame and thus reinforces identification for a racialized gaze. Depending on the spectator's worldview, the racialized gaze can be oppositional and critical, or it can be mimetic and conciliatory. When the two arrive, the camera is positioned at street level, framing the two buddies in a single frame looking up, with Mann's Chinese Theater in the background. Carter says, "but I want to show you something," and functions as the buddy who shows, translates, and confirms what the audience is soon expecting: the inauthentic representation of "Chineseness," Mann's Chinese Theater, collides with the martial arts hero, who is supposedly the authentic personification of "Chineseness." In this hyperreal collision between simulacra and authenticity, the black buddy functions to show just how incompatible the martial arts hero is with the collective U.S. national mythology that incorporates Hollywood cultural imperialism. Therefore, when Carter exclaims, "just like home ain't it," his hands widespread showcasing the monument in all its glory, the spectator through the process of suture is cued to laugh at the incongruence. In true Hollywood caricature, the humor derives from two sources: both Carter's overdetermined ignorance ("ain't never been to China, but I bet it looks just like this, don't it") and Lee's overdetermined sense of loss in seemingly his own world of "Chineseness." Through the full shot of Mann's Chinese Theater, Lee's naïveté and Carter's ignorance produce the desired effect. As such, the racialization of both men is disabled, Lee culturally and Carter intellectually. Both ignite the humor and pleasure the spectator is asked to enjoy at their expense.

Showcasing the collective cultural memory of white national manhood, the Asian-black buddies encounter the sidewalk footprints of John Wayne. For so many, Wayne is the ubiquitous icon and embodiment of the Western hero—or, simply put, the representative cultural imperialist par excellence. After portraying throughout his extensive movie career the genocide of Native Americans, the repulsion of General Santa Anna, and the defeat of the Japanese in World War II, the Duke gets immortalized with his footprints in concrete. Insofar as the Duke is a heroic embodiment of U.S. imperial power, his presence in the frame literally concretizes classic Hollywood cinema's exclusion of Asians in the United States from cultural representability. The camerawork brings alive the cultural myth of the Duke, his grandiose persona, which is framed in a closeup shot of his larger-than-life feet at a tourist attraction symbolizing U.S. cultural power.

In this defining scene of cultural crisis, the camera works in the classic shot–reverse shot, moving from the gazes of the racialized men and from, unbelievably, the gaze of the footprints! Finally, as spectators, we are sutured to identify with the racialized men, but it is in relation to the Duke, whose feet are literally and figuratively too large for the martial arts hero to fill. Inspector Lee's first words in English, "John Wayne," are telling because they represent the collision between the two kinds of hero traditions outlined earlier in this essay. Symbolically, Carter informs the martial arts hero that his feet are not big enough to fit into the collective memory of the nation-state. The scene depicts the exclusion of Asian men from "standing in" as representatives of U.S. masculinity by reminding the nation of its collective memory in wars against Japan in World War II, China and North Korea during the Korean conflict, and the Viet Cong in Vietnam. Thus the logics in the scene show how masculinity works within this homosocial world, including idealizing white subjectivity, making invisible Chineseness, and negating women of color from representation.

Because of this incommensurability between assimilation and racial exclusion, the Asian-black buddy team constructs an alliance based on the common ground of racial oppression and thus forms alternative sites of disidentification for citizenship. More specifically, the Asian-black team routes this inclusion through African American culture and history. However, this trajectory neglects to emphasize the places where Asian American culture and history have resisted cultural erasure or where Asian-black shared history has created subversive forms of alternative social relations. In this way, a mural on a background brick wall depicting African American blues musicians and singers foreshadows later scenes in which Tucker functions to construct citizenship through the perspective of black history, trauma, and culture.

Framed by a consistent two-shot, Lee requests a ride to Counsel Han's location; Carter responds, "Man, just sit there and shut up, this ain't no democracy." In "'Something's Missing Here!' Homosexuality and Film Reviews during the Production Code Era, 1934–1962," Chon Noriega suggests that the Production Code Administration censored homosexuality in all filmmaking. Critical reviews along with audience responses influenced the reception of homoerotic films and muted the homosexual content within.[62] Likewise, martial arts buddy pictures conformed to certain Hollywood production codes and sanitized political and homoerotic content to a more individualized and thematic paradigm. Lee urgently responds to Carter's declaration: "Yes, it is," whereby Carter admonishes, "I'm Michael Jackson, you Tito." Inspector Lee ignores the power dynamic infused in the remark and queries, "why wouldn't they want my help?" Finally, Carter lays it all on the line, referencing literally the FBI, but more generally the United States: "Because they don't give a damn about you."

The two-shot frames the homosociality in this scene, positioning the racialized gaze as an outsider/insider binary representing citizenship. The cinematic apparatus does not suture the spectator to the racialized buddies, and the spectator is not asked by the cinematic shots to identify as "that's me" but instead to listen in, to eavesdrop on the conversation. Afterward, the buddies are seated in the car again, listening to the radio and discussing the politics of national culture. Inspector Lee hears the Beach Boys as an interpellative form of U.S. national culture, in this case the popular music of U.S. cultural imperialism disseminated to all parts of the globe. He says: "Ah, Beach Boys great American music," whereby Carter abruptly switches the radio station to hip-hop, saying, "don't ever touch a black man's radio."

In a reworking of Louis Althusser's classic formulation of interpellation, the state hails Lee through "great American music."[63] Nevertheless, while Lee begins to misrecognize the promises of the state as an illusory promiser of political embodiment, Carter watches the intoxicating power of American national culture mesmerizing his partner. He then disrupts Lee's subjection to the state/culture power axis. As a technological arm of cultural expression, the radio signifies the cultural space in which African Americans are able to resist the silencing of their voice.[64] Carter's warning, "Beach Boys going get you a great ass whipping," reflects the history of white violence and terror directed toward African American men. Realizing the missteps of blacks caught up in racial uplift without critiquing whiteness and democracy, Carter continues his commentary: "You can do that in China, but you get yourself killed over here man. I'll show you some real music. Hear." The camera finally utilizes the classic shot–reverse shot between Lee and Carter, which begins the process of identification suturing the spectator to the buddy team, while Carter says, "now that's music." This is by no means a coincidence. While the Beach Boys' music represents a demographic audience of largely white listeners, hip-hop has its origins in African American and Caribbean traditions of blues, reggae, and bebop, pressure-cooked under urban renewal that called attention to racism, poverty, and the police state.[65]

Some may argue that hip-hop has been co-opted by the homogenizing influence of capital, yet *Rush Hour* represents this cultural expression as a critique of equating U.S. national culture with whiteness. Once Althusser's ideological state apparatuses have been systematically broken down, the coalition building begins for an interracial alliance, through an Asian-black interface of cultural translation and politicized unity. Carter moves in a breakdance style, showcasing the "snake" move, and shouts: "Can you do that to the Beach Boys?" He then answers emphatically: "Hell, nah." As a subtext using certain production codes, the looks between Carter and Lee intersect with various racialized gazes from the audience and construct an oppositional gaze through cultural translation and collective historical remembrance.

The quintessential "bonding scene" between Lee and Carter breaks down the pillar of U.S. cultural imperialism through a communal, critical kind of interracial social engagement within a transpacific interracial conversation based on a shared history of dialogic racialization. The lone martial arts hero, no longer rooted in self-alienation, forges political bonds with members of other excluded groups. Before encountering the Asian gang that has kidnapped Counsel Han's daughter for ransom, Lee and Carter are at the Foo-Chow restaurant in a two-shot, waiting outside for the right opportunity to "bum rush" the Asian gang. While sitting in the car, the camera positions a shot–reverse shot, suturing the spectator to Lee when he hears on the radio Bruce Springsteen's rendition of "War." Still in that frame, Lee sings verbatim the song's lyrics: "War! Huh! / What is it good for?/ Absolutely nothing." In this pivotal scene for cinematic citizenship, the song's lyrics suture the audience to interracial solidarity through the soundtrack and corresponding singing.

On one level, the song's lyrics function to call into question the role of U.S. imperialism in Asia while, in the context of the film, highlighting the return of the martial arts hero to the imperial center. Lee's ventriloquism of an antiwar song performed in the wake of the Vietnam and Persian Gulf Wars calls into question the twin ideological fences of market democracy and militarism spread throughout the world that culminated in various wars in the "Far" and "Middle" East.[66] In many ways, the refusal of the Asian male body, as the discursive site where U.S. cultural imperialism and militarism are etched, denies complicity in such systems of violence and global hegemony and also challenges unreflective patriotism. On another level, the song's lyrics are used to underline thematically the tensions between Asian American and African American cultures, a conflict-ridden history with its volcanic eruption in the Los Angeles riots of 1992. Following this, Detective Carter adds his own flavor, recoding the song through black cultural expressions. Showcasing hip-hop dance moves, his response is a dialogic engagement with Lee's implicit extension of friendship. War in the form of social division is definitely not an effective response to racial divisions. The camera works to suture the audience in this scene, using comedic energy in framing a two-shot, then the all-important shot–reverse shot. Through racialized suture, Carter works off Lee's humorous rendition and adds a performance of hip-hop moves with the martial arts hero. Elevating the humor through mutual teamwork and Asian-black codes of affect culture, Carter's performance stabilizes the homosocial space by educating and translating the politics of culture and citizenship for the martial arts hero through the active body of black racialization. Thus, this maneuver produces a more egalitarian equation than that of the standard buddy format seen in Hollywood. It creates a common bond based upon common exclusions, and constructs their race and masculinity based upon mutual respect for each other. At the end of this scene, the two members of the buddy team teach each other their respective cultural traditions, kung-fu and hip-hop moves, as a means to unearth the compromises and knowledge needed to be culturally engaged and mutually respectful of each other.

Forming a politics of reflexivity, interracial alliance engenders a critique of the social and cultural structures that keep buddies marginal. Through the process of cultural exchange, the shot–reverse shot affirms this newfound cohesion. The buddy picture genre, then, is reworked by a move toward egalitarian traditions evoking civic republicanism and the need for community-based solidarity. At the end of the hilarious scene, after teaching each other hip-hop and kung-fu moves, the two mockingly point guns at each other in order to snatch the guns away. As an oppositional gaze about power, the two-shot here works to produce spectatorial identification with the buddies' newfound friendship. While boisterously laughing together, Carter and Lee point guns at each other's throats and acknowledge the foolishness of "war." As the pair dances in synchronicity, the audience sees them moving down the sidewalk, arms pumping up and down in unison. From the third eye, with their backs turned to the audience, the political gaze is racialized, disrupted, and destabilized.

This "rule of equality" is represented, once again, by the incorporation of the "dozens," an oral tradition in black folk culture that is also an antecedent to the raps of hip-hop MCs. This oral form entails participants creating lyrical lists back and forth in order to masculinize their verbal messages with punch lines, dramatic effect, wit, and humor. Realizing that both their fathers were police officers, Carter and Lee try to "outdo" each other through hyperbole by narrating their fathers' exploits. The shot–reverse shot works to suture the audience into the space of fantasy and wish fulfillment: "My daddy arrested fifteen people"; "My father arrested twenty-five people"; "My daddy saved five crack heads from a burning building"; "My father caught a bullet with his own hand"; "My daddy kick your daddy's ass." Aside from the Oedipal subtext in all this talk about fathers, the playful quid pro quo exchange finalizes Lee's ability to comprehend and take part in U.S. national culture. Using black folk culture and verbal assault, this exchange is much like a poetry slam. While on an equal footing with Carter, Lee can definitely "speakuh English," and he thus has gained Carter's respect and admiration. Carter formalizes this interracial alliance by exclaiming in the ensuing fight with the Asian gang: "I'm Blackanese." As the buddies talk together, dance together, and now fight side by side, Carter instantiates a linguistic and symbolic hybridity that underlines the meaningful cultural exchange in Asian-black spectatorship.

This relationship is not as well determined in *Romeo Must Die* because of the different dynamics between Han and Trish, but their symbolic union can have empowering connotations in relation to state power, property relations, and interracial romance. The first major fight scene between Han and his black counterparts demonstrates the utilization of interracial mimesis as a means to create a sense of solidarity. Between the fight scenes are suggestive interracial looks through the shot–reverse shot technique, suturing the audience to both Han and Trish. The martial arts hero's individualism, his lone trek to solve his brother's lynching, transforms with an interracial alliance with Trish O'Day, the crime boss's daughter. Here, sexuality and violence intertwine with Hollywood production codes of antimiscegenation in containing the overdetermined bodily agency of the martial arts hero.

On the one hand, the deployment of model minority masculinity is evident in the ways in which Han Sing defeats the O'Day gang through specific strategies and techniques of the state apparatus. Reflecting the problems of racial profiling today, the police have incorporated more sophisticated surveillance techniques and tried-and-true methods of apprehending black males for the prison-industrial complex.[67] In this scene, Han enters Trish's private space when he comes unannounced into her apartment. Trish does not feel threatened by his presence, instead offering to help him. After a discussion about the tracing of his brother's last telephone call, Han has secured aid from Trish in finding out that the telephone calls were made to her clothing shop. As though a romantic gaze were in place, they then smile at one another when the O'Day gang drives up, headed by the comic figure of Maurice. Han then racially masquerades as a foreign Chinese delivery boy as Maurice and his associates come to the front doorway. Maurice apprehends that Han is not a delivery boy because there is a lack of an "oriental" aroma in the air. Obviously, we then have the much-anticipated martial arts fight scene.

From Han's vantage point, his gaze is the one the audience sutures to, especially in being the recipient of Maurice's wisecracks such as calling him "dim sum." While performing the flying crane position made famous in *The Karate Kid*, Maurice's representation of masculinity as excessive and overdetermined is the main engine of humor and clownish behavior. Through his racial mimesis of Ralph Macchio's famous climactic moment in whitewashed martial arts films, Maurice racializes Han as a Chinatown caricature. The overdetermined ignorance, much like Carter's, elicits some form of punishment and retribution. Han transforms into a fighting dynamo, and we enter the space/time of the martial arts fight scene. Maurice's excessive masculinity, his large body size and even larger verbosity, is in contrast to Han's small frame and few words. In this way, the misrecognition of blacks of the law and police authority is routed through the heavy-handedness of the Asian martial arts disciplinarian. As distinctly opposite the black masculinity of Maurice, we are asked to marvel at Han's somersault over the stairwell and subsequent flying low kick because the camera is positioned from the vantage point of a third eye. Each punch from the gang is reciprocated with a block, synchronized in a predictable pattern of force-counterforce. Accordingly, the martial arts sequences serve to suture the spectator to the hero, but their "unreality" also reminds the spectator that he or she is in the realm of the imaginary. Indeed, the sheer athleticism and production value of the shots might cause the viewer to ask, "How do they do that?," thereby taking the spectator out of the reverie of visual pleasure.[68] Because dialogue is nonexistent, facial expressions of awe and dismay, frustration and pain are the main visual cues in the martial arts fight scenes. Similar to pornography, the visual culture of martial arts fights is embellished with facial contortions, close-ups, and exaggerations, adding humor and spectator affect to the physical acrobatics.[69] In this case, the next round of fighting down the staircase showcases the police tactics of apprehending criminals (and in the process subjecting black males to the prison system). The police tactics are acted out in an overdetermined manner, highlighting the absolute, extraterritorial force and dominance of militarized state power.

The camera follows Han's gaze as he unleashes plastic hand restraints on his combatants and then goes about whipping them like animals. Such treatment had been popular among slave owners and overseers during the slave trade and on slave plantations, thus showing the unique coupling of an Asian male hero and black "whipping boys." When Han undresses one of the gang members, hog-ties him, and exposes his gold bikini underwear, the figure of the Asian martial arts hero emasculates black men for their excessive virility. Later, when Han apprehends the black gun from Maurice, unclips the ammunition, and drives off in a black sports utility vehicle, his containment of blackness via African American bodies is total and complete. Through color symbolism, he takes away their virile firepower, he drives off in their ride, and he does all this without breaking a sweat. Trish smiles, and Han's performance as disciplinarian and racial policeman is complete.

In *White Screens, Black Images*, James Snead outlines three master codes that provide foundational logics for the production of black representation in classic cinema. From D. W. Griffith's *The Birth of a Nation* to Shirley Temple's blackface, Snead argues that mythification, marking, and omission were constitutive components for the production codes.[70] Mythification is a phantasmagoric relationship constructed in the white imaginary; marking is the construction of blackness through costume, lighting, and contrast; and omission is a reversal, distortion, or some other form of censorship, of the racialization of the black body in cinema. In this sense, these processes use the camera as the liminal spatial and temporal mediator between the image and spectator in designating racialized gazes. In such a construction, it produces the gaze as political through cinematic citizenship.[71] As such, right before the line of credits, the moment in mainstream cinema when the nuclear white family is consolidated through the classic Hollywood kiss, we see a hug between Han and Trish. The camera then marks the two buddies, walking together over a bridge. This image is significant in reformulating how a major Hollywood production can end. Han takes Trish's hand and gives her a hug that subverts media representations of Asian-black conflict. As a new political gaze, Asian-black spectatorship, among spectator and screen images, redefines the meaning associated with crossing over, transcending the liminal spaces of symbolic bridges.

4. Afro-Asian Rhythms and Rhymes

The Hip-Hop and Spoken Word Lyricists of I Was Born with Two
Tongues and the Mountain Brothers

The pairing of a martial arts hero and a hip-hop buddy, as considered in the
previous chapter, reveals a genealogy between Asian and black communities
in post–civil rights culture, referring back to the heyday of kung-fu fever and
the origins of hip-hop music. In this chapter, I continue to examine the urban
dynamic of Afro-Asian cultures but shift the conversation to alternative and
digital spheres of Asian American cultural production—the realm of spoken word and underground hip-hop music. This chapter diverges from the
commodity form of Hollywood cinema and redirects our attention to youth
subcultures and the Asian male body on the stage, a transformative space for
revolutionary critique.

In November 2001, Porter's Pub at the University of California, San Diego,
a usually sleepy hangout for hungry and thirsty students, housed a spectacular live performance by the pan-Asian spoken word group I Was Born with
Two Tongues. On their nationwide tour, sponsored by AsianAvenue.com, the
Chicago-based wordsmiths occupied the imaginations and heartstrings of a
captivated audience famished for voices different from the post-9-11 rhetoric of patriotism and American exceptionalism. With a standing-room-only
crowd of mostly Asian Americans, the performance by I Was Born with Two
Tongues offered students of color an alternative space for exploring issues of
identity, stereotypes, gender relations, and U.S. imperialism by recognizing
their lives performed on stage.

Enter Dennis Kim, aka Denizen Kane—a Korean American twenty-some-
thing with shaved head, hooded athletic jersey, and gifted powerhouse voice.
Sharing the stage with him was the rest of his crew: Anida Yoeu Esguerra,
a Cambodian Muslim immigrant; Marlon Esguerra, a second-generation
Filipino American; and Darius Savage, a black American musician who often accompanies 2Tongues, as they are affectionately known. Prior to this
performance, Jessica Hagedorn had praised the release of their debut album,
Broken Speak, with the following observation: "2Tongues is about brains, po-

ems, beauty, wit and a powerhouse performance style that breathes fire and kicks ass."[1] What distinguished Kim was his spectacular fusion of freestyle hip-hop, Rastaman third world reggae chants, Korean folk music, and traditional poetic free verse, accompanied by Savage's upright jazz bass. Passionately unique, Denizen Kane represented the dynamism of race, the Asian male body, and the performance of Afro-Asian cultural expression on the live stage. Using urban and third world aesthetics, he revolutionized the relationship between the Asian American male body and blackness and thus inspired his audiences to see through the looking glass of racial magnetism.

Outside lecture halls and classrooms, the coffee houses, pubs, and college venues for spoken word poetry capture, even beyond the theatrical stage, the possibilities of political activism and dissemination of knowledge through the power of the speech act, what Saul Williams calls "incantations." Additionally, new identities and social consciousness emerge from the dialectical engagement between artist and audience when poetry, sound, and political thought reverberate the moments of history. For instance, Kim's spoken word performance of masculinity and race, using "the spells laced into poetry," challenged white supremacist history and dispelled myths about culturally invisible Asian American men.[2] But he did so by crafting a passionate desire for self-determination for both men and women, culturally and politically, using his body and voice as a canvas for expressing the contradictions of imperialism, capitalism, and ethnocentrism in, to borrow a page from bell hooks, a white supremacist heteropatriarchal capitalist society. In such an enactment of artistic expression and political critique, Kim's performance of the Asian male body in the public space of Porter's Pub can reveal the power of what Walter Benjamin calls "the shock effect." In "A Work of Art in the Age of Mechanical Reproduction," Benjamin evinces the power of cultural production to create the propulsion of contemplation and critical self-reflection; to enlarge the social function of critical inquiry and awareness; and to have "presence of mind" or, in today's hip-hop parlance, to know what time it is and where you're at. Keeping this need in mind, the "shock effect" of spoken word is its voices speaking forth from the underbelly of capitalist and imperialist projects as we know them, one audience and one present moment at a time.

As such, this chapter addresses the conductive intersection of live performance by Asian American men in hip-hop music and spoken word and links the possibilities of Asian-black cultural fusions and Internet productions as their main medium of communication. It calls attention to the role of public intellectuals such as Dennis Kim and the role of art, activism, and culture intertwined with Asian American urban cultures and black musical expressions. Importantly, this chapter focuses on emergent yet highly significant cultural practices taking place in Asian American communities, especially among youth and on the Internet. Altogether, it emphasizes the Asian-black interface of spoken word and hip-hop as a revolutionary practice as the practitioners claim, one that disrupts the constancy of racial magnetism in matters of social policy and public discourse. Dennis Kim's alias in his hip-hop crew Typical Cats is Denizen Kane, as mentioned above; the term "denizen" connotes someone who has taken up permanent residence in a foreign country and who is given some rights there. His name marks the characterization of Asian Americans in theater, film, and music as habitual outsiders—the ways Asian Americans are excluded from mainstream U.S. visual culture. Denizen Kane, much like its filmic specter, haunts the North American racial imaginary, one stage and one audience at a time, each ephemeral moment abolishing history and space, what Karen Shimakawa exposes as the "phantasms of orientalness through and against which an Asian American performer must struggle to be seen."[3]

Circa August 2005, in Tampa, Florida, more than twelve thousand curious museum-going voyeurs attended a four-day exhibit of cadavers and body parts of preserved Chinese men and women. Called "Bodies: The Exhibition," the display featured twenty cadavers and 260 various body parts that had been preserved at Dalian Medical University's Plastination Company in China. Tampa's Museum of Science and Industry had procured the rights to display the dead, but not without creating a controversy because permission had not been granted by the deceased or their families. Breaking an attendance record set by the 2003 *Titanic* exhibition, the excavation and preservation of Chineseness from their morbid death produced widespread interest; as CNN reported, "similar exhibitions have drawn millions of visitors around the world."[4] This perverse fascination to see the Asian male body as spectacle, detached from his humanity and personhood, has been a trademark of white supremacy's narcissistic impulse to construct "the Oriental" in circus sideshows, vaudeville acts, minstrelsy comedies, popular film, mass literature, and, most recently, the Broadway stage.

During the mid-nineteenth century, Chang and Eng, conjoined twins from Siam, were main showstoppers for Barnum and Bailey's Circus because of their rare "freak" entertainment value for white audiences. Like Afong Moy, the "Chinese Lady," Chang and Eng toured throughout North America and Europe, displaying their bodies as oddities for spectator consumption and pleasure.[5] Indeed, the term "Siamese twin" originates from the spectacle of Chang's and Eng's Asian male bodies, which became constituted by a white imperial gaze. What James Moy calls "the panoptic empire of the gaze," this visual representation of Asianness as fixed and immutable and often as living, breathing dramatis personae, had centralized the power to look as part of America's Manifest Destiny, from the eastern seaboard to the western frontier, to an imagined East full of mystery and monstrosity. Moy asserts:

> By the middle of the nineteenth century two forms of the empowering gaze became clear, the serial and voyeuristic. The popular form of the serial, or survey, offered amusements which brought together, apparently authoritative series and collocations of objects to create the *potential* for meaning.[6]

Indeed, the potential on stage for the creation of meaning over and beyond the humanity of the Asian male body often encompassed viewing white men pretending to be Asian men. In this sense, minstrelsy shows first began to appear after the novelty and spectacle of museum dioramas became a relic of consumptive pastimes. Robert Lee illumines: "Many minstrel shows had made 'Siamese twins' part of their comedy routines. . . . Minstrelsy was a powerful vehicle for constructing the Chinaman as a polluting racial Other in the popular imagination," including such wildly popular shows as Charley Fox's *Minstrel Songster*.[7] Often discussed in terms of blackface, minstrelsy had been much more complex and expansive in its construction of racialized bodies including stock characters such as Zip Coon, John Chinaman in yellowface, and various Indians. Unlike the consumption of Asianness in museums for middle-class white gazes, the performance of yellowface began as entertainment for white working-class audiences, who had recently emerged as a class during the expansion of U.S. industrial capitalism. Through songs, comedy skits, and stump speeches that distorted accents and dialects, yellowface in minstrelsy allowed for Anglo-Americans to represent Asian American masculinity. As Alexander Saxton and George Rawick have explained, minstrelsy functioned to contain the racial crisis of immigration, slavery, industrial capitalism, and Manifest Destiny by consolidating a white supremacist whole, which continually needed reassurance of its moral and racial certitude.[8]

These representations of white supremacy dressed in the garments of orientalism continued to be expressed in popular film and literature. Films such as D. W. Griffith's *Broken Blossoms* (1919), originally titled *The Yellow Man and the Girl*, Frank Capra's *The Bitter Tea of General Yen* (1933), George Pal's *7 Faces of Dr. Lao* (1964), and the 1961 Blake Edwards classic *Breakfast at Tiffany's* represent this obsessive desire through yellowface to contain visually the threat of Asianness. For example, popular visual representations of the Asian male body for white spectatorial pleasure include the evil figure Fu Manchu and the comic figure Charlie Chan. Denied self-representation in performance, production, and creative expression, Asian American men were represented through the mediated body of Werner Oland, a white male actor who played both the world conqueror Fu and the bumbling eunuch Chan. Mary Douglass states: "The body becomes a particularly salient symbolic referent in the context of boundary crisis, the physical body mirroring the boundaries of the social body."[9] As such, the visual containment of Asian masculinity through the spatial containment of the representational field (e.g., the stage, diorama, movie screen, or cropped photograph) is indicative of the invisibility of Asian American men in U.S. national culture. This invisibility references the dehumanization of the Asian male body and thus the metonymic function required of American empire to objectify and marginalize Asianness in order to reconstitute itself as whole, coherent, and modern. Thus, like "Bodies: The Exhibition," the historical racialization of Asian male bodies, knowable by the gaze of white supremacy, shows the development of consumption patterns and racial hierarchies that conjoin race and space, all for the exclusion of Asianness from self-representation and, ultimately, self-determination.

In Asian American studies, the study of race, performance, and the body has allowed for rigorous and continued examination of Asian Americans excluded from national culture and citizenship. One important study in the emerging field of Asian American performance is Karen Shimakawa's *National Abjection*. As highlighted in the title of her monograph, abjection characterizes the politically situated repulsion of Asianness from the U.S. national body, the "collapsing of nationality, race, ethnicity, and bodily identity."[10] Borrowing from Julia Kresteva's theorization, Shimakawa traces, through the character Tam in Frank Chin's play *The Chickencoop Chinaman*, the process of abjection, "an attempt to circumscribe and radically differentiate something that, although deemed repulsively *other* is, paradoxically, at some fundamental level, an undifferentiated part of the whole."[11] Looking at Asian American theater, Shimakawa's work enables us to understand abjection as a constitutive process of white supremacy (although she euphemizes white power, like many Asian Americanists, as the "dominant group"). In particular, her ethnographic work in interviewing Asian American theater artists and companies, especially Mako Iwamatsu and the East West Players, reveals the persistent institutional obstacles for Asian American actors in obtaining roles that do not fall prey to exoticism, stereotypes, and mythification. As Iwamatsu narrates: "The older generation [of Asian American actors] had been used to getting disciplined or being taught by non-Asians, white men. . . . It was very difficult to . . . break them away from what they were used to [racist stereotypes of orientalness]."[12]

In addition, Shimakawa's work on live performance distinguishes theater from other cultural practices because it focuses on understanding the relationship between artists, audience, and performance within a specific temporality and space. She proposes: "Live theater—even at its most seamlessly realist/naturalist—cannot help but flaunt its presentational qualities: a live audience unavoidably participates in the artifice onstage to a degree greater than in perhaps any other artistic medium."[13] For Shimakawa, live theater is a powerful medium for thespians to play a fictional role, with artifice as a tool, to expand the senses of reception, perceiving movements, voices, emotions, and spectacles that are not mediated by the director's camera or the producer's sound recording. How do we then conceptualize the live performance of spoken word or hip-hop artists who supposedly are trying to produce the "real?" What are the differences in live performativity that must be differentiated, based on questions of authenticity, theatricality, and place? In one sense, Walter Benjamin's theory of "shock effect" allows us to think about the concept of critical engagement and its elevation of *the political* in spoken word and hip-hop.

In *Speak It Louder*, Deborah Wong observes in the primacy of rebellion and performance that "scholars working in postindustrial, postmodern contexts look intently for signs of *revolt*, and performance has been identified by some as a means for locating agency."[14] On the spoken word and hip-hop stage, racialized bodies and revolt are interconnected, maintaining a direct link between audience and artists to the political. In contrast to live theater, the separation between artifice and suspension of disbelief is not requested. In fact, the elevation of belief or a quality of nonfiction is maintained in order for the audience to respond to the perceived genuineness of thought, expression, and persona. To exhibit artifice, not to say performance, is seen by audience members as contrivance, as trying too hard to appeal to the audience without heartfelt depth or vulnerability. The performative, raced body becomes transparent for the audience, each thought critically evaluated at different temporal speeds, each whimsical joke collectively enjoyed or rejected, each moment of emotional catharsis delimiting time and place. Such a manner of live performance is the production of a different reality, a process of estrangement that counters the normalizing process of alienation of social life and daily existence under transnational capitalism and U.S. empire. Whereas realist theater incorporates properties that reproduce the effects of the real, "these props index the failure of representation to reproduce the real. . . . The real inhabits the space that representation cannot reproduce."[15]

Walter Benjamin's idea of the aura helps us understand the centrality of history, art, and representational realness. For Benjamin, in "The Work of Art in the Age of Mechanical Reproduction," the aura is the uniqueness of artistic expression in a particular moment of time and place, "its presence in time and space, its unique existence at the place where it happens to be."[16] Furthermore, he explains that "the adjustment of reality to the masses and of the masses to reality is a process of unlimited scope, as much for thinking as for perception."[17] With the visceral aspects of live performance, the spectator is not limited to the visual sense of perception, and this critical lens is not confined by a two-dimensional space. Unlike film spectatorship, the audience actively views each other, gauging the reception and emotional barometer of the event through smell, touch, and unrestricted visual movement—all ensconced in ephemerality. In this sense, Benjamin conjectures a powerful connection between aura, live presence, and active perception: "if while resting on a summer afternoon, you follow with your eyes a mountain range on the horizon or a branch which cast its shadow over you, you experience the aura of those mountains, of the branch."[18] However, when he says that "mechanical reproduction emancipates the work of art from its parasitical dependence on ritual. . . . [I]nstead of being based on ritual, it begins to be based on another practice—politics," he fails to acknowledge the full possibilities of live performance, that its uniqueness in artistic ritual could be a politicized space.

Conversely, Wong's and Shimakawa's ethnographic work on Asian American hip-hop and repertory theater imagines new political possibilities rooted in challenging the hegemony of racial stereotypes and white spectatorship. Indeed, as Dorinne Kondo suggests, "it matters centrally who is writing, who is performing in what venue for what audience."[19] Narrating the performative function of home, community, and identity in the production of Perry Miyake's play *Doughball* in 1991, Kondo illumines: "Asian Americans never laugh the laughter of recognition because we are systematically erased from view. We never see ourselves portrayed the way *we* see ourselves."[20] Furthermore, Kondo's explication of Asian American recognition in live performance is in stark contrast to Josephine Lee's pathologizing of Asian American masculinity and preference to highlight "any Asian American enjoyment of plays that employ exaggerated, stereotypical, or exotic Asian or Asian American characters."[21] Lee's work ignores the pervasiveness of white spectatorial supremacy and disregards the need to examine and emphasize a politics of spectatorship and production that has self-determined Asian American writers, actors, and producers. As such, the intersection of Asian American studies and performance studies has produced paradigms of cultural ethnography that link politics and present temporalities, and that actively engage with questions of cultural autonomy and revolutionary practice. Resisting poststructuralist suspicions of authenticity and authorship, I want to privilege and explore what Kondo calls "the effects of authenticity or verisimilitude." What is it about the aura of live performance that produces a politics of recognition from audiences? How can Asian American men in hip-hop and spoken word create new possibilities of masculinity that produce shock, contemplation, and critical inquiry? My readings of I Was Born with Two Tongues and the Mountain Brothers challenge Asian American performance studies, which has predominantly constructed the idea of Asian American live performance as "primarily Chinese and Japanese American, upper-middle class, and English-speaking."[22]

On the North Side of Chicago, away from the glamour and tradition of Air Jordan, the Daley political machine, and Harpo Productions, Dennis Kim was an introverted teenager, navigating his way through the emerging spoken word scene during the mid-1990s. At the age of seventeen, he started attending the mostly African American open-mic events around Chicago, including famed spots such as the Mad Bar, Another Level, and X. One night, at a live performance, serendipity came along. Kim saw Seattle spoken word group Isangmahal perform, their name being a Tagalog word referencing Bob Marley's third world anthem "One Love." Describing his moment of inner transformation, Kim recalls the night he saw Isangmahal:

> I saw some of them perform and they were just fucking sick. My friends and I, we were writing too. We were part of the hip-hop generation, and we were writing our little raps, thinking we were fresh. But I went to check these guys and they were fucking sick. . . . There was self-love there.[23]

After enrolling at the University of Chicago, Kim met Marlon Esguerra, Anida Yoeu Esguerra, and Emily Chang; all passionate about spoken word, they kept bumping into each other at performances and frequented the same hangouts. Soon, the group formed a collective pan-Asian spoken word troupe of their own, calling themselves I Was Born with Two Tongues.

With its blend of hip-hop culture, political activism, and powerful oral performance, spoken word has been an underground art form for socially, culturally, and politically voiceless people to express their discontent with the Ivory Tower protectionism of text-based poetry, the corporatization of artistic expression, and the right-wing counterrevolution in U.S. national politics.[24] But more than this, spoken word allows many "to be seen," and "to be who they want to be."[25] Emerging from this politicized and racialized context, Asian American spoken word artists and groups such as 2Tongues, Ishle Yi Park, Beau Sia, Eighth Wonder, Staceyann Chin, Yellow Fist, and Freedom Writers, to name a few, have used spoken word to challenge the contradictions of white supremacist heteropatriarchal capitalist domination. Moreover, the fusion of hip-hop music and spoken word has been literally conjoined through HBO's *Def Jam Poetry Slam*, films such as *Love Jones* and *Slam*, and television shows like *Oz* and MTV's *Lyricist Lounge*. Indeed, 2Tongues' Yellow Technicolor Tour with the Asian American group the Pacifics, another Chicago-based hip-hop collective, facilitated their popularity and widespread critical acclaim.

Sponsored by AsianAvenue.com, an Internet site geared toward Asian American youths and young professionals, the Yellow Technicolor Tour created a whirlwind word-of-mouth buzz in 2002, due to standing-room-only audiences and raw visceral performances. Across college campuses, sponsored primarily by Asian American student organizations and fraternities, the Yellow Technicolor Tour brought up issues affecting Asian American communities, as *EM* magazine announced, to "educate the masses on the plight of the Asian person in the midst of a pseudo-equal rights-for-all millennial dream."[26] College tour stops included a wide array of public, private, liberal arts, and science-oriented institutions of higher learning including Lawrence University, Columbia College, Arizona State University, the University of Pittsburgh, Wellesley College, and the University of California, Riverside. Most remarkable about the tour is that much of the publicity and press was disseminated, as early as 2002, through the Internet.

Several websites devoted extensive coverage to both 2Tongues and the Pacifics, showcasing upcoming tour dates, printing interviews with the performers, and presenting forums to discuss blogger-initiated comments and reviews about the tour. From more mainstream Asian American websites such as AsianWeek.com, Goldsea.com, and AsianAvenue.com to more niche-oriented websites like newcitychicago.com, evilmonito.com, and nichibeitimes.com, the effectiveness of the Internet to create buzz and critical evaluation for Asian American cultural practices, at the time, heralded a new era for a decentralized media machinery. This event utilized cyberdistribution patterns that have since been widely adopted by youth subcultures, reminiscent of hip-hop's early days of fliers, posters, and word-of-mouth. Suggestively, even though Asian American websites were the main engine for the success of the Yellow Technicolor Tour, the audiences that turned out were definitely more racially diverse than might at first be assumed. Marlon Esguerra remarked about the composition of audience members: "It's about the struggle . . . the majority of our audience are mixed crowds . . . the Asian, Black, Esas [sic] struggle . . . we're all different but the struggle is the same."[27]

Throughout their national and international tour, members of 2Tongues performed many pieces from their 1999 debut album, *Broken Speak*. Asian

Improv Records, a nonprofit record label based in San Francisco, record-ed and distributed *Broken Speak*. Started by Mark Izu, Jon Jang, Anthony Brown, and Francis Wong—all jazz musicians—Asian Improv initially formed to "bring the African American tradition of improvised music and jazz together with our Asian roots."[28] Not surprisingly, this fusion of Afro-Asian aesthetic forms to fashion new Asian American music reflected the experiences of all the founding members, who had been active during the Asian American movement. Indeed, Asian Improv seeks to develop and nur-ture "Asian American arts and performance," and its landmark recording of 2Tongues expanded its predominant audience base of jazz and blues toward hip-hip culture.

As a result, *Broken Speak* is a musical and poetic testament to nurture and develop Asian American self-love and self-expression. Composed of sev-enteen tracks, *Broken Speak*'s astonishing array of musical influences, from hip-hop scratch DJ mixes and jazz instrumentals to reggae-inflected spoken word, creates a form of cultural communication that blends political activism and art. Pieces such as "Not Your Fetish" showcase Anida Yoeu Esguerra's and Emily Chang's talent to remake Asian American femininity into a form that refuses sexual objectification and exoticism within U.S. popular culture. In addition, Yoeu Esguerra's performance of "Alag" (i.e., "a little Asian girl") is a showstopper due to its wit, humor, and criticism of stereotypes of the demure Asian woman, who then reinvents herself as "that Asian girl, the one who speaks with sharpened instincts and responds with intentional rage."[29] Speaking about her use of rage to express her racial trauma, Yoeu Esguerra explains: "I think people underestimate the power of art as activism. We are political poetry. We are just telling the shit we feel and telling our stories. Actively participating in trying to create a better world and trying to create change, which starts within yourself."[30] Quite remarkably, the performance of Asian American gender and sexuality in *Broken Speak* works to create emer-gent and different kinds of femininity and masculinity. Although this chapter does not have the scope to devote needed attention to the many facets of 2Tongue's oeuvre, the lens of race and masculinity may illuminate some of the creative and political processes and energies in perpetual motion in their collective endeavor.

In this sense, at the 2001 performance of 2Tongues at the University of California, San Diego, Dennis Kim presented a piece entitled "Han," which incorporates Korean *pansori* and *punk-ak* folk music, jazz bass lines, and hip-hop rhyme schemes. Routing his Korean American masculinity through the Korean term *han*, Kim's invocation of a word that connotes deep, lasting trauma in the Korean language reworks traditional ways in which Korean men are expected to express their wounds, pains, and fears. The concept of *han* had been pivotal for the "comfort women" (*chongshindae*), Korean women kidnapped as sex slaves by the Japanese army during World War II, to narrate and expunge their historical legacy of silence and shame; and, in a Korean American context, the documentary film *Sa-I-Gu* chronicles the concept of *han* for Korean American women dealing with the loss of their Koreatown properties and, even more dramatically, their immigrant ideals of the American Dream after the Rodney King verdicts and subsequent riots in Los Angeles. In this way, it is important to note that Korean American women and not Korean American men have been the inspirational and courageous voices to narrate the contradictions of Japanese militarism and U.S. racialization. Therefore, Kim's special performance of "Han" reimagines the possibility of a kind of Korean American manhood that gains dignity and voice by talking about the suffering of Korean people within a transpacific diaspora. Specifically, he responds to the impact of U.S. empire, patriarchy, and white supremacy over Korean American identity by weaving a critical tapestry of *han* through Asian-black musical forms.

On the CD recording, "Han" initiates the sonic experience of 2Tongues in track 1, framing the opening hip-hop poetic verses of "Han" in the traditional Korean folk music of *pansori* storytelling and *punk-ak* drum circles, both styles with roots in shamanism and narrative ritual. The employment of Korean folk music and the spoken word medium allows Kim to reconstruct his Korean American masculinity sans borders, akin to Gloria Anzaldúa's "sans fronteras" of mestiza consciousness.[31] As one critic comments, Kim's body becomes the corporal instrument to mediate sound, word, and diasporic fusions through his "grimace of concentration," "his right hand twist[ing] the bill of his baseball cap back and forth," "left index finger point[ing] to the sky," and "deep and sorrow[ful]" voice.[32] Significantly, the power of agency in remaking the Korean American body contests the coercive forces that shape Korean American bodies in the first place. The audience sees, hears, and touches (through sonic vibrations) the rising crescendo of words: "There is a word—*Han* / that squirms behind the vacuum glass of old photographs—*Han* / is the hungry scent of sorrow on the skin of my people—*Han* / is the sound of a tongue plucked out of a young child's mouth."[33] In weaving Korean American identity through *han*, Kim discovers the process of memory, language, and lineage caused by the violence of immigration enacted through bodily displacement and disfigurement. As Ishle Yi Park comments, Kim challenges audiences to change "the way they see the world by urging them to question identity, history, and roots."[34] Without pretense, Kim employs Korean vernacular in his spoken word.

Not even his "broken speak" can dissuade Kim from singing passionately in the next movement of "Han," wailing the lament of identity, homeland, and U.S. militarism with *pansori* singing and percussion. Commenting on using the Korean language, Kim maintains: "There is something about those words in my mouth, even in my broken speak, that communicates something important to me, and I am hungry to participate in an art where every shade of me is visible."[35] For 2Tongues, the "broken speak," as their CD title suggests, is a vivid reminder of how language and identity are affected by global and political migrations of people due to war and racial trauma, especially in the Korean context of "how the DMZ becomes the barbed line that traces thee / military." Linking the U.S. military presence on the Korean peninsula to the Cold War Korean diaspora *within* post–civil rights race relations, Kim relates: "I get a face full of tchim boy / if you don't step off my mic with that assimilate and distort /ghim becomes kim / and chei becomes choi / and I become the foreigner assimtism [sic] employ." Kim's construction of Korean immigrant identity to the U.S. nation-state challenges wholesale gratitude for the host country, especially when the process of assimilation is a militarized process similar to the situation on the peninsula. Rather, he identifies the difference between diasporas of war and diasporas of flight, so much so that he breaks Khachig Tölölyan's definitional rule that "diasporas may criticize their homelands but not chastise them."[36] Indeed, Kim's performance of Korean American masculinity, as constructed within the Korean diaspora, critiques the post–civil rights "glitter" of the American Dream and mirages of "Gold Mountain" that at once peels his "skin back from the madness of [his] heart." There seems to be less a critique than a radical rejection of a U.S. citizenship that erases his humanity, while he does not wait "for the culture to embrace me yo." Thus, immigration and assimilation are nodal points of cultural disruption and state violence, with the upright bass of Darius Savage as the formal backdrop that gives rhythm to Kim's rhymes.

In this way, "Han" establishes firm roots in black musical traditions that enable a radical critique of the U.S. nation-state and imperialism. Blending Savage's bass lines and including a sampling of a song by Louis Armstrong near the end, "Han" forms a sense of shared racial trauma with black music while at the same time keeping the specificity of Korean American experiences intact. Not only do the jazz and hip-hip forms mesh with Korean folk music but, even more, Kim reimagines, using Afro-Asian musical fusion, broader conceptions of diasporic identity that confront, as Stuart Hall relates, "the fragmented and pathological ways in which that experience has been reconstructed within the dominant regimes of cinematic and visual representation of the West."[37] As a result, working off Gayatri Gopinath's contribution that the nation is but one location within diasporic cultural circuits, the Asian-black cultural crossings of "Han" offer an example of spoken word's multiple exchanges within and without the nation-state itself.[38]

What we receive in the end stanzas of the piece are intersectional dimensions of Korean American identity and gender politics. Continuing with a quicker, up-tempo jazz bass line, Kim questions the construction of gender and race for men and women. Discussing Korean American masculinity and femininity, he remarks: "Can I hold my brother up if his manhood must be defended? Can I see my sister's face clouded make transcendent / to mend I, wipe her eye of surgeries, foundation can't be drawn on / and on your skin I see my *Han*—Dancing." As a means to connect bodies and assimilation, Kim routes *han* through the impact of white supremacy in U.S. national culture, its pop culture of desirable white bodies and its persistent stereotyping of Asian men and women. But in the end, Kim seeks to "paint my freedom with the bruises on my heart / I start by speaking peace," and thus he utters the mantra of overcoming racialized personhood and the abjection of Asianness through live performance, of using the stage and microphone as crafted responses to dehumanization and trauma. As such, *han* is the centralizing concept of displacement and gender formation, transplanted from traditionally Korean women's trauma and reinvented to link both Asian American men's and women's racialization under the umbrella of U.S. militarism and in the "½ peninsula."

Because the tracks on *Broken Speak* cannot adequately portray the live dynamism of 2Tongues, the live-recorded "Tree City Anthem" is an important track to represent Kim's homegrown persona as a live performer in Chicago. Not coincidentally, Kim is the featured member to showcase his ability and talent to generate audience appeal and dialectical critical engagement through his improbable musical and poetic repertoire including KRS-One-inspired reggae chants, free-flow hip-hop rhymes, and the heartache found in rhythm and blues. This particular piece showcases the ability of an Asian male performer and his audience to create new spaces and ways of social awareness and critical interaction that break away from the traditional rigidity of patriarchal, nonreflective Asian masculinities.

Although not his most political piece, "Tree City Anthem" might be Kim's most personal. Addressing the death of his younger brother, the anthem is a centerpiece to Kim's aura of spirituality, which at once acknowledges and critiques his Christian background through the incorporation of "Jah" and "Allah" as legitimate names. At the beginning of his live set, Kim beckons the audience: "This show is for my baby last child, when I say last, you say child / you say last." Thereafter, the crowd responds to his call, and the noise level is clearly at a fever pitch; the audience is ready to be transported or, dare I say, "shocked." "My baby brother flew away from a world that's cold and hostile / left me in this place to preach terrible gospels [audience: come on!]." Singing a cappella, Kim's voice is resonant and full, displaying his range as a musician and artist as the audience encourages him to continue. Throughout the entire piece, audience members can be heard yelling "come with it!" and screaming when Kim switches from a cappella to reggae to hip-hop. As such, there are some breathtaking moments in "Tree City Anthem." On the one hand, we hear third world reggae flows of "we choose death as the kindest / shelter from the teeth of the timeless / now hide this" that hypnotize the audience into a head-bobbing trance. On the other hand, the track features the hip-hop-inspired poetry of "slow a boppin' tangibles-and-tangos / gold tangles and reasoning unravels /and nervous micro-babbles / I'm traveling a path without definite end" that mesmerizes hip-hop connoisseurs with its linguistic acrobatics. Remarking about genres, Kim relates:

> As young artists, there are pressures to obey the conventions of the form that you're working in. But the further I travel and the more I become myself, I realize that it's an impossibility to stay so within the confines of some genre. I only have this lifetime to be who I am. I can't waste time waiting for people to catch up, or waiting for them to agree that what I'm doing is hip-hop.[39]

As a risky gambit, all of this form switching allows the audience to appreciate the Asian male body as a refusal of pretense, as not appropriating but rather employing black forms to speak truth to power. And this lack of pretense and inspiration of genuineness offers a collective audience appreciation of the Asian male body as "real," a real-time performer able to transcend the racialized borders that create racial division and mistrust.

Other pieces like "In America" continue Kim's consideration of U.S. citizenship and Korean immigration through his examination of the ways his mother or *omma* faced hardships both economically and culturally. By redeploying the familiar mother-daughter trope in Asian American literature through the relationship between mothers and sons, Kim's sensitive treatment of how "women must cry many times to be heard" refashions the traditional focus of men's studies on fathers and sons. Finally, in "Race and I'm Running" and "Pillars," Kim works with Marlon Esguerra to question, as Esguerra speaks, "the ill still longing and cursing for belonging to a place of home, of Greystone, of uptown, of industrial corridors, census bureaus, neglected like ghetto stillborns." Using imageries of urban decay and economic destitution, "Pillars" incorporates Islamic prayer chants and hip-hop turntablism to create untraditional sonic cross-fertilizations that express the kind of experimentation taking place in *Broken Speak*. As Esguerra reminds us: "We remember like pop quiz, and pass songs by way of hip-hop." To some degree, all these pieces as well as others by 2 Tongue members ask audiences, especially Asian Americans, to rethink where Asian America positions itself in relation to other racial minorities. This may allow for cultural belonging and agency through a shared determination to formulate new and innovative paradigms of revolutionary cultural practice. In an interview, Kim conveys: "The real story of it is that you can't qualify the experience we're having here. There really isn't a model for what we're doing."[40] Indeed, the spoken word phenomenon has ambassadors such as 2 Tongues who are reconceptualizing not only Asian American performance cultures on the live stage and on the Internet but also the meaning of cultural self-determination and personal actualization.

With common ground between hip-hop and spoken word, I conclude my discussion of Asian American performance cultures by considering underground hip-hop and Asian American masculinity. Old-school Asian American crews like the Seoul Brothers, Yellow Peril, and Fists of Fury laid down demo tracks and gave live performances that used the medium of an emergent hip-hop cultural revolution during the late 1980s and early 1990s. Their cultural works embody a form of political empowerment and cultural expression to call out the contradictions of racial magnetism in the post–civil rights era. Working off these oft-maligned pioneers, new school artists and groups like MC Jin, the Typical Cats (with Denizen Kane), Boo-Yaa T.R.I.B.E., Key Kool, Rono Ise, In-Cite, the Pacifics, and the Far East Movement have elevated the prominence of Asian Americans in hip-hop, often called "GenerAsian hip-hop" in cyberspace. Nevertheless, no other crew can claim to have legitimized the talent, hard work, and persistence of Asian Americans in hip-hop to a greater extent than a Philadelphia-based crew calling themselves the Mountain Brothers.

As chronicled in the classical Chinese novel *Water Margin*, the original Mountain Brothers were Song Dynasty mountain bandits who contested wealthy landowners who were themselves committing corrupt forms of injustice upon poor people. Etched in underground hip-hop mythology, the current-day Mountain Brothers were the first Asian American hip-hop crew signed by a major label, namely Columbia Records/Ruffhouse Records, the home of Cypress Hill and the Fugees. Vanguards in the GenerAsian movement, the Mountain Brothers consist of Scott Jung (Chops), Steve Wei (Styles), and Chris Wang (Peril-L), a trio of former Penn State college stu-

dents who added the MC to Asian America's presence in hip-hop. Soon after forming, the crew gained street credibility and notoriety because of their
mixture of "scratching, themed rhymes, and storytelling."[41] In 1999, the release of their full-length LP, *Self: Volume 1*, was a watershed for Asian American hip-hop, as it signaled the first major critical and underground work
appreciated by mainstream music connoisseurs. Here, I am concerned with
interracial crossover appeal and the marketing of Asian American hip-hop
music in mainstream music and Internet cultures.

A remarkable aspect of the Mountain Brothers is that their fan base is
composed of mostly non-Asian people. Appealing to black, Latino/a, and
white crowds at their performances, the Mountain Brothers have diverse
audiences all across the United States who appreciate their organic Philly-
based sound and link them with other Philadelphia artists like the Roots and
Bahamadia. Nevertheless, in an interview about Asian American fan apathy,
Styles remarks: "I'm sure the majority of our fans are non-Asian. Although
we're completely happy with that, it's kind of unsettling to have non-Asian
people support your music and be all hype at shows, and then do a show for
certain populations of Asian people and have them just not get it at all."[42]
Relating their experiences in front of largely African American crowds, the
Mountain Brothers have had to overcome white supremacy's stereotyping of
Asian American men and their own co-optation of African American music. Moreover, as Deborah Wong informs us, "identifying African American
musics as a source for Asian American expression becomes a way for Asian
American musicians to rescue certain possibilities made so difficult by ra-
cializations that muffle and silence them."[43]

For African American hip-hop audiences, the success of interracial crossover appeal by non–African American artists is fraught with the understand-
able booby traps of suspicion and animosity (think: Vanilla Ice). Yet, even
though the Mountain Brothers have "felt the odd stares and glares when
signifying before a predominately black crowd back east," Chops confident-
ly relates, "we've found that any stereotyping ends in the first ten seconds.
Once they hear us, everything's cool."[44] Signifying an Asian American hip-
hop sound to African American audiences encompasses an understanding
of cultural respect and authentic passion for musical integrity. As George
Lipsitz illumines, "intercultural rap music" builds upon a base of "'prestige
from below' originating in African-American culture."[45] In this respect, the
Mountain Brothers in published interviews have repeatedly honored Afri-
can American hip-hop pioneers like Pete Rock, Diamond D, Timbo, Large
Professor, Jazze Pha, and Mannie Fresh.[46] Drawing inspiration from African
American pioneers, the Mountain Brothers have faced mounting challenges

from industry executives, both white and black, to create their own musical path while still maintaining respect for hip-hop.

The marketing of the Mountain Brothers reveals the tension between artist self-determination and commercial industry. Being Asian American has its disadvantages in the rap game. One big-name music executive praised their music and then bluntly surmised: "There's only one problem: you're Asian." Another music representative "suggested they liven up their stage act with kung-fu kicks, chanting and gongs."[47] After their campaign against music industry orientalism, the Mountain Brothers secured a record deal with Ruffhouse/Columbia Records and released the twelve-inch "Paperchase" backed with "5 Elements" in 1997. The single garnered much underground praise and broke into the CMJ Top 40 rap charts, but the relationship between the group and their label soured and ended in 1998. Commenting on their historic partnership and divorce, Styles says:

> It was creative stuff. We basically signed with them, recorded our whole album and then they wanted to change some stuff to make it more commercial. . . . With Ruffhouse you have to fight through the system in order to do what you want to do and now we're free of those constraints so it's really cool.[48]

Strategies for cultural participation by Asian American men include self-marketing their music before their ethnicity. As part of their goal for hip-hop acceptance on their terms, the Mountain Brothers "have found repeatedly that listeners hear them differently depending on whether they're already known to be Asian American. Indeed, they have found repeatedly that listeners who know they are Asian American beforehand take them much less seriously than when given no racial clues at all."[49] Thus, the conscious marketing of the Mountain Brother has had to privilege musicality over and beyond racial identification due to the lack of Asian American men in U.S. popular culture.

Rather than relying on mainstream avenues for commercial success, the Mountain Brothers signed with Pimpstrut Records to record and distribute their 1998 album, *Self: Volume 1*, and relied on websites and performance word-of-mouth to promote their explosive and successful entry into underground hip-hop legitimacy and, eventually, legendary status. *Self: Volume 1* contains nineteen tracks, each a variation of Chops's signature productions with no samples, original beats, and the unique rhyme structure that all the Mountain Brothers employ. Part of what constitutes the Mountain Brothers' appeal to an underground audience is their staunch desire to maintain control

over their sound, to avoid the trappings of commercialism and musical dilu-
tion. Indeed, this is what separates commercial hip-hop from underground
productions. Nelson George, in *Hip-Hop America*, relates how commercialism and record company hopes for profitable crossover acts have historically
weakened hip-hop: "Hoping for crossover, producers artificially reshaped
and usually diluted the sound of records recorded and released. In many instances, singles were released only with potential crossover paramount in
the label's mind."[50] Once again, marketing and sound were in hypertension,
and for the Mountain Brothers several tracks including "Paperchase," "Brand
Names," "Day Jobs," and "Whiplash" intelligently and sonically shed light on
the effects of corporatization on Asian American self-representation.

In "Paperchase," the Mountain Brothers critique the ubiquitous centrality of post–civil rights materialism. When they rhetorically ask, "why must
everything revolve around the penny?," they not only question the turn in
mainstream hip-hop to commodification but also the corporate reality of
hip-hop that attempts to divest its historical and political origins in subcul-
tural disidentification with capitalist alienation. Peril-L raps with expert delivery and original word play: "Lemme state my case about the paperchase / I
know it's hard trying to escape the pace / of the fast lane situated in gold-plat-
ed Camry, Lex, or Benz / But what about some perk-related family checks
for friends."[51] Challenging the ideology of liberal individualism, Peril-L situates his masculinity not on the superficiality of material objects but rather
on a sense of shared community where everyone benefits from individual
gains. Moreover, commenting on the hip-hop recording industry, Peril-L
criticizes the underlying logic of the profit motive: "The fall of hip-hop it's
gonna be / fucking ceo's don't see what it means to be original / seems to me
they fiend to see residual, I reckon smash flow's gettin' paid for half-assed
shows."[52] When the Mountain Boys were trying to break into the business of
hip-hop, many observers noted that "they represent a principled attempt to
enter the mainstream music industry on their own terms."[53] For Peril-L, the
mainstream trappings of "selling out" is one of musical death, of not remaining true to underground hip-hop's spirit of dismissing, or rather *dissin'*, the
cultural logic of transnational capitalism. Nevertheless, because the Mountain Brothers are Asian American pioneers in hip-hop, they have the added
responsibility to refuse orientalist gimmicks and instead uphold more control over their sound. As they remark: "If we don't have a big say—if not final
say—it could really hurt, not just us, but other Asian groups that might come
along in the future. So that's really important to us."[54]

Continuing, Chops, his voice deep and rich, offers a distinctive way to
understand how hip-hop's paper chase of greenbacks and fetishistic materi-

alism affects the social relations of people within transnational capitalism. At its incipient moment of germination, when hip-hop was not a mass-market commodity or career advancement, hip-hop artists staged block parties and free concerts that attempted, as Tricia Rose explains, "to negotiate the experiences of marginalization, brutally truncated opportunity, and oppression within the cultural imperatives of African-American and Caribbean history, identity, and community."[55] Of course, many of the Jamaican bass and drum beats that were crucial to the genesis of hip-hop had been created by Chinese Jamaican producers. In this way, the Mountain Brothers are only continuing the Afro-Caribbean-Asian roots of hip-hop, a time when crossracial relationships trumped crossover appeal. Using original internal rhyme schemes and distinctive one-line punch lines, Chops relates the superficiality of so-called friends who "rob and leech tryin' livin' life somethin' rich and famous, you're making me sick / because you're shameless, plus you see me like pomegranates."[56] Considering that Asian Americans have not had a significant impact on the U.S. recording industry and that hip-hop is the cultural language of transnational social life, the tour de force of the Mountain Brothers to fashion their own sonic experience and maintain their own commitment to Asian American identity is quite remarkable. Chops rides the beat in a certain way, distinct from other hip-hop MCs, and the Mountain Brothers incorporate creative wordplay and unusual diction. In general, the MBs, as they are affectionately called, know the importance of paying due respect to African American hip-hop while at the same time promoting an Asian American sensibility. To be sure, the Asian male body (or, in this case, trio) on the grandest stage of global culture gives legitimacy to Asian American culture in general. And to fashion that identity on progressive underground politics of community, respect, and loyalty ensures the continuation of Asian American cultural integrity and self-representation without appropriating African American history and culture.

The conclusion of "Paperchase" features Styles commenting on the global character of the paper chase. He insightfully comments: "It's true that gold rules the whole globe, diamond no close / well, there were art of inlays with gold fixtures / 'til I remain a bitch to the dollar . . . / Rockin' dashin' fashions and stashin' cash hits, but what is this am I a business man or just a heavy spendage?"[57] Refusing to act as creative labor for financial markets, Styles performs the Asian male body as antimaterialist. This approach contrasts with Asian American entrepreneurship or middle-class (white) acculturation. Indeed, Styles remarks, "we just rap about things that are important to us or that we feel strongly about. We don't like to write about things that aren't true to us."[58] Materialistic braggadocio and hip-hop have always gone together, often toward remasculinist absurdity (we need only think of the evolution of bling-bling). Yet, the entry of Asian American MCs who portray the rap game as deeply penetrated by transnational corporations finds common ground with underground pioneers the Wu-Tang Clan, who assert in *Enter the Wu-Tang (36 Chambers)* that "cash rulz everything around me."

Other tracks on *Self: Volume 1* have memorable references to African American history. In "Ain't Nuthin," Chops raps: "Not with a noose and an apple tree / you wouldn't have juice enough to hang with me." His juxtaposition of lynch mobs to his superior ability as an MC showcases his respect for African American racial trauma. However, perhaps to their detriment, the Mountain Brothers limit their engagement of interracialism to exclude a revolutionary politics of black liberation. Kara Keeling reminds us that today's iconography of hip-hop's race rebels, most notably the "star text" of Tupac Shakur, is embedded in the logic of transnational commodification, as a general trend "highlighting the ways in which recent business literature and marketing schemes have adopted much of the rhetoric and strategies of 1960s-style rebellion not only in order to sell products, but also as a means by which to ensure the consolidation of already existing structures of power."[59] It is this relationship between hip-hop and social movements, the leverage sustaining the antiestablishment credibility from its street base, that is often ignored even in the underground movement. In many published interviews, the MBs pay homage to African American hip-hop pioneers, from Scott La Rock to KRS-One to Public Enemy; they elevate the discussion of Asian American appropriation of a presumably authentic black cultural form. Yet, they lack more imaginative and revolutionary theorization.

One such aspect of the Mountain Brothers' music is their performance of heterosexual boasts of sexual conquests. On the one hand, the employment of hip-hop's tradition of sexual boasting is perhaps a normalized industry marker of manhood and masculinity, especially for black male MCs. On the other hand, as Asian American men, the Mountain Brothers occupy a different racial/sexual identity in U.S. racial hierarchy than do their black counterparts. Thus, I want to analyze the ways in which the Mountain Brothers reproduce heterosexist representations while simultaneously sexualizing the Asian male body. Complicating reductive binarisms in political discussions about hip-hop, Tricia Rose maintains that "male rappers' sexual discourse is not consistently sexist, and female sexual discourse is not consistently feminist."[60] In addition, bell hooks teaches: "The sexist, misogynistic, patriarchal ways of thinking and behaving that are glorified in gangsta rap are a reflection of the prevailing values in our society, values created and sustained by white supremacist capitalist patriarchy."[61] Clearly, judgments of sexual boasts in Mountain Brothers tracks such as "Love Poetry," "Things to Do," and "Whiplash" are not complete without what George Lipsitz calls "dialogic criticism":

> Popular music is nothing if not dialogic, the product of an ongoing histori-
> cal conversation in which no one has the first or last word. The traces of the
> past that pervade the popular music of the present amount to more than
> mere chance: they are not simply juxtapositions of incomparable realities.
> They reflect a dialogic process, one embedded in the collective history and
> nurtured by the ingenuity of artists interested in fashioning icons of op-
> position.[62]

In this way, the project of remasculinization in the Mountain Brothers' music reflects the historical erasure of Asian American male sexuality, especially in popular culture. Indeed, the knot of U.S. national culture/sexism of hip-hop, and the Mountain Brothers, is intricate and interrelated, a dialogic process continually refashioning itself.

Three central themes dominate the work of sexism in the Mountain Brothers' music: the importance of sexual conquest, the mastery of punch lines, and the employment of humor. In "Whiplash," a sequence of scratch-ing and funky beats inspired by early African American hip-hop opens the MBs' most explicit track of sexual boasting. All three MCs take their turn to dismiss the state of hip-hop (a popular theme) by sexual allegory. Styles taunts other MCs: "I slide your girl just cause you're bothering me / While you're bangin' on the door she talking / 'How 'bout some privacy?' / I'm quite humorous, women bag numerous."[63] Styles raps about stealing another MC's girlfriend, even admitting his arrogance in the theft. All the while, he ap-plauds his own intellectual verbal skills and sense of humor in a perceived game of masculinity in which women are the spoils of men who battle as MCs.

As a master of punch lines, Chops distinguishes his use of boasts to pro-claim sexual prowess in quantity and ability. He incorporates innovative uses of metaphors and imagery that promote a "hardcore" masculinity. Under funk beats and scratch synthesizers, he brags: "Cats don't want to see no part of Chops / I get more trim than barbershops / Tag your ass like I was a graph-head . . . / I'm like a sumo gettin' the drawers, because I'm fat as fuck."[64] For Asian American MCs, tales of sexual domination, like those of their black counterparts, are an industry mainstay. When the television channel BET sponsored the show *106 & Park* featuring freestyle battles, millions of rap fans saw another influential Asian American rapper, Jin, "telling another kid on rap's marquee channel to ask his girl how 'she had my egg roll and my dumplings in her mouth'?"[65] The ability of the MBs to use sharp wit and confident delivery contains the paradox of sexism and sexuality, especially for mainstream audiences, who rely on certain codes of signification and receive pleasure from such lines.

Peril-L steps up to the microphone to offer an unusual admixture of gender-bending in which the listener hears fears of same-sex relations and even asexual hip-hop subjects. The finality of "Whiplash" leaves little doubt about the remasculinization of the MBs through a heteropatriarchal framework: "Great enough to bless since the erogenous / The misogynous, I wouldn't have to step up on virgin MCs, androgynous / They don't have sex, dodge my fist, came to reclaim my properties."[66] Here, Peril-L symbolizes inept MCs through sexual naïveté or, worse, gender confusion in which feminine qualities corrupt the masculinity of violence-prone and propertied MCs.

That the MBs incorporate a paradox of sexism/sexuality cannot be ignored. But tracks such as "Love Poetry" and "Things to Do" show elements of humor, romance, and storytelling that attenuate their macho role as battle MCs. Satirizing the voice of Barry White (another R&B influence in old-school hip-hop), "Love Poetry" is a syrupy hip-hop ballad dedicated to women (again a heterosexual motif) but emphasizing the MBs' ability not to take themselves too seriously: "Girl if you were a newspaper / Then I would be your ink (that sounds nice) / If you were a piece of doo doo, then I would be your stink / We go together like Abbott and Costello, Bill Cosby and Jello (j-e-l-l-o)."[67] Not many MCs employ humor to construct masculinities of playfulness and sharp wit effectively. By doting "I wanna dig you like a mole and hump you like a camel / And then commence to suckin' out all your tooth enamel," the MBs contradict their previous invocation of hypermasculinity in "Whiplash." As sexual boasting morphs into hip-hop's version of stand-up comedy, "Love Poetry" illustrates the complex Asian American masculinity of the Mountain Brothers to show that, indeed, part of rap's game is to perform masculinity, to give audiences what they want—all of which has been produced within a heteropatriarchal reality.

Finally, within such a reality, the ability of Asian American MCs to forge new as well as old masculinities signals Asian American men entering national and global dialogues about race and masculinity. While spoken word artists are certainly more mindful of sexism and homophobia (perhaps because more women and queer people are in such spaces), hip-hop is the dominant cultural language of our youth. I think it is always important to question the dialogues, performances, and trajectories in which these daily practices are occurring, while also not dismissing too quickly any *one* practice. Thus, the close kinship between spoken word and hip-hop has been a powerful and influential relationship for Asian American masculinities to question their current reality as marginal men and to assert their rightful (although flawed) ability to self-determine their understandings of the "human" in neoliberal America.

Conclusion

Critical Reflections on Race, Class, Empire, and the "Pains of Modernity"

Broadcast all over the world, by stations from CNN to Al Jazeera, the scene of Saddam Hussein's statue tumbling down in Baghdad's Firdos Square was a symbol of U.S. military "shock and awe." As the image of Iraqi citizens and U.S. soldiers collectively toppling the remnants of the Ba'athist regime was shown in media outlets repeatedly ad nauseam, little attention was given to Corporal Edward Chin, the Chinese American soldier who had physically tied the noose around Saddam's neck. Chin climbed up the outstretched crane of an M88 recovery vehicle to fasten a cable around the statue's neck, and, while he was there, he briefly covered its face with an American flag. Representing the exemplary citizen-soldier, Corporal Chin rendered service that dutifully mirrors Roland Barthes's famous account of an Algerian soldier saluting the colonial French flag. Corporal Chin, his body and service, sutures the Western expansion of U.S. imperialism across the Pacific and the Atlantic, the archipelagos, peninsulas, and Asian and European continents themselves. For "an Army of One," his incorporation into empire building parallels the neoconservative incorporation of people of color into centers of power, best represented by Condoleezza Rice, Alberto Gonzalez, Colin Powell, John Yoo, Viet Dinh, and Barack Obama—all architects of U.S. global militarism.[1] While the post–civil rights era is a contradictory period of U.S. racialization between notions of de jure freedom and de facto racial hierarchy, this book has argued that its temporality is simultaneous with the global phenomena of U.S. militarism and transnational capitalism. In this sense, Corporal Chin's service also mirrors the subaltern silence of Bhuvaneswari Bhaduri and her familial legacy, one of whose descendants now works for a transnational corporation and thus "can speak" the tongue of the free market.[2]

The parable of racial magnetism is the story of how Asian Americans fit into the logic of white supremacy vis-à-vis class relations within and between racial minorities, and how this accommodation constitutes the subjectification and denial of black liberation. The editors of *Aiiieeeee!* challenge this density of post–civil rights racial ideology that would make them "feel better off than blacks"; Denizen Kane and the Mountain Brothers find manhood and cultural self-determination in the black musical forms of hip-hop and reggae, saying "never let the oppressor take away your peace," in this instance the ability to make magnificent words and musical incantations and render live audiences spellbound; and Jackie Chan and Chris Tucker discover that "war" is definitely not the answer in Asian-black political and cultural interactions. Rather, Chan understands the history of U.S. racial trauma and cultural integrity through the lens of black U.S. history.

This reality of black racial subjectification forms the basis for Asian American citizenship in the post–civil rights era, and Corporal Chin's body and service exemplify both the complex interconnections between proper national manhood and racial exclusion, and to what extent the Asian male body consents to the proliferation of imperial aspirations, wittingly or unwittingly. Just as the Irish and Italians had claimed their entitlement to U.S. citizenship through the adoption of the ideology of white supremacy, the logic of racial magnetism asks constituent Asian and black communities to identify with the project of post–civil rights imperial and market-based supremacy by refusing to identify with or promote black liberation in any area of U.S. political or material life. Simply put, in the spirit of Kanye West, the discourse of racial magnetism asks Asian Americans to not care about black people, but instead, in order to constitute a unified Asian American whole, to see black communities as what they are not, weighted by a density of ideology that blinds and deafens one to the dehumanization of class exploitation and racial hierarchy that is seemingly not all around us. This condition in and of itself constitutes the whole system of hegemony that relies upon racial hierarchy, in such a form as racial magnetism, in order to maintain cross-racial hostilities, cross-racial alienation, and ultimately the "pains of modernity"—the alienation of modernity's underbelly, namely the working-class peoples and peasants who show the anger, resentment, hunger, shame, and guilt associated with poverty, dispossession, and invisibility.

Out of sight and out of mind does not constitute a meaning of out of modernity, although many would have us follow this black hole of disavowal. Rather, race and class seem to have organized in fundamental ways American life and the American fictions of material opportunity and the equality of the property system. Take, for instance, the headlines of this century: Hurricane Katrina, the Duke University rape scandal, the Iraq War, immigration reform, the Occupy movement, Stop and Frisk, NSA surveillance, and Gitmo. As we initially immerse ourselves in the twenty-first century, the contradictions of modernity, the spiral of race and class divisions, have seemingly combusted together, explosively and decisively, on both an international and a domestic scale. How, then, do we take the first baby steps, and hopefully later leaps, out of this volatile concoction of the "pains of modernity"? Of course there are no easy answers, but I do think that the multiplicity of voices shared in this book can add something valuable to this conversation. And it is with another voice, John Okada's, that I'd like to end this study.

Although first published in 1957, John Okada's first and only novel, *No-No Boy*, did not gain notoriety until its introduction in *Aiiieeeee!* sixteen years later. Okada deals with important social relations in critical Asian-black social spaces inhabited by black and Asian men. In *No-No Boy*, the lead protagonist, Ichiro Yamada, returns home from federal prison after refusing to serve in the U.S. military and forswearing unqualified allegiance to the nation, two stipulations asked in the 1943 Leave Clearance Application Form (a "loyalty questionnaire" administered to Japanese Americans interned during the war). Despondency and confusion riddle the novel; Ichiro develops a philosophical outlook toward his American and masculine status, often through interactions with blacks in his neighborhood, and he falls into self-loathing. At the end of the novel, Okada describes a flashback scene in which Ichiro and his friend Tommy attend a predominantly white church in the Idaho town adjacent to their internment camp. By the sixth or seventh Sunday of their attendance, members of the congregation make Ichiro feel at home, asking him questions and "conversing endlessly." However, Ichiro experiences a pivotal moment of clarity, one that shows him the limits of U.S. citizenship, one that shows him how his welcome came at the expense of black people:

> He [Ichiro] saw the white-haired Negro standing in the back. He wondered then why the usher hadn't gotten out one of the folding chairs which were often used when bench space ran out. . . . There was no whispering, no craning as there had been in the other church. Yet, everyone seemed to know of the colored man's presence. The service concluded, the minister stood silent and motionless on the stage. The congregation remained seated instead of disintegrating impatiently as usual into a dozen separate chattering groups. Very distinctly through the hollowness of the small church echoed the slow, lonely footsteps of the intruder across the back, down the stairs, and out into the hot sun. As suddenly, the people came back to life like actors on a screen who had momentarily been rendered inanimate by some mechanical failure of the projector.[3]

This passage represents Okada's most memorable national allegory: Ichiro's refusal to accept the invitation of the white congregation, as he is imprisoned in a wartime relocation camp, underscores his refusal of Asian ethnic assimilation that would be given only through the exclusion and dehumanization of a "white-haired Negro." His identification with the old black man, seemingly when the white congregation wants to make the unwelcomed stranger invisible, illustrates an Asian American masculinity that is cognizant of social relations—who sits where, who ignores whom—and the superficiality of false overtures of inclusion not informed on a consistent and equal distribution of democracy for all, with the tenets of antiblackness at its heart. The black man's "slow, lonely footsteps" symbolize the historical development of racialized modernity, the "pains" of a modernity in which the emergence of citizenship and manhood has occurred differently for black and Asian men and often in conflict with each another. The congregation can be seen as the post–civil rights congregation of white supremacy in general, often seeking Asian American complicity and silence when matters of race and class emerge; the silence of the congregation is the silence of those who lack all conviction when the moment arises to speak against racial dictatorship, when the worst have such passionate intensity. Okada underscores our national amnesia and the silences that fill the hollow of our everyday spaces, the loss of our old racial skins, and the forward vision of true social justice, the best of what the humanities has to offer—requiring knowledge and skill.

There is no easy way out in Okada's text, only situational and relational representations of race and masculinity in the social milieu. Yet, Ichiro meets a person who shows him something different than the Idaho church congregation, a person named Gary, a fellow No-No boy, at the Christian Rehabilitation Center, where jobs are available for ex-convicts and poor men. Gary represents the No-No boy that Ichiro is not, somewhat well adjusted and, most importantly, not bitter or angry. He narrates to Ichiro a story about his friendship with a black coworker named Birdie:

> There were a number of vets in the same shop, even a couple I'd known pretty well at one time. They steered clear of me. Made it plain that I wasn't welcome. But, hell, I have to eat too. I guess they spread the word around because, pretty soon, the white guys weren't talking to me either. Birdie knew about it too, but it didn't seem to matter to him. Birdie's a colored fellow. He took a liking to me. He let everybody know that anyone wanting to give me a rough time would have to deal through him. I heard he used to spar with Joe Louis some years back. I had plenty of protection.[4]

The figure of Birdie is an inspiration for Gary because he, under the sedimented pressure of black racialization, steps outside of racial magnetism's force and decisively supports Gary's anti-imperialist masculinity. Birdie refuses to reproduce capital's division of racialized labor by protecting Gary from men who mimic and seek the approval of proper national manhood. In fact, we can say that there is a third "no" to the double No-No of antiwar Japanese American men who answered in the negative to the loyalty oath questions. It comes from the outside, from someone we might not expect—black men saying "no" to aggression and intimidation predicated upon militarized domination and violence. For this kind act, the men at the work camp punish Birdie by sabotaging his car, making it roll over. Yet, the story of Birdie's heroism is not forgotten; it is passed on to Ichiro, who finds optimism to counter his modernist spiral of melancholia and disbelief. There comes belief in the project of democracy, belief in closing the alienations of modernity—a belief in others; and Okada illustrates, for any interracial dialogue, the power relations that are involved, the mistakes made, and the faith in humanity instilled. In so doing, his novel reimagines alternative forms of social life and collectivity as much as understanding the processes of racial formation that route through constellations of masculinity as different as the social spaces they inhabit.

As an Asian Americanist whose scholarly work is situated in institutions of knowledge that often remain silent or invisible in U.S. mainstream political discourse, I am awestruck by the courage and conviction of voices of disidentification from the national imperial project such as Birdie and Ichiro. Hopefully, these voices found in cultural works can have something meaningful to teach those of us in and outside the academy. If we are truly committed to the project of decolonizing the mind and fulfilling the promise of modernity's social contract, then we must become flexible in our approaches and daily commitments. For Asian American studies, what this means is that we must do more—we must stay relevant. For we live in the face of Empire every day, but it is as Joseph Conrad said in *Heart of Darkness*: we refuse to see the reflection of the mirror staring in front of us, without pause and without patience. Hopefully, this book has moved the reader in the direction of Afro-Asian thought as a necessary intervention and forward practice for social transformation.

Notes

Introduction

1. Dana Nelson, *National Manhood: Capitalist Citizenship and the Imagined Fraternity of White Men* (Durham, NC: Duke University Press, 1998).

2. Support systems, personal ambition, willpower, hard work, role modeling, and institutional relations of power explain only a little of this stratification of race and masculinity. Thus, surface-level visual difference seals commonsense understandings of racialized masculinities.

3. Stuart Hall, "Racist Ideologies and the Media," in *Media Studies: A Reader*, ed. Sue Thornham, Caroline Basset, and Paul Marris (New York: New York University Press, 2000): 271.

4. Barack Obama, *Dreams from My Father: A Story of Race and Inheritance* (New York: Three Rivers Press, 2004): 121.

5. David Eng, *Racial Castration: Managing Masculinity in Asian America* (Durham, NC: Duke University Press, 2001).

6. Ibid., 4.

7. Michael Omi and Howard Winant, *Racial Formation in the United States: From the 1960s to the 1990s*, 2nd ed. (New York: Routledge, 1994): 78–81.

8. Daniel Kim, *Writing Manhood in Black and Yellow: Ralph Ellison, Frank Chin, and the Literary Politics of Identity* (Stanford, CA: Stanford University Press, 2006).

9. Michel Foucault, *The Order of Things: An Archaeology of the Human Sciences* (New York: Pantheon Books, 1971).

10. R. W. Connell, *Masculinities* (Berkeley: University of California Press, 1995); Nelson, *National Manhood*; Gail Bederman, *Manliness and Civilization* (Chicago: University of Chicago Press, 1995); Susan Jeffords, "The Big Switch: Hollywood Masculinity in the Nineties," in *Film Theory Goes to Hollywood*, ed. Jim Collins et al. (New York: Routledge, 1993); and Richard Dyer, "White Man's Muscles," in *Race and the Subject of Masculinities*, ed. Harry Stecopoulos and Michael Uebel (Durham, NC: Duke University Press, 1997).

11. Judith Halberstam, *Female Masculinity* (Durham, NC: Duke University Press, 1998).

12. Lisa Lowe, *Immigrant Acts: On Asian American Cultural Politics* (Durham, NC: Duke University Press, 1996): 24.

13. Ibid., 22.

14. Ibid., 10.

15. Ibid., 12.

16. Ibid., 15.

17. Christine So, *Economic Citizens: A Narrative of Asian American Visibility* (Philadelphia: Temple University Press, 2008): 14.

18. Ibid., 3.

19. See erin Khuê Ninh, *Ingratitude: The Debt-Bound Daughter in Asian American Literature* (New York: New York University Press, 2011): 8.

20. James remarks: "[S]tage by stage, we have seen the revolution and the counter-revolution develop in Europe over the centuries," where "at each new stage of development, both the revolution and the counterrevolution assume a new quality with the new quality of the social development." See C. L. R. James, "Dialectical Materialism and the Fate of Humanity," in *Spheres of Existence: Selected Writings* (Westport, CT: Lawrence Hill, 1980): 76.

21. *A Girl Like Me*, dir. Kiri Davis, Reel Works Teen Filmmaking, 2005.

22. Omi and Winant, *Racial Formation*, 78.

23. Helen Heran Jun, *Race for Citizenship: Black Orientalism and Asian Uplift from Pre-emancipation to Neoliberal America* (New York: New York University Press, 2011): 95.

24. Laura Pulido, *Black, Brown, Yellow, and Left: Radical Activism in Los Angeles* (Berkeley: University of California Press, 2006): 24.

25. Quoted in Susan Koshy, "Morphing Race into Ethnicity: Asian Americans and Critical Transformations of Whiteness," *boundary* 2 28:1 (2001): 152.

26. Gerald Horne, *Fire This Time: The Watts Uprising and the 1960s* (Charlottesville: University of Virginia Press, 2005): 98.

27. Paul Ong, Edna Bonacich, and Lucie Cheng, "The Political Economy of Capitalist Restructuring and the New Asian Immigration," in *The New Asian Immigration in Los Angeles and Global Restructuring*, ed. Paul Ong, Edna Bonacich, and Lucie Cheng (Philadelphia: Temple University Press, 1994): 5–6.

28. David Harvey, *The Condition of Postmodernity: An Enquiry into the Origins of Cultural Change* (Oxford: Blackwell Publishers, 1990): 141.

29. David Harvey, "Neoliberalism as Creative Destruction," *Geografiska Annaler*, ser. B, 88 (2006): 145–158; David Harvey, *A Brief History of Neoliberalism* (Oxford: Oxford University Press, 2005): 19.

30. Jun, *Race for Citizenship*, 124.

31. Kwame Nkrumah, *Class Struggle in Africa* (London: Panaf Books, 1970): 17.

32. Stuart Hall et al., *Policing the Crisis: Mugging, the State, and Law and Order*

(Basingstoke, England: Macmillan, 1979); Michael Denning, *The Cultural Front: The Laboring of American Culture in the Twentieth Century* (London: Verso, 1998); Toni Negri, *Revolution Retrieved: Writings on Marx, Keynes, Capitalist Crisis and New Social Subjects, 1967–83* (London: Red Notes, 1988).

33. Stanley Cohen, *Folk Devils and Moral Panics* (Saint Albans, England: Paladin, 1973): 16.

34. Quoted in Denning, *The Cultural Front*, 22.

35. Hall, *Policing the Crisis*, 11.

36. Negri, *Revolution Retrieved*, 34.

37. Charles Hurst, *Social Inequality: Forms, Causes, Consequences*, 8th ed. (Upper Saddle River, NJ: Pearson Press, 2012): 31–34.

38. Todd Gitlin, *The Sixties: Years of Hope, Days of Rage* (New York: Bantam Books, 1993); Todd Gitlin, *The Whole World Is Watching: Mass Media in the Making and Unmaking of the New Left* (Berkeley: University of California Press, 2003); George Katsiaficas, *The Imagination of the New Left: A Global Analysis of 1968* (Boston: South End Press, 1987).

39. Dylan Rodríguez, *Forced Passages: Imprisoned Radical Intellectuals and the U.S. Prison Regime* (Minneapolis: University of Minnesota Press, 2006): 1–16.

40. Catherine Lutz, "Making War at Home in the United States: Militarization and the Current Crisis," *American Anthropologist*, n. ser., 104:3 (2002): 723.

41. Chandan Reddy, *Freedom with Violence: Race, Sexuality, and the U.S. State* (Durham, NC: Duke University Press, 2011).

42. Negri, *Revolution Retrieved*.

43. Horne, *Fire This Time*, 64, 141.

44. Ibid., 230.

45. Daniel Patrick Moynihan, "The Negro Family: The Case for National Action," U.S. Department of Labor, Office of the Assistant Secretary for Policy, March 1965, at http://www.dol.gov/asp.

46. In *Race Rebels*, Robin D. G. Kelley writes about his days cooking burgers and bagging fries at a McDonald's restaurant. He discusses working in the service sector, an emerging labor market that transformed job opportunities for communities of color in Pasadena, California, in proximity to declining aerospace and shipbuilding industries. In a humorous account, Kelley admits to "criminal behavior": "because we were underpaid and overworked, we accepted consumption as just compensation—though in hindsight eating Big Macs and fries to make up for low wages and mistreatment was probably closer to self-flagellation." Reflecting on his working-class experience, Kelley understands through time and self-reflection that "we were part of the 'working class' engaged in workplace struggles." Kelley's narrative evokes two powerful statements. On the one hand, personal behavior usually seen at the workplace as laziness or thievery can also be viewed as survival strategies, depending on

one's perspective. This is not to suggest some form of moral relativism but rather the intersection between race and cultural behavior and the ways they inform the transfer of morals or humanity onto the skin. Kelley's narrative responds to the discourse of cultural pathology that places black men as culturally deficient and bankrupt of values needed for political assimilation and economic success. See Robin D. G. Kelley, *Race Rebels: Culture, Politics, and the Black Working Class* (New York: Free Press, 1994): 2.

47. See George Lipsitz, *The Possessive Investment in Whiteness: How White People Profit from Identity Politics* (Philadelphia: Temple University Press, 1998).

48. Ibid., 3.

49. Quoted in ibid., 2.

50. Ibid., 3.

51. Lois Parkinson Zamora, ed., *The Apocalyptic Vision in America: Interdisciplinary Essays on Myth and Culture* (Bowling Green, OH: Bowling Green State University Popular Press, 1982): 4.

52. Roderick Ferguson, *Aberrations in Black: Toward a Queer of Color Critique* (Minneapolis: University of Minnesota Press, 2004): 122.

53. William Ryan, *Blaming the Victim* (New York: Vintage Books, 1971).

54. Sander L. Gilman, *Difference and Pathology: Stereotypes of Sexuality, Race, and Madness* (Ithaca, NY: Cornell University Press, 1985): 23.

55. William Peterson, "Success Story: Japanese-American Style," *New York Times Magazine*, January 9, 1966, 22.

56. Ibid.

57. Ibid.

58. Ibid.

59. Ibid., 21.

60. Ibid., 40.

61. Elaine Kim, *Asian American Literature: An Introduction to the Writings and Their Social Context* (Philadelphia: Temple University Press, 1982): 18.

62. Keith Osajima, "Asian Americans as the Model Minority: An Analysis of the Popular Press Image in the 1960s and 1980s," in *Contemporary Asian America: A Multidisciplinary Reader*, ed. Min Zhou and James Gatewood (New York: New York University Press, 2000): 449–458; Won Moo Hurh and Kwang Chung Kim, "The 'Success' Image of Asian Americans: Its Validity, and Its Practical and Theoretical Implications," *Ethnic and Racial Studies* 12 (1989): 514–561; Stanley Sue and Harry H. L. Kitano, "Stereotypes as a Measure of Success," *Journal of Social Issues* 29 (1973): 83–98; Bob H. Suzuki, "Asian-American as the Model Minority," *Change*, November 1989, 13–19; Frank Wu, *Yellow: Race in America beyond Black and White* (New York: Basic Books, 2002).

63. Viet Thanh Nguyen, *Race and Resistance: Literature and Politics in Asian America* (New York: Oxford University Press, 2002): 146.

64. Lowe, *Immigrant Acts*, 27. Tule Lake was a crucial interment camp for Japanese American resistance to mass incarceration by the U.S. military. The prison opened on May 26, 1942, and had a peak population of 18,700. Those placed in the maximum security camp were classified as threats to national security because they refused to swear unqualified allegiance to the United States via a loyalty questionnaire.

65. Ibid., 43.

66. Cited in Robert Lee, *Orientals: Asian Americans in Popular Culture* (Philadelphia: Temple University Press, 1998): 151.

67. Ibid.

68. Nayan Shah, *Contagious Divides: Epidemics and Race in San Francisco's Chinatown* (Berkeley: University of California Press, 2001).

69. Ann Laura Stoler, *Race and the Education of Desire: Foucault's History of Sexuality and the Colonial Order of Things* (Durham, NC: Duke University Press, 1995); Gauri Viswanathan, *Masks of Conquest: Literary Study and British Rule in India* (New York: Columbia University Press, 1989).

70. Stefi San Buenaventura, "The Colors of Manifest Destiny in the Philippines," in *Major Problems in Asian American History*, ed. Lon Kurashige and Alice Yang Murray (Boston: Houghton Mifflin, 2003): 167.

71. James Kyung-Jin Lee, *Urban Triage: Race and the Fictions of Multiculturalism* (Minneapolis: University of Minnesota Press, 2004): 2.

72. David Palumbo-Liu, *Asian/American: Historical Crossings of a Racial Frontier* (Stanford, CA: Stanford University Press, 199): 156.

73. Lutz, "Making War at Home," 743.

74. Chang-rae Lee, *Native Speaker* (New York: Riverhead Books, 1995): 195.

75. Lowe, *Immigrant Acts*, 103.

76. Chang-rae Lee, *Native Speaker*, 195.

77. Ibid.

78. Ibid., 153.

79. Ibid., 193.

80. Gary Okihiro, "Is Yellow Black or White?," in *Margins and Mainstreams: Asians in American History and Culture* (Seattle: University of Washington Press, 1994).

81. Diane Fujino, "The Black Liberation Movement and Japanese American Activism: The Radical Activism of Richard Aoki and Yuri Kochiyama," in *Afro Asia: Revolutionary Political and Cultural Connections between African Americans and Asian Americans*, ed. Fred Ho and Bill Mullen (Durham, NC: Duke University Press, 2008): 165–197; Daryl Maeda, *Chains of Babylon: The Rise of Asian America* (Minneapolis: University of Minnesota Press, 2009); Pulido, *Black, Brown, Yellow, and Left*; Fred Ho,

ed., *Legacy to Liberation: Politics and Culture of Revolutionary Asian Pacific America* (Oakland, CA: AK Press, 2000); Steven Louie and Glenn Omatsu, eds., *Asian Americans: The Movement and the Moment* (Los Angeles: UCLA Asian American Studies Center Press, 2001).

82. Katsiaficas, *The Imagination of the New Left*, 29–82.

83. See issues of *Gidra* published from 1969 to 1974 by the University of California, Los Angeles, and Gidra, Inc.; see also I Wor Kuen's publication *Getting Together*, vol. 2, no. 6.

84. James Boggs, *A Black Radical's Notebook: A James Boggs Reader*, ed. Stephen M. Ward (Detroit: Wayne State University Press, 2011): 171–179.

85. Fujino, "The Black Liberation Movement and Japanese American Activism," 165–197.

86. Louie and Omatsu, *Asian Americans*; Amy Tachiki, Eddie Wong, Franklin Odo, and Buck Wong, eds., *Roots: An Asian American Reader* (Los Angeles: UCLA Asian American Studies Center Press, 1971).

87. Alan Nishio, "The Oriental as a 'Middleman Minority,'" *Gidra*, April 1969, 3.

88. Yen Le Espiritu, *Asian American Panethnicity: Bridging Institutions and Identities* (Philadelphia: Temple University Press, 1992).

89. Junot Díaz, *The Brief Wondrous Life of Oscar Wao* (New York: Riverhead Books, 2007): 81.

90. Louie and Omatsu, *Asian Americans*, 7.

91. Bobby Seale, *Seize the Time: The Story of the Black Panther Party and Huey P. Newton* (New York: Random House, 1968): 79.

92. Ibid., 211.

93. Walter Benjamin, *Illuminations: Essays and Reflections*, ed. Hannah Arendt, trans. Harry Zohn (New York: Schocken Books, 1968).

94. Judith Butler, *The Psychic Life of Power: Theories in Subjection* (Stanford, CA: Stanford University Press, 1997).

95. Fredric Jameson, *The Political Unconscious: Narrative as a Socially Symbiotic Act* (Ithaca, NY: Cornell University Press, 1981).

96. Lisa Lowe and David Lloyd, *The Politics of Culture in the Shadow of Capital: Worlds Aligned* (Durham, NC: Duke University Press, 1997): 1.

97. Quoted in Robin D. G. Kelley, *Freedom Dreams: The Black Radical Imagination* (Boston: Beacon Press, 2002): x.

Chapter 1

1. Larry Neal, "The Black Arts Movement," *Drama Review* 12 (Summer 1968): 29–39.

2. Al Young, "Interview: Ishmael Reed," *Changes*, November 1972, 12.

3. Ibid., 16.

4. Ibid.

5. Kandice Chuh, *Imagine Otherwise: On Asian Americanist Critique* (Durham, NC: Duke University Press, 2003).

6. Frank Chin, Jeffrey Paul Chan, Lawson Fusao Inada, and Shawn Wong, eds., *Aiiieeeee! An Anthology of Asian-American Writers* (Washington, DC: Howard University Press, 1974); Frank Chin and Shawn Wong, eds., *Yardbird Reader*, vol. 3 (Berkeley, CA: Yardbird Publishing, 1974).

7. William J. Harris, "The *Yardbird Reader* and the Multi-Ethnic Spirit," *MELUS* 8:2 (Summer 1981): 72.

8. Kalamu ya Salaam, "Black Arts Movement," in *Oxford Companion to African American Literature*, ed. W. L. Andrews et al. (New York: Oxford University Press, 1997).

9. Denning, *The Cultural Front*, 6.

10. Maeda, *Chains of Babylon*; Daniel Kim, *Writing Manhood in Black and Yellow*.

11. Daniel Kim, *Writing Manhood in Black and Yellow*, 128.

12. Ibid., 125.

13. Chin et al., *Aiiieeeee!*, 3.

14. Vijay Prashad, *Everybody Was Kung Fu Fighting: Afro-Asian Connections and the Myth of Cultural Purity* (Boston: Beacon Press, 2001): 65.

15. See, for example, King-Kok Cheung, "The Woman Warrior versus the Chinaman Pacific: Must a Chinese American Critic Choose between Feminism and Heroism?," in *Conflicts in Feminism*, ed. Marianne Hirsch and Evelyn Fox Keller (New York: Routledge, 1990): 234–251.

16. Frank Chin, letter to Maxine Hong Kingston, July 1976, Frank Chin Papers, Special Collections, University of California, Santa Barbara.

17. Eve Kosofsky Sedgwick, *Epistemology of the Closet* (Berkeley: University of California Press, 1990).

18. Claire Jean Kim, "The Racial Triangulation of Asian Americans," *Politics and Society* 27 (1999): 105–137.

19. These works highlighted the genesis of Asian American literary thought and consciousness at the moment of incipient panethnicity and flexible accumulation of transnational capitalism, converging once again in a hyperbolic fashion. The anthologies responded to the contradiction of racialized masculinities in an era of neoliberal and multicultural enforcement.

20. Maeda, *Chains of Babylon*, 75.

21. *Newsweek*, "Japanese Success Story: Outwhiting the Whites," June 21, 1971, 24–25.

22. Shirley Hune, "Asian American Studies and Asian Studies: Boundaries and Borderlands of Ethnic Studies and Area Studies," in *Color-Line to Borderlands: The*

Matrix of American Ethnic Studies, ed. Johnnella E. Butler (Seattle: University of Washington Press, 2001): 236.

23. *Aiiieeeee!* was published in 1974, at a moment of immense upheaval and social change in the economic, political, and cultural order both in the United States and abroad. We must interrogate the divergence of these radical ethnics from the theoretical vision of their grassroots political arm. During the early 1970s, third world liberation had conjoined the *global* and the *political*. Such a limitation to their political horizon illustrates not only an unfaithful departure from the superstructure of third world liberation but also a communicative alienation from their material, community base. Geographer David Harvey states in *The Condition of Postmodernity* that 1973 signaled a crisis in Fordist capitalism in which corporations rapidly transformed their production modes to "flexible accumulation." This new strategy transformed, among many other things, the labor pool of factory production from working-class men to third world women of color. Post-Fordist capital created a crisis in the labor pool, which shifted from factory production jobs in domestic cities, mainly held by men, to the outsourcing of those jobs to deregulated production zones in Asia and Latin America. Corporations sought greater profits, and national boundaries eroded in the economic sphere at the same time that racial minorities were invoking cultural nationalism in the political and cultural spheres. These changes illustrate some limitations and contradictions in the radical democratic project evinced by cultural nationalism. See Harvey, *The Condition of Postmodernity*, 141–172.

24. Chin et al., *Aiiieeeee!*, xvi.

25. Frantz Fanon, "Concerning Violence," in *The Wretched of the Earth* (New York: Grove Press, 1963): 35–106.

26. Elaine Kim, *Asian American Literature*.

27. Chin et al., *Aiiieeeee!*, xlviii.

28. Lowe and Lloyd, *The Politics of Culture*, 26.

29. Roberta Palm, letter to Frank Chin, March 1974, Frank Chin Papers, Special Collections, University of California, Santa Barbara.

30. Chin et al., *Aiiieeeee!*, 9–10. The editorial collective, with Chin as the lead tactician, writes: "The ideal racial stereotype is a low maintenance engine of white supremacy whose efficiency increases with age, as it becomes authenticated and historically verified." See Chin et al., *Aiiieeeee!*, xxvii.

31. Lipsitz, *The Possessive Investment in Whiteness*, 1.

32. Chin et al., *Aiiieeeee!*, 9.

33. Stephen Sumida, "The More Things Change: Paradigm Shifts in Asian American Studies," *American Studies International* 38:2 (June 2000): 97.

34. Chin et al., *Aiiieeeee!*, 14.

35. Frank Chin, letter to Maxine Hong Kingston, October 20, 1976, Frank Chin Papers, Special Collections, University of California, Santa Barbara.

36. When the editors attack writers such as Jade Snow Wong, Virginia Lee, and Pardee Lowe for their assimilationist writing, they are targeting the ideological engine of white supremacy. See Chin et al., *Aiiieeeee!*, 3.

37. Chin et al., *Aiiieeeee!*, xxxviii.

38. Daniel Kim, "Do I, Too, Sing America? Vernacular Representations and Chang-rae Lee's *Native Speaker*," *Journal of Asian American Studies* 6:3 (2004): 232.

39. Chin et al., *Aiiieeeee!*, xxvi.

40. Until 1943, U.S. immigration law designated Asian Americans as "aliens ineligible to citizenship," even though Asian immigrants were vital in building the backbone of U.S. capitalism, serving as cheap labor for the construction of railroads, agriculture, and mining. Culturally, figurations such as the pollutant, coolie, the Yellow Peril, the deviant, the model minority, and gook have utilized race, gender, and sexuality in order to alienate Asian American masculinity from U.S. national culture. Furthermore, Asian Americans have served as soldiers during wartime, sacrificing their lives for the United States while simultaneously being branded with state-sanctioned labels such as "enemies of the state." See Robert Lee, *Orientals*, 8.

41. Ling's analysis suggests the utility of a rights discourse enabling the editors to frame their racial emasculation. The scope of their critique is the nation-state, which narrows possibilities for transnational affiliations. Although this framework departed from third world liberation movements calling for cross-continental mobilization beyond national borders, the editors were correct in pointing out that the nation-state indeed mediated geographically, linguistically, and militarily the symbolic ordering of U.S. third world men's racialized alienation and national belonging. See Jinqi Ling, *Narrating Nationalisms: Ideology and Form in Asian American Literature* (New York: Oxford University Press, 1998): 25.

42. Wendy Brown, *States of Injury: Power and Freedom in Late Modernity* (Princeton, NJ: Princeton University Press, 1995): 97.

43. Rogin states that blackface freed white audiences from their communities of origin. He emphasizes the ritual discarding of identity markers by whites who chose accoutrements directly opposite their own. Further, he analyzes the making of an audience's racial identity, formed through collective distancing in the cultural imaginary that reflected the harsh Jim Crow segregation in material life. Just as minstrelsy freed Jewish communities from their designation as nonwhite, performing blackface allowed the *Aiiieeeee!* editors mobility to move from categories designated by the state and by knowledge industries. See Michael Rogin, *Blackface, White Noise: Jewish Immigrants in the Hollywood Melting Pot* (Berkeley: University of California Press, 1996): 125.

44. I want to thank Lisa Lowe for her assistance in helping me mark this idea in our Asian American Literature course, Spring 2003.

45. Chin et al., *Aiiieeeee!*, xxi.

46. Raymond Williams describes "mediated" as an active process that is a "necessary of the making of meanings and values, in the necessary form of general social process of signification and communication." See Raymond Williams, *Marxism and Literature* (Oxford: Oxford University Press, 1977): 95–100; see also Gwendolyn Brooks, *Maud Martha* (Chicago: Third World Press, 1993).

47. Stuart Hall, "Ethnicity: Identity and Difference," in *Becoming National: A Reader*, ed. Geoff Eley and Ronald Grigor Suny (New York: Oxford University Press, 1999): 339–349.

48. Looking at the construction of emergent Asian American identities, Glenn Omatsu states that Asian American neoconservatives are "new because they are creatures born from the Reagan-Bush era of supply-side economics, class and racial polarization, and the emphasis on elitism and individual advancement." This definition describes ideological processes that produce Asian Americans who do not understand the legacy of African American politics, which has, ironically, enabled Asian American legal entry and subsequent economic success. In contrast, the editors had earlier theorized the importance of black America for any understanding of Asian America's precarious relationship to whiteness and the nation-state. They interrogated the range of racial pathways Asian American communities choose to citizenship and national belonging. In our post–civil rights moment, Asian America, a political construct that *Aiiieeeee!*'s editors critiqued in their preface, has diverged into the "country" and the "city," two worlds in which poor and professional and English deficient and English proficient have created politically distinct communities. This dichotomy has greatly affected the neighborhoods in which we live, the people whom we associate with as friends and colleagues, and those whom we find commonality with in our "politics of everyday oppression." Unfortunately, neoconservative and professional Asian Americans have aligned themselves with those who are most privileged in society and have eschewed their political responsibility to sympathize with those who do not have such opportunities and life chances. This pathway has immense racial implications for imagining a socially conscious community. See Glenn Omatsu, "The 'Four Prisons' and the Movements of Liberation," in *The State of Asian America: Activism and Resistance in the 1990s*, ed. Karin Aguilar-San Juan (Boston: South End Press, 1994): 42–43.

49. Ishle Yi Park, "Sa-I-Gu," *Def Poetry*, season 5, episode 4, 2005.

50. Chin and Wong, *Yardbird Reader*.

51. Ibid., back cover.

52. Ibid., iv.

53. Ibid.

54. Ibid., vi.

55. Peter Taylor, *Modernities: A Geohistorical Interpretation* (Minneapolis: University of Minnesota Press, 1999): 102.

56. Chin and Wong, *Yardbird Reader*, vi.

57. Laura I. Rendón Linares and Susana M. Muñoz, "Revisiting Validation Theory: Theoretical Foundations, Applications, and Extensions," *Enrollment Management Journal* 5:2 (Summer 2011): 12–33.

58. Jordan Churchill, "Validation," *Journal of Philosophy* 56 (February 26, 1959): 203.

59. Chin and Wong, *Yardbird Reader*, vii.

60. Russell Leong, "Lived Theory," *Amerasia Journal* 21:1–2 (1995): v–x.

Chapter 2

1. Mia Penta, "Ichibobs Invade Seattle," *Morning News* (Seattle), July 26, 2001, 2B.

2. Films such as D. W. Griffith's *Broken Blossoms* (1919), originally titled *The Yellow Man and the Girl*, Frank Capra's *The Bitter Tea of General Yen* (1933), George Pal's *7 Faces of Dr. Lao* (1964), and the 1961 Blake Edwards classic *Breakfast at Tiffany's* represent this obsessive desire through yellowface to contain visually the threat of Asianness. For example, popular visual representations of the Asian male body for white spectatorial pleasure include the evil figure Fu Manchu and the comic figure Charlie Chan. Denied self-representation in performance, production, and creative expression, Asian American men were represented through the mediated body of Werner Oland, a white male actor who played both the world conqueror Fu and the bumbling eunuch Chan.

3. Michel Foucault, *"Society Must Be Defended": Lectures at the Collège de France, 1975–1976*, trans. David Macey (New York: Picador, 2003): 61.

4. Ibid., 76.

5. Yvonne Tasker, "Fists of Fury," in *Race and the Subject of Masculinities*, ed. Harry Stecopoulos and Michael Uebel (Durham, NC: Duke University Press, 1997): 317–320; Robert Lee, *Orientals*; Daniel Kim, *Writing Manhood in Black and Yellow*.

6. Halberstam, *Female Masculinity*, 2.

7. See also Sedgwick, *Epistemology of the Closet*.

8. Bederman, *Manliness and Civilization*, 7.

9. Ibid., 7–8.

10. Brian Pronger, *The Arena of Masculinity: Sports, Homosexuality, and the Meaning of Sex* (New York: St. Martin's Press, 1990): 19.

11. Michael Messner and Donald Sabo, eds., *Sport, Men, and the Gender Order: Critical Feminist Perspectives* (Champaign, IL: Human Kinetics, 1990): 1–13.

12. Jim McKay, Michael Messner, and Donald Sabo, eds., *Masculinities, Gender Relations, and Sport* (Thousand Oaks, CA: Sage Publications, 2000): 6.

13. Toby Miller, Geoffrey Lawrence, Jim McKay, and David Rowe, eds., *Globalization and Sport* (London: Sage Publications, 2001): 1–5.

14. Alfred Chandler, *Scale and Scope: The Dynamics of Industrial Capitalism* (Cambridge: Harvard University Press, 1990).

15. Karl Marx, "Economic and Philosophic Manuscripts of 1844," in *The Marx-Engels Reader*, trans. and ed. Robert C. Tucker (New York: W. W. Norton, 1978): 73.

16. Susan Faludi, *Stiffed: The Betrayal of the American Man* (New York: William Morrow, 1999).

17. I use the term "feminization" to express the trepidation of white men, specifically their sense of becoming like women. The gendering of women as weak, passive, irrational, feeble, and hysterical dialectically produced meanings of what manhood was not.

18. Harvey Green, *Fit for America: Health Fitness, Sport, and American Society* (New York: Pantheon Books, 1986).

19. Michael S. Kimmel, "Consuming Manhood," in *The Male Body: Features, Destinies, Exposures*, ed. Laurence Goldstein (Ann Arbor: University of Michigan Press, 1994): 26.

20. Boxing as America's newest sports craze was a cultural site married to race and class. John L. Sullivan was perhaps "the greatest American hero of the late nineteenth century." His muscled body and other accoutrements of manhood, like his famous well-waxed moustache, signified "the growing desire to smash through the fluff of bourgeois gentility and the tangle of corporate ensnarements to the throbbing heart of life." Sullivan's fame shaped the cultural identity of the emergent working class, and one could hear daily conversations about his exploits in workplaces, saloons, and public discourse. His successor as the protector of white manhood, Jim Jeffries, had to negotiate the difficult road of America's newfound doctrine of "separate but equal" sanctioned by the 1898 *Plessy v. Ferguson* case. In this turbulent era of de facto segregation and the spectacle of public lynchings in the Deep South, Jeffries fought one of the most remarkable championship fights in boxing history. Of course, to Jeffries's Iago there was his Othello—Jack Johnson. Johnson, the first African American heavyweight champion of the world, dethroned Jeffries in a media event that sent shockwaves throughout the nation. His sport body as public spectacle produced an alternative cultural formation to the lynched bodies of the Jim Crow South and thus represented a masculinized body that physically and symbolically defeated its white enslavers in a critical public space. Johnson caroused with white prostitutes, openly flaunted his black sexuality, and enjoyed performing the figure of the black brute. His assault on white manhood aroused the African American community to celebrate in the streets when he defeated Jeffries, "the Great White Hope," and drew the ire of white supremacists for his racial transgressions. His racialized black body was the quintessence of racial and sexual mobility and represented the impact of popular sport in challenging rigid antimiscegenation laws and codes of racial hierarchy. As popular sport became entrenched in America, pugilism came to represent the dy-

namics of the color line that Du Bois predicted would become the quagmire of the twentieth century. See Elliott Gorn, *The Manly Art: Bare-Knuckle Prize Fighting in America* (Ithaca, NY: Cornell University Press, 1986): 247.

21. Gorn, *The Manly Art*.

22. Thorstein Veblen, *The Theory of the Leisure Class* (New York: Modern Library, 1911).

23. C. L. R. James, *Beyond a Boundary* (Durham, NC: Duke University Press, 1993): 66.

24. Richard Wright, "Joe Louis Uncovers Dynamite," *New Masses*, October 8, 1935, 18–19.

25. Arnold Rampersad, *Jackie Robinson* (New York: Alfred A. Knopf, 1997): 150.

26. White masculinity, assaulted by several communities including feminist, queer, and various ethnic groups, had an identity crisis. It failed to benefit from multiculturalism's "ethnic pride" and feminism's "gender pride," to which the white men's movement along with white supremacy responded in virulent ways. Primal screams in the woods met Nazi tattoos in efforts to cope with the new situation in which whiteness no longer held the dominant prestige it once did. To add insult to injury, black male athletes commanded center stage, dominated their white counterparts, and became the identity that signified legitimate styles, language, and masculine performance. All these different movements helped shape national masculinity. See Michael Omi, "Racialization in the Post–Civil Rights Era," in *Mapping Multiculturalism*, ed. Avery Gordon and Christopher Newfield (Minneapolis: University of Minnesota Press, 1996): 181.

27. Rather than dismissing wholesale white masculinity's role, I argue against the *centrality* afforded to white masculinity in cultural production and ideological work. Insofar as white masculinity holds a crucial position of power and domination, minority masculinities in global sport have developed playing styles, iconic symbols, and methods of interracial teamwork that resist the dominance of whiteness as the ideological core of American life. See Halberstam, *Female Masculinity*, 3.

28. See Harry Edwards, *Sociology of Sport* (Homewood, IL: Dorsey Press, 1973): 202. The conservative backlash co-opted multiculturalism's emphasis on diversity but responded by producing "racelessness," a color-blind politics that ignored institutional and cultural forms of racism. Thus, the wholesale contraction of civil society channeled African American men into racialized institutional and cultural spaces that were relatively open and acceptable. Additionally, Toni Negri has aptly associated the rise of the warfare state in post-Keynesian nation-states with the increased domestic militarization of urban space. See Angela Davis, "Race and Criminalization: Black Americans and the Punishment Industry," in *The House That Race Built*, ed. Wahneema Lubiano (New York: Pantheon Books, 1997). A weak multiculturalism failed miserably up to the 1990s and will need to progress further in its development,

maybe toward Wahneema Lubiano's idea of "transformative multiculturalism," a discursive practice that begins to dismantle state power and institutional inequities. See Wahneema Lubiano, "Like Being Mugged by a Metaphor: Multiculturalism and State Narratives," in *Mapping Multiculturalism*, ed. Avery Gordon and Christopher Newfield (Minneapolis: University of Minnesota Press, 1996): 64–75; Negri, *Revolution Retrieved.*

29. Richard Majors, "Cool Pose: Black Masculinity and Sports," in *Sport, Men, and the Gender Order: Critical Feminist Perspectives*, ed. Michael Messner and Donald Sabo (Champaign, IL: Human Kinetics, 1990): 109.

30. Paul Gilroy, *Against Race: Imagining Political Culture beyond the Color Line* (Cambridge, MA: Belknap Press, 2000): 21.

31. Ibid., 7.

32. Kobena Mercer, *Welcome to the Jungle: New Positions in Black Cultural Studies* (New York: Routledge, 1994): 133.

33. Popular sport has inherited this legacy of colonial typologies of the body, which still functions in dominant and powerful ways. In his classic work *Black Skin, White Masks*, Frantz Fanon explained that the black man in any white society is not simply perceived as merely racially different. His "darkness" represents the savagery of the jungle; he becomes an "uncontrollable beast," or the embodiment of lustful hypersexuality. "One is no longer aware of the Negro, but only of a penis; the Negro is eclipsed. He is turned into a penis. He is a penis." In composing a narrative of how race and sexuality hinge on bodily synecdoche, conflating anatomy and symbols offers Fanon a powerful lens through which to understand his racializing physicality, his civilization, and his figure as the Negro rapist. See Frantz Fanon, *Black Skins, White Mask* (New York: Grove Weidenfeld, 1952): 170.

34. Lipsitz, *The Possessive Investment in Whiteness.*

35. Jon Entine, *Taboo: Why Black Athletes Dominate Sports and Why We're Afraid to Talk About It* (New York: Public Affairs, 1995): 19.

36. Robyn Wiegman, *American Anatomies: Theorizing Race and Gender* (Durham, NC: Duke University Press, 1995).

37. Schematizing the body, predicated upon quantifying individual traits such as "aggressiveness," "strength of sex drive," "anxiety," and "rule-following," Rushton tries to legitimate the relative characteristics of "Orientals," "Whites," and "Blacks." He correlates his data on these character traits and then asks *only* "Orientals" and "Whites" (it seems that blacks were not qualified to participate in this "research" study") to assess themselves and their "opposite number," and blacks. Relying on specious data gathered from study participants already subject to interpellation by state logics, values, and traits correlates to a cultural-biologistic individuation, a reductive process marred by subjective polling. His methodology focused on matters of race, intelligence, and sexuality, the "Great Chain of Being." He depends on the nonequivalence

of "White" from "nonwhite" and "Blacks" from "Orientals," and the equivalence of "Oriental" masculinity to "lack" and black masculinity to "overdetermined." In the end, this triangulation services a perverse common sense that establishes citizenship based on sexualized definitions of classed and racialized bodies. J. Phillipe Rushton, *Race, Evolution, and Behavior: A Life History Perspective* (New Brunswick, NJ: Transaction Publishers, 1995): 9–12.

38. Eldridge Cleaver, *Soul on Ice* (New York: Dell, 1968): 171.

39. Richard Fung, "Looking for My Penis: The Eroticized Asian in Gay Video Porn," in *Q&A: Queer in Asian America*, ed. David Eng and Alice Hom (Philadelphia: Temple University Press, 1998): 115–134.

40. Mercer, *Welcome to the Jungle*, 178.

41. Ibid.

42. Ibid., 176.

43. Messner and Sabo, *Sport, Men, and the Gender Order*, 23.

44. In other words, the theory of articulation asks how an ideology discovers its subjects, rather than how a subject formulates the necessary and inevitable thoughts of an ideology at its specificities; it empowers subjects to begin to apprehend some sense or intelligibility of their historical positioning without subjecting them to reductive class or socioeconomic categories. See Stuart Hall, *Interviews with Stuart Hall* (New York: Vintage Books, 1996).

45. Dick Hebdige, *Subculture: The Meaning of Style* (London: Methuen, 1979): 18.

46. *Outside the Lines*, ESPN Television, July 1, 2001.

47. Albert G. Spalding, *America's National Game* (New York: American Sports Publishing Company, 1911): 4. Indeed, baseball's rules and competition perfectly embodied the social organization of American modernity by reproducing ideologies of consumption, obedience, hard work, and nationalism. In this way, the game of baseball contained the contradictions of American modernity with its racial hierarchy, gender divisions, and focus on capitalist sociality that are the bedrock of U.S. liberal democracy.

48. *Major League Baseball All-Star Game*, Fox Television, July 8, 2001.

49. For a discussion of fandom and leisure using class analysis, see Pierre Bourdieu, "How Can One Be a Sports Fan?," in *The Cultural Studies Reader*, ed. Simon During (New York: Routledge, 1993): 339–356.

50. S. L. Price, "The Ichiro Paradox," *Time*, July 15, 2002.

51. Ibid., 1.

52. Robert Falkoff, "Same Scenario, Different Outcome," MLB.com, February 2, 2003, at http://www.mlb.com.

53. Major League Baseball International, 2001 Annual Report, 2–3.

54. Major League Baseball International, "Baseball Tonight" (advertisement), ESPN, August 3, 2001.

55. Stuart Elliott, "A Sales Pitch Tries to Connect Fans as Baseball Season Starts," *New York Times*, March 28, 2001, C6.

56. Jeffrey Denberg, "Q&A with David Stern," *Atlanta Journal-Constitution*, June 2, 2003.

57. ESPN, advertisement, *Sports Illustrated*, October 28, 2002.

58. In linking the important congruence of "Asian" to "American," it is through Asian male bodies that the collective naming of Asian American men can be made culturally embodied, institutionally represented, and sexually regulated. Likewise, it is over and against Asian American men's bodies that Asian masculinities can be understood as formally equivalent to one another. Asian manhood has been historically and discursively equivalent to Asian American men. Each have signaled in differential ways a shift in Asian American masculinity, nation, and citizenship; it is the landscape where the transition from "Asian foreigner" to "Asian immigrant" to "Asian American male citizen" must be understood in the context of African American masculinity, racialization, and nationalisms.

59. Todd Boyd and Kenneth L. Shropshire, eds., *Basketball Jones: America above the Rim* (New York: New York University Press, 2000): 3.

60. Fox Sports Television, *Best Damn Sports Show Period*, hosted by Tom Arnold, John Salley, and John Kruk, June 28, 2002.

61. Robert Lee, *Orientals*.

62. Jonathan Feigen, "Shaq Dismisses Yaomania," *Houston Chronicle*, June 21, 2002.

63. Ric Butler, "Yao Knows How to Strike a Pose with Media," *ESPN the Magazine*, December 3, 2002.

64. The issue of nationalism is the predominant mode of analysis in sport theory, but this particularity of nationalism has parameters and points of difference that vary from studies dealing with, for example, British identity in soccer or Australian fandom in rugby. See Alan Bairner, *Sport, Nationalism, and Globalization* (Albany: State University of New York Press, 2001).

65. Ibid., 1.

66. For an interesting discussion on masochism and sadomasochism and their implication for the construction of masculinity, see David Savran, *Taking It Like a Man: White Masculinity, Masochism, and Contemporary American Culture* (Princeton, NJ: Princeton University Press, 1998).

67. Irwin Tang, "APA Community Should Tell Shaquille O'Neal to 'Come Down to Chinatown,'" *AsianWeek*, January 3, 2003.

68. Ibid., 1.

69. Ibid., 3.

70. L. A. Chung, "Media Looked the Other Way on Shaq's Slur," *San Jose Mercury News*, January 17, 2003.

71. *Talk Back Live*, moderated by Arthel Neville, CNN, January 23, 2003; *The Tavis Smiley Show*, National Public Radio, January 24, 2003.

72. Miller et al., *Globalization and Sport*, 16.

73. Stefan Fatsis, Peter Wonacott, and Maureen Tkacik, "Chinese Basketball Star Is Big Business for NBA," *Wall Street Journal*, October 22, 2002.

74. To offer Yao to the NBA was meant as a symbolic gesture signifying China's opening of Asia's biggest market to unrestricted transnationalism. What this means in the figure of Yao is that he had the potential to create a billion-dollar industry in China and worldwide, thus producing a node in the transnational circuit different from Ichiro's and perhaps much more spectacular. Yao stood at a crossroads of an insular past that created superb athletes for nationalist glory, and a stark future that cannot smile without seeing seven-foot-five dollar signs: the communist legacy of Mao and the future of China immersed in capitalist sociality.

75. *San Jose Mercury News*, "Yao Wins Showdown with Shaq," January 18, 2003.

76. C. L. R. James, *American Civilization*, ed. Anna Grimshaw and Keith Hart (Oxford: Blackwell Publishers, 1993): 27–29.

Chapter 3

1. David Desser, "The Kung Fu Craze," in *The Cinema of Hong Kong: History, Arts, Identity*, ed. Poshek Fu and David Desser (Cambridge: Cambridge University Press, 2000): 19–44.

2. Tasker, "Fists of Fury," 317–320.

3. W. E. B. Du Bois, *Black Reconstruction in America, 1860–1880* (New York: Atheneum, 1935): 728. Lowe, *Immigrant Acts*, 2–10.

4. Paul Gilroy, *The Black Atlantic: Modernity and Double Consciousness* (Cambridge: Harvard University Press, 1993).

5. Halberstam, *Female Masculinity*; Judith Butler, *Bodies That Matter: On the Discursive Limits of "Sex"* (New York: Routledge, 1993); Siobhan B. Somerville, *Queering the Color Line: Race and the Invention of Homosexuality in American Culture* (Durham, NC: Duke University Press, 2000); Stoler, *Race and the Colonial Education of Desire*.

6. Stuart Hall, "Gramsci's Relevance for the Study of Race and Ethnicity," in *Stuart Hall: Critical Dialogues in Cultural Studies*, ed. David Morley and Kuan-Hsing Chen (London: Routledge, 1996): 428.

7. Robert Lee, *Orientals*, 145–155.

8. The theory of racial formation inveighs against a seminal recasting of how the state is structured as racial—how an interventionist state, as witnessed during the Civil Rights Movement, may induce a misconception of the state as intervened, as preeminently racialized from within. The institutions of the United States, as in most

capitalist states, are composed of policy trajectories, ambient factors and codes that support and justify them, and social relationships in which that bedrock is embedded. See Omi and Winant, *Racial Formation*, 84–88.

9. C. B. Macpherson, *The Political Theory of Possessive Individualism* (Oxford: Oxford University Press, 1962).

10. In framing a foundational text for market democracy, John Locke in *Two Treatises of Government* inaugurated an understanding of the political relations among citizens living within the dynamic of civil society through the idea of the social contract. From his conceptualization of a natural state of "man" living under the paternal powers of fathers to one where social contracts and rules of engagement are explicitly stated and enforced by the state, Locke describes his defining concepts of personal liberty and forms of government, property rights and their efficient maintenance, and the role of consent and individual autonomy for an ordered political society that ensures the protection of property and freedoms originating in nature. John Locke, *Two Treatises of Government* (London: Orion Publishing Group, 1993); John Locke, *An Essay Concerning Human Understanding* (London: Orion Publishing Group, 1993).

11. For a discussion of liberalism as a failure for individual freedoms and rights, see Jean-Jacques Rousseau, *The Basic Political Writings*, trans. Donald A. Cress (Indianapolis: Hackett Publishing, 1987).

12. Karl Marx, "On the Jewish Question," in *The Marx-Engels Reader*, trans. and ed. Robert C. Tucker (New York: W. W. Norton, 1978).

13. Antonio Gramsci, *Selections from the Prison Notebooks*, trans. and ed. Quintin Hoare and Geoffrey Nowell Smith (New York: International Publishers, 1971): 181.

14. Ibid., 175–185.

15. W. E. B. Du Bois, *The Souls of Black Folk* (New York: Penguin Books, 1995): 85.

16. Alexander Saxton, *The Indispensable Enemy: Labor and the Anti-Chinese Movement in California* (Berkeley: University of California Press, 1971); David Roediger, *The Wages of Whiteness: Race and the Making of the American Working Class* (London: Verso, 1990): 59–60.

17. No other example reinforces this discontinuity of "nonwhite" better than the Supreme Court decisions involving Takao Ozawa and Bhagat Singh Thind. Ronald Takaki writes that in 1923 the Supreme Court ruled on the disenfranchisement of Asian Indians from land ownership and citizenship because they were classified as "nonwhite." Because Asian Indians were classified anthropologically as Indo-Caucasian, Thind advocated the right of naturalized citizenship based on scientific evidence that was held to be valid at that time. Thereafter, the Court conflated the term "Caucasian" with "white person" and showcased its loyalty to the creed of white civilization, arguing that the intention of the Founding Fathers was to "confer the privilege of citizenship upon that class of persons they knew as 'white.'" See Ronald Takaki, *Strangers from a Different Shore: A History of Asian Americans* (New York: Penguin

Books, 1989): 299. The Chinese Exclusion Act of 1882, by excluding and disenfranchising the Chinese, appeased the lobbying of the state by its white constituents and thus reinscribed the notion of "whiteness" as the marker for citizenship. This legislative act is a specific legal restriction in a historical lineage dating all the way back to the 1790 Naturalization Act. The genealogical record of exclusion for foreign and racial others, a formation with a wide and extensive lineage—from the Chinese in 1882 to Asian Indians in 1917, Japanese in 1924, and Filipinos in 1934—bespeaks a history of prohibition from the categories of citizenship and property ownership in which the markers of race configure as the primary criterion.

18. I want to specify for my argument that the two martial arts heroes in my analysis are designated as male, but there are female martial arts heroines who follow parallel trajectories yet diverge in their gender performance. See, for instance, *Crouching Tiger, Hidden Dragon*, dir. Ang Lee, Miramax, 2000.

19. Kaja Silverman, *The Subject of Semiotics* (New York: Oxford University Press, 1983).

20. bell hooks, "The Oppositional Gaze: Black Female Spectators," in *Black American Cinema*, ed. Manthia Diawara (New York: Routledge, 1993): 290.

21. Manthia Diawara, "Black British Cinema: Spectatorship and Identity Formation in *Territories*," *Public Culture* 3:1 (Summer 1989): 33–48.

22. hooks, "The Oppositional Gaze," 300–302.

23. Hall, "Ethnicity: Identity and Difference," 339–349.

24. Blake French, "*Rush Hour* Review," FilmCritic.com., March 1, 2005, at http://filmcritic.com; Simon O'Ryan, "*Rush Hour* Review," Boxoffice.com, February 28, 2005, at http://www.boxoffice.com; Anthony Leong, "*Rush Hour* Movie Review," Mediacircus.net, February 28, 2005, at http://www.meidacircus.net.

25. Janet Maslin, "Kicks, Swivels, and Wisecracks on Hollywood Boulevard," *New York Times*, September 18, 2001, at http://movies2.nytimes.com/mem/movies/review.html.

26. Bob Graham, "'Rush Hour' Speeds Right Along: Chan, Tucker Star in Action Comedy," *San Francisco Examiner*, January 29, 1999, D12.

27. Maitland McDonagh, "On the Waterfront," *TV Guide*, February 28, 2005, at http://www.tvguide.com.

28. Wesley Morris, "'Romeo' Just Dies at End," *San Francisco Examiner*, March 22, 2000, C3.

29. Dennis Lim, "Demographic Violence," *Village Voice*, March 22, 2000, at http://www.villagevoice.com.

30. Savran, *Taking It Like a Man*.

31. The tragic hero of Greek drama, in the works of Aeschylus, Sophocles, and Euripides, through no obvious fault of his own, finds himself in conflict with the principles of a particular society, not a conflict between good and evil but between man

and community. The Greek word *demos*, "populace," signifies the linguistic roots that were foundations for the influence of democratic ideals, an ethic within the community advocating active participation and dialogue in all facets of daily life.

32. Américo Paredes, *With His Pistol in His Hand* (Austin: University of Texas Press, 1958): 169.

33. Benedict Anderson, *Imagined Communities: Reflections on the Origin and Spread of Nationalism* (London: Verso, 1991).

34. Roberto Alejandro, *Hermeneutics, Citizenship, and the Pubic Sphere* (Albany: State University of New York Press, 1993): 1–5.

35. Lisa Odham Stokes and Michael Hoover, *City on Fire: Hong Kong Cinema* (London: Verso, 1999): 90.

36. Ibid.

37. Bey Logan, *Hong Kong Action Cinema* (Woodstock, NY: Overlook Press, 1995): 10.

38. Ibid., 90.

39. Ibid., 11.

40. Stephen Teo, "The 1970s," in *The Cinema of Hong Kong: History, Arts, Identity*, ed. Poshek Fu and David Desser (Cambridge: Cambridge University Press, 2000): 98.

41. Ibid., 24–25.

42. I am thinking of a panel at the 2004 American Studies Association convention with scholars such as Deborah Whaley.

43. Amy Ongiri, "'He Wanted to Be Just Like Bruce Lee': African Americans, Kung Fu Theater and Cultural Exchange at the Margins," *Journal of Asian American Studies* 5:1 (2002): 25.

44. Ibid., 39.

45. Laura Mulvey, "Visual Pleasure and Narrative Cinema," in *Visual and Other Pleasures* (Bloomington: Indiana University Press, 1989).

46. Ibid., 251.

47. In most buddy pictures, women are relegated to the margins in the diegetic. Especially in the martial arts films of Hollywood, one asks: where are the representations of strong Asian women, and why are white women excluded from these films entirely? Obviously, antimiscegenation taboos concerning sexuality still regulate discourses about racialized men and white femininity in film as well as making invisible even same-race romance through the workings of the martial arts buddy genre. This male-dominated genre, which has prescribed through homosociality a range of models of manhood including active, violent agents, sets the stage for an evaluation of the reproduction of hegemonic masculinity.

48. Rogin, *Blackface, White Noise*.

49. Lisa Lowe suggests that immigration thus can be seen as the single most important site of the Asian American collective memory, a discursive and historical

terrain where the economic, cultural, and legal confrontation with American capital and racial ideology informs us of the global and national narratives that form the immigrant subject. The form takes on a racialized configuration, where inclusion and exclusion expressed through legislation is the discursive and ideological formation by the nation-state. This complicated and contradictory dynamic of American culture, a desire and repulsion of the immigrant alien and the processes of disciplining the immigrant citizen as a subject to ameliorate ambivalence through specific immigration acts, tells the history of our racial intersection with globalism and our needs to modulate our economy in the wake of the last century and a half of economic expansion. See Lowe, *Immigrant Acts*, 2–20.

50. Rising anti-Korean sentiment within the African American community because of declining black economic power and cultural misunderstandings led to prominent rap artists, most notably Ice Cube, to castigate Korean American grocers, with their allegedly standoffish business practices, in a song entitled "Black Korea." Jeff Chang said that the conflict was turned into a black-against-Korean conflict, although the relative lack of power held by either group rendered the conflict a nonissue among white media institutions. In other words, the strife between the two marginalized groups negated any meaningful critique of the larger economic and ideological structures that give rise to interethnic conflicts. Instead of African Americans and Korean Americans forming an alliance and standing in cross-cultural unity against white material oppression, the African Americans, in a binary axis of dialogue, assumed the position of whites, and the Korean Americans took the position of blacks in relative social-political power. This led to the boycott by the Korean American Grocers Association (KAGRO) of St. Ides malt liquor, of which Ice Cube was a prominent endorser, showcasing the power of economic pressure to obstruct the political-social agenda of a prominent African American voice. See Jeff Chang, "Race, Class, Conflict and Empowerment: On Ice Cube's 'Black Korea,'" *Amerasia Journal* 19:2 (1993): 87–107.

51. However, racializing the function of fetish, Trish acts as both object and subject in the scene. The fetishistic deployment of Trish's face is the formal backdrop to Han's foreign status. As an individual marked as foreign, his mimesis of a South Asian cab driver expresses this contrast. A South Asian figure who appeared earlier in the plot, the cab driver Achebar, scolded Han for not noticing his posted "off duty" sign with the remark, "understand English?" Later, Han steals his cab and, while pretending to be Achebar, drives Trish away. From the inception of the scene, Han performs the limitations, linguistically and culturally, of his incorporation into citizenship by being pitted against Achebar, who occupies a South Asian working-class position. At the end of the scene, found out by Trish to be an imposter, he ogles her, enacting the male gaze in an over-the-shoulder two-shot. From this shot, the audience is made aware of his racialized gaze. It is overextended, positioning both sets of looks as exclusive from the viewpoint of both the film and the spectator.

52. Chris Straayer, "Redressing the 'Natural': The Temporary Transvestite Film," in *Deviant Eyes, Deviant Bodies: Sexual Re-Orientation in Film and Video* (New York: Columbia University Press, 1996): 56.

53. See Jacquie Jones, "The Construction of Black Sexuality: Towards Normalizing the Black Cinematic Experience," in *Black American Cinema*, ed. Manthia Diawara (New York: Routledge, 1993): 251.

54. Lowe and Lloyd, *The Politics of Culture*, 3.

55. Lalitha Gopalan, "Avenging Women in Indian Cinema," *Screen* 38:1 (Spring 1997): 42–59.

56. Tasker, "Fists of Fury," 315–317.

57. Prashad, *Everybody Was Kung Fu Fighting*, 42–47; see also Lipsitz, *The Possessive Investment in Whiteness*.

58. Harris rightly sees the racialized conception of property from a historical and legal analysis. She examines the emergence of whiteness as property and traces the evolution of whiteness from color to race to status to property as a progression historically rooted in white supremacy and economic hegemony. See Cheryl Harris, "Whiteness as Property," *Harvard Law Review* 106:8 (June 1993): 1710–1791. See also Ian F. Haney López, *White by Law: The Legal Construction of Race* (New York: New York University Press, 1996).

59. Sedgwick, *Epistemology of the Closet*, 254.

60. Ibid., 77.

61. Wiegman, *American Anatomies*.

62. Chon Noriega, "'Something's Missing Here!' Homosexuality and Film Reviews during the Production Code Era, 1934–1962," *Cinema Journal* 30:1 (Fall 1990): 21–39.

63. Louis Althusser found slippages in orthodox Marxism in terms of repression and subjugation that he wanted to rework. He rejected the idea of ideology as false consciousness, instead firmly holding to the role of ideology as a social reality: that it structures social relationships, that it raises the importance of the "real." What Althusser revolutionized in the field of orthodox class analysis regarding the impact of ideology on social institutions and subjects was his elucidation of the concept of ideological hailing. He attempted to formulate that "all ideology hails or interpellates concrete individuals as concrete subjects, by the functioning of the category of the subject." What hailing entails is the formation of citizens into subjects through the acts or functions of ideology. Althusser espouses that ideology recruits subjects from among individuals (where there are no individuals who are not hailed), and that it transforms individuals into subjects (where there are no individuals who are not transformed). The precise operation of ideological hailing is analogically compared to the hailings of everyday police officers when they yell, "Hey, you there!" The hailed individual will turn around—and it is in "this mere one-hundred-and-eighty-degree

physical conversion, [that] he becomes a subject." The subject turns around because he or she realizes that it was he or she who was really being addressed, that it was really he or she being hailed. Moreover, Althusser argues that the primary functioning power of ideology is its capacity to veil its very true character as Ideology: "Ideology never says, 'I am ideological.'" See Louis Althusser, "Ideology and Ideological State Apparatuses," in *Lenin and Philosophy and Other Essays*, trans. Ben Brewster (New York: Monthly Review Press, 1971): 127–186; quotations, 174.

64. Gilroy, *The Black Atlantic*, 72–110. Gilroy maintains that there has always been a politics of utopia in all black cultural expression, especially in the musical forms of blues and spirituals.

65. See Tricia Rose, *Black Noise: Rap Music and Black Culture in Contemporary America* (Lebanon, NH: University Press of New England, 1994).

66. The wars in the Philippines, Korea, Vietnam, and Cambodia all tell of a history of foreign intervention. This repressed memory from the national polity comes full circle when emigrants from the colonized periphery migrate to the imperial center. Therefore, the history of Asian Americans traverses the history of racial formation and U.S. imperial and colonial engagements in Asia. As Amy Kaplan says, the absence of empire in the collective pedagogy, memory, and stories of genesis in such fields as American studies shows the erasure of America's penetration into Asian culture both on a systemic and a cultural terrain. See Amy Kaplan, "Left Alone with America: The Absence of Empire in the Study of American Culture," in *Cultures of United States Imperialism*, ed. Amy Kaplan and Donald E. Pease (Durham, NC: Duke University Press, 1993); Lisa Yoneyama, *Hiroshima Traces: Time, Space, and the Dialectics of Memory* (Berkeley: University of California Press, 1999).

67. See, for instance, Davis, "Race and Criminalization." She addresses the discussions by those who are leading the call for more prisons and employ statistics in the same fetishistic and misleading way that Thomas Malthus did more than two centuries ago. The rising enterprise of the prison industrial complex and the use of transnational corporation capital in some sweetheart deals conceptualize the fusion of flexible modes of accumulation and the racialization of a super-surplus labor. Deindustrialization accelerated this process, which occurred during the 1970s and 1980s, and the subsequent explosion of the informal drug economy in which many black people were displaced.

68. I want to thank Judith Halberstam for conversations concerning this idea.

69. Fung, "Looking for My Penis," 115–134.

70. James Snead, *White Screens, Black Images: Hollywood from the Dark Side*, ed. Colin MacCabe and Cornel West (New York: Routledge, 1994).

71. hooks, "The Oppositional Gaze," 288–290.

Chapter 4

1. Asian Improv Records, press release for I Was Born with Two Tongues, *Broken Speak*, 1999.

2. Saul Williams, "The Future of Language," in *The Spoken Word Revolution*, ed. Mark Eleveld (Naperville, IL: Sourcebooks, 2003): 58–59.

3. Karen Shimakawa, *National Abjection: The Asian American Body Onstage* (Durham, NC: Duke University Press, 2002): 17.

4. CNN, "Human Cadaver Exhibit," August 23, 2005, at http://www.cnn.com.

5. Robert Lee, *Orientals*, 30.

6. James Moy, *Marginal Sights: Staging the Chinese in America* (Iowa City: University of Iowa Press, 1993): 8.

7. Robert Lee, *Orientals*, 32.

8. George Rawick, *From Sundown to Sunup: The Making of the Black Community* (Westport, CT: Greenwood Press, 1972); Saxton, *The Indispensable Enemy*.

9. Quoted in Robert Lee, *Orientals*, 32.

10. Shimakawa, *National Abjection*, 2.

11. Ibid.

12. Quoted in ibid., 59.

13. Ibid., 69.

14. My emphasis. Deborah Wong, *Speak It Louder: Asian Americans Making Music* (New York: Routledge, 2004): 164.

15. Quoted in Shimakawa, *National Abjection*, 70.

16. Walter Benjamin, "The Work of Art in the Age of Mechanical Reproduction," in *Illuminations: Essays and Reflections*, ed. Hannah Arendt, trans. Harry Zohn (New York: Schocken Books, 1968): 220.

17. Ibid., 223.

18. Ibid., 222–223.

19. Dorinne Kondo, *About Face: Performing Race in Fashion and Theater* (New York: Routledge, 1997): 16.

20. Ibid., 195.

21. Josephine Lee, *Performing Asian America: Race and Ethnicity on the Contemporary Stage* (Philadelphia: Temple University Press, 1997): 41.

22. Ibid., 23.

23. Dennis Kim, interview by Chong Chon-Smith, August 29, 2005.

24. Mark Eleveld, ed., *The Spoken Word Revolution* (Naperville, IL: Sourcebooks, 2003): 10–12.

25. Dennis Kim, interview by Chong Chon-Smith, September 18, 2005.

26. See Rickey Kim, "Speaking in Tongues," *EM* magazine, August 29, 2005.

27. Ibid., 8.

28. Quoted in Deborah Wong, *Speak It Louder*, 240.

29. I Was Born with Two Tongues, "Alag," *Broken Speak*, Asian Improv Records, 1999.

30. Quoted in Neela Banerjee, "Slam Poets Mix Words and Music and Mojo and Intellect into Political Performance Art," *AsianWeek*, August 29, 2005, at http://www.asianweek.com.

31. Gloria Anzaldúa, *Borderlands/La Frontera: The New Mestiza* (San Francisco: Aunt Lute Books, 1987): 245.

32. Ibid., 1.

33. I Was Born with Two Tongues, *Broken Speak*, Asian Improv Records, 1999.

34. Ishle Yi Park, "Asian Word Warriors," *A Gathering of the Tribes*, May 31, 2005, at http://www.tribes.org.

35. Ibid., 2.

36. See Khachig Tölölyan, "Rethinking Diapora(s): Stateless Power in the Transnational Moment," *Diaspora* 5:1 (Spring 1996): 7.

37. Stuart Hall, "Cultural Identity and Diaspora," in *Colonial Discourse and Post-Colonial Theory: A Reader*, ed. Patrick Williams and Laura Chrisman (New York: Columbia University Press, 1994): 194.

38. Gayatri Gopinath, "'Bombay, U.K., Yuba City': Bhangra Music and the Engendering of Diaspora," *Diaspora* 4:3 (Winter 1995).

39. Quoted in David Jakubiak, "Denizen Kane Returns from the West a Changed Man," *Chicago Sun-Times*, August 29, 2005, at http://www.suntimes.com.

40. Dennis Kim, interview by Chong Chon-Smith, August 29, 2005.

41. "Mountain Brothers Interview," Asiatic Theory Project, June 19, 2003.

42. Dennis Smith, "*Asian Pacific Review* Interviews the Mountain Brothers," *Asian Pacific Review*, September 6, 2005.

43. Deborah Wong, *Speak It Louder*, 179.

44. Todd Inoue, "Mountain Grown: Asian American Rappers the Mountain Brothers Step Out from the Speakers and Turntables," *MetroActive*, September 6, 2005, at http://www.metroactive.com.

45. George Lipsitz, "We Know What Time It Is: Race, Class and Youth Culture in the Nineties," in *Microphone Fiends: Youth Music and Youth Culture*, ed. Andrew Ross and Tricia Rose (New York: Routledge, 1994): 17–28.

46. FD, "Interview with Super-Producer Chops of Mountain Brothers," Aznraps.com, January 28, 2004.

47. Quoted in Monica Anke Hahn-Koenig, "The Dope Slope," *Philadelphia City Paper*, September 5, 2005, at http://citypaper.net.

48. Qwest, "Mountain Brothers," *Elements*, September 9, 2005, at http://www.hiphop-elements.com.

49. Deborah Wong, *Speak It Louder*, 252.

50. Nelson George, *Hip-Hop America* (New York: Penguin Books, 1999): 4.

51. Mountain Brothers, "Paperchase," *Self: Volume 1*, Pimpstrut Records, 1998.

52. Ibid.

53. Deborah Wong, *Speak It Louder*, 235.

54. Quoted in ibid., 236.

55. Rose, *Black Noise*, chapter 2.

56. Mountain Brothers, "Paperchase."

57. Ibid.

58. "Mountain Brother Interview," *Philadelphia City Paper*, August 29, 2005, at http://www.philadelphiacitypaper.com.

59. Kara Keeling, "'A Homegrown Revolutionary'? Tupac Shakur and the Legacy of the Black Panther Party," *Black Scholar* 29:2–3 (1999): 59–63.

60. Rose, *Black Noise*, 150.

61. bell hooks, *Outlaw Culture: Resisting Representations* (New York: Routledge, 1994): 116.

62. Quoted in Rose, *Black Noise*, 149.

63. Mountain Brothers, "Whiplash," *Self: Volume 1*, Pimpstrut Records, 1998.

64. Ibid.

65. Kevin Kim, "Repping Chinatown," *Colorlines* 7:4 (Winter 2004–2005).

66. Mountain Brothers, "Whiplash."

67. Mountain Brothers, "Love Poetry," *Self: Volume 1*, Pimpstrut Records, 1998.

Conclusion

1. Melani McAlister, *Epic Encounters: Culture, Media, and U.S. Interests in the Middle East since 1945* (Berkeley: University of California Press, 2001).

2. Bhuvaneswari Bhaduri was a young Bengali girl whom Gayatri Spivak gives as an example of subaltern silence in 1926 India. Refusing to follow orders to kill someone, Bhaduri instead committed suicide, waiting until her menstrual period to do so. This silent resistance was her attempt to challenge the official narrative of Indian politicians and journalists, who she knew would attribute the suicide to an illegitimate pregnancy. Her subaltern expression defied the ritual codes of purity for suttee, in which a woman must be "pure" for four days before jumping onto the funeral pyre of her husband, and disputed the fabricated reason of illegitimate pregnancy as the cause of her death. However, the pregnancy story given by political and media elites nevertheless became the commonsense story believed by the general population. Spivak connects Bhaduri and her granddaughter to a genealogy of subaltern silence: the grandmother, within caste and gender oppression, and her granddaughter, a dedicated worker for a transnational conglomerate.

3. John Okada, *No-No Boy* (Seattle: University of Washington Press, 1976): 231.

4. Ibid., 225–226.

Works Cited

Alejandro, Roberto. *Hermeneutics, Citizenship, and the Pubic Sphere*. Albany: State University of New York Press, 1993.

Althusser, Louis. "Ideology and Ideological State Apparatuses." In *Lenin and Philosophy and Other Essays*. Translated by Ben Brewster. New York: Monthly Review Press, 1971.

Anderson, Benedict. *Imagined Communities: Reflections on the Origin and Spread of Nationalism*. London: Verso, 1991.

Anzaldúa, Gloria. *Borderlands/La Frontera: The New Mestiza*. San Francisco: Aunt Lute Books, 1987.

Arteaga, Alfred, ed. *An Other Tongue: Nation and Ethnicity in the Linguistic Borderlands*. Durham, NC: Duke University Press, 1994.

Bairner, Alan. *Sport, Nationalism, and Globalization*. Albany: State University of New York Press, 2001.

Banerjee, Neela. "Slam Poets Mix Words and Music and Mojo and Intellect into Political Performance Art." *AsianWeek*, August 29, 2005. At http://www.asianweek.com.

Baseball Tonight. Advertisement. ESPN, August 3, 2001.

Bederman, Gail. *Manliness and Civilization*. Chicago: University of Chicago Press, 1995.

Bell, Derrick. "Brown v. Board of Education and the Interest-Convergence Dilemma." *Harvard Law Review* 93 (1980): 518–533.

Benjamin, Walter. *Illuminations: Essays and Reflections*. Edited by Hannah Arendt. Translated by Harry Zohn. New York: Schocken Books, 1968.

Bercovitch, Sacvan. *The Rites of Assent: Transformations in the Symbolic Construction of America*. New York: Routledge, 1993.

Bluestone, Barry, and Bennett Harrison. *The Deindustrialization of America: Plant Closings, Community Abandonment, and the Dismantling of Basic Industry*. New York: Basic Books, 1982.

Boggs, James. *A Black Radical's Notebook: A James Boggs Reader*. Edited by Stephen M. Ward. Detroit: Wayne State University Press, 2011.

Bourdieu, Pierre. "How Can One Be a Sports Fan?" In *The Cultural Studies Reader*. Edited by Simon During. New York: Routledge, 1993.

———. *Language and Symbolic Power*. Edited by John B. Thompson. Translated by Gino Raymond and Matthew Adamson. Cambridge: Polity Press, 1991.

Boyd, Todd, and Kenneth L. Shropshire, eds. *Basketball Jones: America above the Rim*. New York: New York University Press, 2000.

Brooks, Gwendolyn. *Maud Martha*. Chicago: Third World Press, 1993.

Brown, Wendy. *States of Injury: Power and Freedom in Late Modernity*. Princeton, NJ: Princeton University Press, 1995.

Butler, Judith. *Bodies That Matter: On the Discursive Limits of "Sex."* New York: Routledge, 1993.

———. *The Psychic Life of Power: Theories in Subjection*. Stanford, CA: Stanford University Press, 1997.

Butler, Ric. "Yao Knows How to Strike a Pose with Media." *ESPN the Magazine*, December 3, 2002.

Césaire, Aimé. "Notebook of a Return to the Native Land." In *The Collected Poetry*. Translated by Clayton Eshleman and Annette Smith. Berkeley: University of California Press, 1983.

Chan, Sucheng. *Asian Americans: An Interpretive History*. Boston: Twayne Publishers, 1991.

Chandler, Alfred. *Scale and Scope: The Dynamics of Industrial Capitalism*. Cambridge: Harvard University Press, 1990.

Chang, Jeff. "Race, Class, Conflict and Empowerment: On Ice Cube's 'Black Korea.'" *Amerasia Journal* 19:2 (1993): 87–107.

Cheung, King-Kok. "The Woman Warrior versus the Chinaman Pacific: Must a Chinese American Critic Choose between Feminism and Heroism?" In *Conflicts in Feminism*, edited by Marianne Hirsch and Evelyn Fox Keller. New York: Routledge, 1990.

Chin, Frank. Letter to Maxine Hong Kingston, July 1976. Frank Chin Papers. Special Collections, University of California, Santa Barbara.

———. Letter to Maxine Hong Kingston, October 20, 1976. Frank Chin Papers. Special Collections, University of California, Santa Barbara.

Chin, Frank, Jeffrey Paul Chan, Lawson Fusao Inada, and Shawn Wong, eds. *Aiiieeeee! An Anthology of Asian-American Writers*. Washington, DC: Howard University Press, 1974.

Chin, Frank, and Shawn Wong, eds. *Yardbird Reader*. Vol. 3. Berkeley, CA: Yardbird Publishing, 1974.

Chuh, Kandice. *Imagine Otherwise: On Asian Americanist Critique*. Durham, NC: Duke University Press, 2003.

Chung, L. A. "Media Looked the Other Way on Shaq's Slur." *San Jose Mercury News*, January 17, 2003.

Churchill, Jordan. "Validation." *Journal of Philosophy* 56 (February 26, 1959): 200–208.

Cleaver, Eldridge. *Soul on Ice*. New York: Dell, 1968.

Cohen, Stanley. *Folk Devils and Moral Panics*. Saint Albans, England: Paladin, 1973.

Connell, R. W. *Masculinities*. Berkeley: University of California Press, 1995.

Corber, Robert. *In the Name of National Security: Hitchcock, Homophobia, and the Political Construction of Gender in Postwar America*. Durham, NC: Duke University Press, 1993.

Crouching Tiger, Hidden Dragon. Directed by Ang Lee. Miramax, 2000.

Davis, Angela. "Race and Criminalization: Black Americans and the Punishment Industry." In *The House That Race Built*, edited by Wahneema Lubiano. New York: Pantheon Books, 1997.

Dead Prez. "Psychology." *Let's Get Free*. Loud Records, 1996.

Denberg, Jeffrey. "Q&A with David Stern." *Atlanta Journal-Constitution*, June 2, 2003.

Denning, Michael. *The Cultural Front: The Laboring of American Culture in the Twentieth Century*. London: Verso, 1998.

Desser, David. "The Kung Fu Craze." In *The Cinema of Hong Kong: History, Arts, Identity*, edited by Poshek Fu and David Desser. Cambridge: Cambridge University Press, 2000.

Diawara, Manthia. "Black British Cinema: Spectatorship and Identity Formation in *Territories*." *Public Culture* 3:1 (Summer 1989).

Díaz, Junot. *The Brief Wondrous Life of Oscar Wao*. New York: Riverhead Books, 2007.

Douglass, Frederick. *Narrative of the Life of Frederick Douglass*. In *The Classic Slave Narratives*, edited by Henry Louis Gates Jr. New York: Penguin Books, 2002.

Du Bois, W. E. B. *Black Reconstruction*. New York: Atheneum, 1935.

———. *The Souls of Black Folk*. New York: Penguin Books, 1995.

Dudziak, Mary L. "Desegregation as a Cold War Imperative." *Stanford Law Review* 41:1 (1988): 61–120.

Dyer, Richard. "White Man's Muscles." In *Race and the Subject of Masculinities*, edited by Harry Stecopoulos and Michael Uebel. Durham, NC: Duke University Press, 1997.

Edwards, Harry. *Sociology of Sport*. Homewood, IL: Dorsey Press, 1973.

Ehrenreich, Barbara. *The Hearts of Men: American Dreams and the Flight from Commitment*. New York: Anchor Books, 1983.

Eleveld, Mark, ed. *The Spoken Word Revolution*. Naperville, IL: Sourcebooks, 2003.

Elliott, Stuart. "A Sales Pitch Tries to Connect Fans as Baseball Season Starts." *New York Times*, March 28, 2001.

Eng, David. *Racial Castration: Managing Masculinity in Asian America*. Durham, NC: Duke University Press, 2001.

Espiritu, Yen Le. *Asian American Panethnicity: Bridging Institutions and Identities.* Philadelphia: Temple University Press, 1992.

ESPN. Advertisement. *Sports Illustrated,* October 28, 2002.

Falkoff, Robert. "Same Scenario, Different Outcome." MLB.com, February 2, 2003. At http://www.mlb.com.

Faludi, Susan. *Stiffed: The Betrayal of the American Man.* New York: William Morrow, 1999.

Fanon, Frantz. *Black Skins, White Masks.* New York: Grove Weidenfeld, 1952.

———. "Concerning Violence." In *The Wretched of the Earth.* New York: Grove Press, 1963.

Fatsis, Stefan, Peter Wonacott, and Maureen Tkacik. "Chinese Basketball Star Is Big Business for NBA." *Wall Street Journal,* October 22, 2002.

Feigen, Jonathan. "Shaq Dismisses Yaomania." *Houston Chronicle,* June 21, 2002.

Ferguson, Roderick. *Aberrations in Black: Toward a Queer of Color Critique.* Minneapolis: University of Minnesota Press, 2004.

Foucault, Michel. *The Order of Things: An Archaeology of the Human Sciences.* New York: Pantheon Books, 1971.

———. *"Society Must Be Defended": Lectures at the Collège de France, 1975–1976.* Translated by David Macey. New York: Picador Press, 2003.

Fox Sports Television. *Best Damn Sports Show Period.* Hosted by Tom Arnold, John Salley, and John Kruk. June 28, 2002.

Fujino, Diane. "The Black Liberation Movement and Japanese American Activism: The Radical Activism of Richard Aoki and Yuri Kochiyama." In *Afro Asia: Revolutionary Political and Cultural Connections between African Americans and Asian Americans,* edited by Fred Ho and Bill Mullen, 165–197. Durham, NC: Duke University Press, 2008.

Fung, Richard. "Looking for My Penis: The Eroticized Asian in Gay Video Porn." In *Q&A: Queer in Asian America,* edited by David Eng and Alice Hom. Philadelphia: Temple University Press, 1998.

George, Nelson. *Hip-Hop America.* New York: Penguin Books, 1999.

Gidra Incorporated and the University of California, Los Angeles. *Gidra,* various issues, 1969–1974.

Gilman, Sander L. *Difference and Pathology: Stereotypes of Sexuality, Race, and Madness.* Ithaca, NY: Cornell University Press, 1985.

Gilroy, Paul. *Against Race: Imagining Political Culture beyond the Color Line.* Cambridge: Belknap Press, 2000.

———. *The Black Atlantic: Modernity and Double Consciousness.* Cambridge: Harvard University Press, 1993.

Girl Like Me, A. Directed by Kiri Davis. Reel Works Teen Filmmaking, 2005.

Gitlin, Todd. *The Sixties: Years of Hope, Days of Rage.* New York: Bantam Books, 1993.

———. *The Whole World Is Watching: Mass Media in the Making and Unmaking of the New Left*. Berkeley: University of California Press, 2003.

Gopalan, Lalitha. "Avenging Women in Indian Cinema." *Screen* 38:1 (Spring 1997): 42–59.

Gopinath, Gayatri. "'Bombay, U.K., Yuba City': Bhangra Music and the Engendering of Diaspora." *Diaspora* 4:3 (Winter 1995): 303–321.

Gorn, Elliott. *The Manly Art: Bare-Knuckle Prize Fighting in America*. Ithaca, NY: Cornell University Press, 1986.

Gramsci, Antonio. *Selections from the Prison Notebooks*. Translated and edited by Quintin Hoare and Geoffrey Nowell Smith. New York: International Publishers, 1971.

Green, Harvey. *Fit for America: Health Fitness, Sport, and American Society*. New York: Pantheon Books, 1986.

Hahn-Koenig, Monica Anke. "The Dope Slope." *Philadelphia City Paper*, September 5, 2005. At http://citypaper.net.

Halberstam, Judith. *Female Masculinity*. Durham, NC: Duke University Press, 1998.

Hall, Stuart. "Cultural Identity and Diaspora." In *Colonial Discourse and Post-Colonial Theory: A Reader*, edited by Patrick Williams and Laura Chrisman. New York: Columbia University Press, 1994.

———. "Ethnicity: Identity and Difference." In *Becoming National: A Reader*, edited by Geoff Eley and Ronald Grigor Suny. New York: Oxford University Press, 1999.

———. "Gramsci's Relevance for the Study of Race and Ethnicity." In *Stuart Hall: Critical Dialogues in Cultural Studies*. Edited by David Morley and Kuan-Hsing Chen. London: Routledge, 1996.

———. *Interviews with Stuart Hall*. New York: Vintage Books, 1996.

———. *Policing the Crisis: Mugging, the State, and Law and Order*. Basingstoke, England: Macmillan, 1979.

———. "Racist Ideologies and the Media." In *Media Studies: A Reader*, edited by Sue Thornham, Caroline Basset, and Paul Marris. New York: New York University Press, 2000.

———. "The Whites of Their Eyes: Racist Ideologies and the Media." In *Silver Linings: Some Strategies for the Eighties*, edited by George Bridges and Rosalind Brunt. London: Lawrence and Wishart, 1981.

Haney López, Ian F. *White by Law: The Legal Construction of Race*. New York: New York University Press, 1996.

Harris, Cheryl. "Whiteness as Property." *Harvard Law Review* 106:8 (June 1993): 1710–1791.

Harris, William J. "The *Yardbird Reader* and the Multi-Ethnic Spirit." *MELUS* 8:2 (Summer 1981): 72–75.

Harvey, David. *A Brief History of Neoliberalism*. Oxford: Oxford University Press, 2005.

———. *The Condition of Postmodernity: An Enquiry into the Origins of Cultural Change*. Oxford: Blackwell Publishers, 1990.

Hebdige, Dick. *Subculture: The Meaning of Style*. London: Methuen, 1979.

Hing, Bill Ong. *Making and Remaking Asian America through Immigration Policy, 1850–1990*. Stanford, CA: Stanford University Press, 1993.

Ho, Fred, ed. *Legacy to Liberation: Politics and Culture of Revolutionary Asian Pacific America*. Oakland, CA: AK Press, 2000.

Ho, Fred, and Bill Mullen, eds. *Afro Asia: Revolutionary Political and Cultural Connections between African Americans and Asian Americans*. Durham, NC: Duke University Press, 2008.

Hong, Grace Kyungwon. "'Something Forgotten Which Should Have Been Remembered': Private Property and Cross-Racial Solidarity in the Work of Hisaye Yamamoto." *American Literature* 71:2 (June 1999): 291–310.

hooks, bell. *Killing Rage: Ending Racism*. New York: Henry Holt, 1995.

———. "The Oppositional Gaze: Black Female Spectators." In *Black American Cinema*, edited by Manthia Diawara. New York: Routledge, 1993.

Horne, Gerald. *Fire This Time: The Watts Uprising and the 1960s*. Charlottesville: University of Virginia Press, 2005.

Hune, Shirley. "Asian American Studies and Asian Studies: Boundaries and Borderlands of Ethnic Studies and Area Studies." In *Color-Line to Borderlands: The Matrix of American Ethnic Studies*, edited by Johnnella E. Butler. Seattle: University of Washington Press, 2001.

Hurh, Won Moo, and Kwang Chung Kim. "The 'Success' Image of Asian Americans: Its Validity, and Its Practical and Theoretical Implications." *Ethnic and Racial Studies* 12 (1989): 514–561.

Hurst, Charles. *Social Inequality: Forms, Causes, Consequences*. 8th ed. Upper Saddle River, NJ: Pearson Press, 2012.

Inoue, Todd. "Mountain Grown: Asian American Rappers the Mountain Brothers Step Out from the Speakers and Turntables." *MetroActive*, September 6, 2005. At http://www.metroactive.com.

I Was Born with Two Tongues. *Broken Speak*. Asian Improv Records, 1999.

I Wor Kuen. *Getting Together* 2:6.

Jakubiak, David. "Denizen Kane Returns from the West a Changed Man." *Chicago Sun-Times*, August 29, 2005. At http://www.suntimes.com.

James, C. L. R. *American Civilization*. Edited by Anna Grimshaw and Keith Hart. Oxford: Blackwell, 1993.

———. *Beyond a Boundary*. Durham, NC: Duke University Press, 1993.

———. "Dialectical Materialism and the Fate of Humanity." In *Spheres of Existence: Selected Writings.* Westport, CT: Lawrence Hill, 1980.

Jameson, Fredric. *The Political Unconscious: Narrative as a Socially Symbiotic Act.* Ithaca, NY: Cornell University Press, 1981.

———. *Postmodernism, or, The Cultural Logic of Late Capitalism.* Durham, NC: Duke University Press, 1992.

Jeffords, Susan. "The Big Switch: Hollywood Masculinity in the Nineties." In *Film Theory Goes to Hollywood,* edited by Jim Collins et al. New York: Routledge, 1993.

Jones, Jacquie. "The Construction of Black Sexuality: Towards Normalizing the Black Cinematic Experience." In *Black American Cinema,* edited by Manthia Diawara. New York: Routledge, 1993.

Jun, Helen Heran. *Race for Citizenship: Black Orientalism and Asian Uplift from Pre-emancipation to Neoliberal America.* New York: New York University Press, 2011.

Kang, Laura Hyun Yi. *Compositional Subjects: Enfiguring Asian/American Women.* Durham, NC: Duke University Press, 2002.

Kang, Younghill. *East Goes West: The Making of an Oriental Yankee.* New York: Charles Scribner's Sons, 1937.

Kaplan, Amy. *The Anarchy of Empire in the Making of U.S. Culture.* Cambridge: Harvard University Press, 2002.

———. "Left Alone with America: The Absence of Empire in the Study of American Culture." In *Cultures of United States Imperialism,* edited by Amy Kaplan and Donald E. Pease. Durham, NC: Duke University Press, 1993.

Katsiaficas, George. *The Imagination of the New Left: A Global Analysis of 1968.* Boston: South End Press, 1987.

Keeling, Kara. "'A Homegrown Revolutionary'? Tupac Shakur and the Legacy of the Black Panther Party." *Black Scholar* 29:2–3 (1999): 59–63.

Kelley, Robin D. G. *Freedom Dreams: The Black Radical Imagination.* Boston: Beacon Press, 2002.

———. *Race Rebels: Culture, Politics, and the Black Working Class.* New York: Free Press, 1994.

Kim, Claire Jean. "The Racial Triangulation of Asian Americans." *Politics and Society* 27 (1999): 105–137.

Kim, Daniel. "Do I, Too, Sing America? Vernacular Representations and Chang-rae Lee's *Native Speaker*." *Journal of Asian American Studies* 6:3 (2004): 231–260.

———. *Writing Manhood in Black and Yellow: Ralph Ellison, Frank Chin, and the Literary Politics of Identity.* Stanford, CA: Stanford University Press, 2006.

Kim, Dennis. Interview by Chong Chon-Smith, August 29, 2005.

———. Interview by Chong Chon-Smith, September 18, 2005.

Kim, Elaine. *Asian American Literature: An Introduction to the Writings and Their Social Context.* Philadelphia: Temple University Press, 1982.

Kim, Illsoo. *New Urban Immigrants: The Korean Community in New York City* Princeton, NJ: Princeton University Press, 1981.

Kim, Kevin. "Repping Chinatown." *Colorlines* 7:4 (Winter 2004–2005).

Kim, Rickey. "Speaking in Tongues." *EM* magazine, August 29, 2005.

Kimmel, Michael S. "Consuming Manhood." In *The Male Body: Features, Destinies, Exposures*, edited by Laurence Goldstein. Ann Arbor: University of Michigan Press, 1994.

Kochiyama, Yuri. *Shades of Power*. Newsletter of the Institute for MultiRacial Justice. Spring 1998. At http://modelminority.com.

Kondo, Dorinne. *About Face: Performing Race in Fashion and Theater*. New York: Routledge, 1997.

Koshy, Susan. "Morphing Race into Ethnicity: Asian Americans and Critical Transformations of Whiteness." *boundary* 2 28:1 (2001): 153–194.

Lee, Chang-rae. *Native Speaker*. New York: Riverhead Books, 1995.

Lee, James Kyung-jin. *Urban Triage: Race and the Fictions of Multiculturalism*. Minneapolis: University of Minnesota Press, 2004.

Lee, Josephine. *Performing Asian America: Race and Ethnicity on the Contemporary Stage*. Philadelphia: Temple University Press, 1997.

Lee, Robert. *Orientals: Asian Americans in Popular Culture*. Philadelphia: Temple University Press, 1998.

Lemke-Santangelo, Gretchen. "Deindustrialization, Urban Poverty, and African American Community Mobilization in Oakland, 1945 through the 1990s." In *Seeking El Dorado: African Americans in California*, edited by Lawrence de Graaf, Kevin Mulroy, and Quintard Taylor. Seattle: University of Washington Press, 2001.

Leong, Russell. *The Country of Dreams and Dust*. Boston: West End Press, 1993.

———. "Lived Theory." *Amerasia Journal* 21:1–2 (1995): v–x.

Lim, Shirley Geok-lin, and Amy Ling, eds. *Reading the Literatures of Asian America*. Philadelphia: Temple University Press, 1992.

Ling, Jinqi. *Narrating Nationalisms: Ideology and Form in Asian American Literature*. New York: Oxford University Press, 1998.

Lipsitz, George. *The Possessive Investment in Whiteness: How White People Profit from Identity Politics*. Philadelphia: Temple University Press, 1998.

———. "We Know What Time It Is: Race, Class and Youth Culture in the Nineties." In *Microphone Fiends: Youth Music and Youth Culture*, edited by Andrew Ross and Tricia Rose. New York: Routledge, 1994.

Liu, John M. "The Contours of Asian Professional, Technical and Kindred Work Immigration, 1965–1988." *Sociological Perspectives* 35:4 (Winter 1992): 673–704.

Lloyd, David. "Race under Representation." *Oxford Literary Review* 13:1–2 (July 1991): 62–94.

Locke, John. *An Essay Concerning Human Understanding*. London: Orion Publishing Group, 1993.

——. *Two Treatises of Government*. London: Orion Publishing Group, 1993.

Logan, Bey. *Hong Kong Action Cinema*. Woodstock, NY: Overlook Press, 1995.

Louie, Steven, and Glenn Omatsu, eds. *Asian Americans: The Movement and the Moment*. Los Angeles: UCLA Asian American Studies Center Press, 2001.

Lowe, Lisa. *Immigrant Acts: On Asian American Cultural Politics*. Durham, NC: Duke University Press, 1996.

Lowe, Lisa, and David Lloyd. *The Politics of Culture in the Shadow of Capital: Worlds Aligned*. Durham, NC: Duke University Press, 1997.

Lubiano, Wahneema. "Like Being Mugged by a Metaphor: Multiculturalism and State Narratives." In *Mapping Multiculturalism*, edited by Avery Gordon and Christopher Newfield. Minneapolis: University of Minnesota Press, 1996.

Lutz, Catherine. "Making War at Home in the United States: Militarization and the Current Crisis." *American Anthropologist*, n. ser., 104:3 (2002): 723–735.

Macpherson, C. B. *The Political Theory of Possessive Individualism*. Oxford: Oxford University Press, 1962.

Maeda, Daryl. *Chains of Babylon: The Rise of Asian America*. Minneapolis: University of Minnesota Press, 2009.

Major League Baseball All-Star Game. Fox Television, July 8, 2001.

Major League Baseball International. 2001 Annual Report.

——. "Baseball Tonight" (advertisement). ESPN, August 3, 2001.

Majors, Richard. "Cool Pose: Black Masculinity and Sports." In *Sport, Men, and the Gender Order: Critical Feminist Perspectives*, edited by Michael Messner and Donald Sabo. Champaign, IL: Human Kinetics, 1990.

Malcolm X with Alex Haley. *The Autobiography of Malcolm X*. New York: Grove Press, 1965.

Marx, Karl, and Friedrich Engels. *The Marx-Engels Reader*. Translated and edited by Robert C. Tucker. New York: W. W. Norton, 1978.

McAlister, Melani. *Epic Encounters: Culture, Media, and U.S. Interests in the Middle East since 1945*. Berkeley: University of California Press, 2001.

McKay, Jim, Michael Messner, and Donald Sabo, eds. *Masculinities, Gender Relations, and Sport*. Thousand Oaks, CA: Sage Publications, 2000.

Mercer, Kobena. *Welcome To The Jungle: New Positions in Black Cultural Studies*. New York: Routledge, 1994.

Messner, Michael, and Donald Sabo, eds. *Sport, Men, and the Gender Order: Critical Feminist Perspectives*. Champaign, IL: Human Kinetics, 1990.

Miller, Toby, Geoffrey Lawrence, Jim McKay, and David Rowe, eds. *Globalization and Sport*. London: Sage Publications, 2001.

Mouffe, Chantal. *The Return of the Political*. London: Verso, 1993.

Mountain Brothers. *Self: Volume 1*. Pimpstrut Records, 1998.

Moy, James. *Marginal Sights: Staging the Chinese in America*. Iowa City: University of Iowa Press, 1993.

Moynihan, Daniel Patrick. "The Negro Family: The Case for National Action." U.S. Department of Labor, Office of the Assistant Secretary for Policy, March 1965. At www.dol.gov/asp.

Mulvey, Laura. "Visual Pleasure and Narrative Cinema." In *Visual and Other Pleasures*. Bloomington: Indiana University Press, 1989.

Mumford, Kevin. *Interzones: Black/White Sex Districts in Chicago and New York in the Early Twentieth Century*. New York: Columbia University Press, 1997.

Neal, Larry. "The Black Arts Movement." *Drama Review* 12 (Summer 1968): 29–39.

Negri, Toni [Antonio]. *Revolution Retrieved: Writings on Marx, Keynes, Capitalist Crisis and New Social Subjects, 1967–83*. London: Red Notes, 1988.

Nelson, Dana. *National Manhood: Capitalist Citizenship and the Imagined Fraternity of White Men*. Durham, NC: Duke University Press, 1998.

Newsweek. "Japanese Success Story: Outwhiting the Whites." June 21, 1971, 24–25.

Nguyen, Viet Thanh. *Race and Resistance: Literature and Politics in Asian America*. New York: Oxford University Press, 2002.

Ninh, erin Khuê. *Ingratitude: The Debt-Bound Daughter in Asian American Literature*. New York: New York University Press, 2011.

Nishio, Alan. "The Oriental as a 'Middleman Minority.'" *Gidra*, April 1969.

Nkrumah, Kwame. *Class Struggle in Africa*. London: Panaf Books, 1970.

Noriega, Chon. "'Something's Missing Here!' Homosexuality and Film Reviews during the Production Code Era, 1934–1962." *Cinema Journal* 30:1 (Fall 1990): 20–39.

Obama, Barack. *Dreams from My Father: A Story of Race and Inheritance*. New York: Three Rivers Press, 2004.

Okada, John. *No-No Boy*. Seattle: University of Washington Press, 1976.

Okihiro, Gary. "Is Yellow Black or White?" In *Margins and Mainstreams: Asians in American History and Culture*. Seattle: University of Washington Press, 1994.

Omatsu, Glenn. "The 'Four Prisons' and the Movements of Liberation." In *The State of Asian America: Activism and Resistance in the 1990s*, edited by Karin Aguilar-San Juan. Boston: South End Press, 1994.

Omi, Michael. "Racialization in the Post–Civil Rights Era." In *Mapping Multiculturalism*, edited by Avery Gordon and Christopher Newfield. Minneapolis: University of Minnesota Press, 1996.

Omi, Michael, and Howard Winant. *Racial Formation in the United States: From the 1960s to the 1990s*. 2nd ed. New York: Routledge, 1994.

Ong, Paul, Edna Bonacich, and Lucie Cheng, eds. *The New Asian Immigration in Los Angeles and Global Restructuring*. Philadelphia: Temple University Press, 1994.

Ong, Paul, and John M. Liu. "U.S. Immigration Policies and Asian Migration." In *The*

New Asian Immigration in Los Angeles and Global Restructuring, edited by Paul Ong, Edna Bonacich, and Lucie Cheng. Philadelphia: Temple University Press, 1994.

Ongiri, Amy. "'He Wanted to Be Just Like Bruce Lee': African Americans, Kung Fu Theater and Cultural Exchange at the Margins." *Journal of Asian American Studies* 5:1 (2002).

Osajima, Keith. "Asian Americans as the Model Minority: An Analysis of the Popular Press Image in the 1960s and 1980s." In *Contemporary Asian America: A Multidisciplinary Reader*, edited by Min Zhou and James Gatewood, 449–458. New York: New York University Press, 2000.

Outside the Lines. ESPN Television, July 1, 2001.

Palm, Roberta. Letter to Frank Chin, March 1974. Frank Chin Papers. Special Collections, University of California, Santa Barbara.

Palumbo-Liu, David. *Asian/American: Historical Crossings of a Racial Frontier*. Stanford, CA: Stanford University Press, 1999.

Paredes, Américo. *With His Pistol in His Hand*. Austin: University of Texas Press, 1958.

Park, Ishle Yi. "Asian Word Warriors." *A Gathering of the Tribes*, May 31, 2005. At http://www.tribes.org.

Penta, Mia. "Ichibobs Invade Seattle." *Morning News* (Seattle), July 26, 2001, 2B.

Peterson, William. "Success Story: Japanese-American Style." *New York Times Magazine*, January 9, 1966.

Prashad, Vijay. *Everybody Was Kung Fu Fighting: Afro-Asian Connections and the Myth of Cultural Purity*. Boston: Beacon Press, 2001.

———. *The Karma of Brown Folk*. Minneapolis: University of Minnesota Press, 2000.

Price, S. L. "The Ichiro Paradox." *Time*, July 15, 2002.

Pronger, Brian. *The Arena of Masculinity: Sports, Homosexuality, and the Meaning of Sex*. New York: St. Martin's Press, 1990.

Pulido, Laura. *Black, Brown, Yellow, and Left: Radical Activism in Los Angeles*. Berkeley: University of California Press, 2006.

Rampersad, Arnold. *Jackie Robinson*. New York: Alfred A. Knopf, 1997.

Rawick, George. *From Sundown to Sunup: The Making of the Black Community*. Westport, CT: Greenwood Press, 1972.

Reddy, Chandan. *Freedom with Violence: Race, Sexuality, and the U.S. State*. Durham, NC: Duke University Press, 2011.

Reich, Robert. *The Work of Nations: Preparing Ourselves for 21st-Century Capitalism*. New York: Albert A Knopf, 1991.

Reimers, David M. *Still the Golden Door: The Third World Comes to America*. New York: Columbia University Press, 1992.

Rendón Linares, Laura I., and Susana M. Muñoz. "Revisiting Validation Theory:

Theoretical Foundations, Applications, and Extensions." *Enrollment Management Journal* 5:2 (Summer 2011): 12–33.

Robinson, Cedric. "Manichaeism and Multiculturalism." In *Mapping Multiculturalism*, edited by Avery Gordon and Christopher Newfield. Minneapolis: University of Minnesota Press, 1996.

Rodríguez, Dylan. *Forced Passages: Imprisoned Radical Intellectuals and the U.S. Prison Regime*. Minneapolis: University of Minnesota Press, 2006.

Roediger, David. *The Wages of Whiteness: Race and the Making of the American Working Class*. London: Verso, 1990.

Rogin, Michael. *Blackface, White Noise: Jewish Immigrants in the Hollywood Melting Pot*. Berkeley: University of California Press, 1996.

Romeo Must Die. Directed by Andrzej Bartkowiak. Silver Pictures, 2000.

Rose, Tricia. *Black Noise: Rap Music and Black Culture in Contemporary America*. Lebanon, NH: University Press of New England, 1994.

Rousseau, Jean-Jacques. *The Basic Political Writings*. Translated by Donald A. Cress. Indianapolis: Hackett Publishing, 1987.

Rush Hour. Directed by Brett Ratner. New Line Cinema, 1998.

Rushton, J. Phillipe. *Race, Evolution, and Behavior: A Life History Perspective*. New Brunswick, NJ: Transaction Publishers, 1995.

Ryan, William. *Blaming the Victim*. New York: Vintage Books, 1971.

Salaam, Kalamu ya. "Black Arts Movement." In *Oxford Companion to African American Literature*, edited by William T. Andrews, Frances Foster, and Trudier Harris. New York: Oxford University Press, 1997.

San Buenaventura, Stefi. "The Colors of Manifest Destiny in the Philippines." In *Major Problems in Asian American History*, edited by Lon Kurashige and Alice Yang Murray. Boston: Houghton Mifflin, 2003.

San Jose Mercury News. "Yao Wins Showdown with Shaq." January 18, 2003.

Sassen, Saskia. *Globalization and Its Discontents*. New York: New York University Press, 1998.

———. *The Mobility of Labor and Capital*. Cambridge: Cambridge University Press, 1988.

Savran, David. *Taking It Like a Man: White Masculinity, Masochism, and Contemporary American Culture*. Princeton, NJ: Princeton University Press, 1998.

Saxton, Alexander. *The Indispensable Enemy: Labor and the Anti-Chinese Movement in California*. Berkeley: University of California Press, 1971.

Seale, Bobby. *Seize the Time: The Story of the Black Panther Party and Huey P. Newton*. New York: Random House, 1968.

Sedgwick, Eve Kosofsky. *Epistemology of the Closet*. Berkeley: University of California Press, 1990.

Shah, Nayan. *Contagious Divides: Epidemics and Race in San Francisco's Chinatown.* Berkeley: University of California Press, 2001.

Shimakawa, Karen. *National Abjection: The Asian American Body on Stage.* Durham, NC: Duke University Press, 2002.

Shklar, Judith. *American Citizenship: The Quest for Inclusion.* Cambridge: Harvard University Press, 1991.

Silverman, Kaja. *The Subject of Semiotics.* New York: Oxford University Press, 1983.

Smith, Dennis. "*Asian Pacific Review* Interviews the Mountain Brothers." *Asian Pacific Review,* September 6, 2005.

Snead, James. *White Screens, Black Images: Hollywood from the Dark Side.* Edited by Colin MacCabe and Cornel West. New York: Routledge, 1994.

So, Christine. *Economic Citizens: A Narrative of Asian American Visibility.* Philadelphia: Temple University Press, 2008.

Somerville, Siobhan B. *Queering the Color Line: Race and the Invention of Homosexuality in American Culture.* Durham, NC: Duke University Press, 2000.

Spalding, Albert G. *America's National Game.* New York: American Sports Publishing Company, 1911.

Stokes, Lisa Odham, and Michael Hoover. *City on Fire: Hong Kong Cinema.* London: Verso, 1999.

Stoler, Ann Laura. *Race and the Education of Desire: Foucault's History of Sexuality and the Colonial Order of Things.* Durham, NC: Duke University Press, 1995.

Straayer, Chris. "Redressing the 'Natural': The Temporary Transvestite Film." In *Deviant Eyes, Deviant Bodies: Sexual Re-Orientation in Film and Video.* New York: Columbia University Press, 1996.

Su, Karen. "Jade Snow Wong's Badge of Distinction in the 1990s." *Critical Mass: A Journal of Asian American Criticism* 2:1 (Winter 1994): 3–52.

Sue, Stanley, and Harry H. L. Kitano. "Stereotypes as a Measure of Success." *Journal of Social Issues* 29 (1973): 83–98.

Sumida, Stephen. "The More Things Change: Paradigm Shifts in Asian American Studies." *American Studies International* 38:2 (June 2000): 97-114.

Suzuki, Bob H. "Asian-American as the Model Minority." *Change,* November 1989, 13–19.

Tachiki, Amy, Eddie Wong, Franklin Odo, and Buck Wong, eds. *Roots: An Asian American Reader.* Los Angeles: UCLA Asian American Studies Center Press, 1971.

Takaki, Ronald. *Strangers from a Different Shore: A History of Asian Americans.* New York: Penguin Books, 1989.

Talk Back Live. Moderated by Arthel Neville. CNN, January 23, 2003.

Tang, Irwin. "APA Community Should Tell Shaquille O'Neal to 'Come Down to Chinatown.'" *AsianWeek,* January 3, 2003.

Tasker, Yvonne. "Fists of Fury." In *Race and the Subject of Masculinities*, edited by Harry Stecopoulos and Michael Uebel. Durham, NC: Duke University Press, 1997.

Tavis Smiley Show, The. National Public Radio, January 24, 2003.

Taylor, Peter. *Modernities: A Geohistorical Interpretation.* Minneapolis: University of Minnesota Press, 1999.

Teo, Stephen. "The 1970s." In *The Cinema of Hong Kong: History, Arts, Identity*, edited by Poshek Fu and David Desser. Cambridge: Cambridge University Press, 2000.

Tölölyan, Khachig. "Rethinking Diapora(s): Stateless Power in the Transnational Moment." *Diaspora* 5:1 (Spring 1996): 3–36.

Ungar, Sheldon. "Moral Panics, the Military-Industrial Complex, and the Arms Race." *Sociological Quarterly* 31:2 (Summer 1990): 165–185.

United States Commission on Civil Rights. "Shutdown: Economic Dislocation and Equal Opportunity." Report prepared by the Illinois Advisory Committee. Washington, DC: Government Printing Office, June 1981.

United States Senate. *Hearings before the Committee on Labor and Human Resources*, 96th Congress. Washington, DC: Government Printing Office, September 17–18, 1980.

Veblen, Thorstein. *The Theory of the Leisure Class.* New York: Modern Library, 1911.

Viswanathan, Gauri. *Masks of Conquest: Literary Study and British Rule in India.* New York: Columbia University Press, 1989.

Wiegman, Robyn. *American Anatomies: Theorizing Race and Gender.* Durham, NC: Duke University Press, 1995.

Williams, Raymond. *Marxism and Literature.* Oxford: Oxford University Press, 1977.

Williams, Saul. "The Future of Language." In *The Spoken Word Revolution*, edited by Mark Eleveld. Naperville, IL: Sourcebooks, 2003.

Wong, Deborah. *Speak It Louder: Asian Americans Making Music.* New York: Routledge, 2004.

Wong, Sau-Ling. "Denationalization Reconsidered: Asian American Cultural Criticism at a Theoretical Crossroads." *Amerasia Journal* 21:1–2 (Winter-Spring 1995): 1–27.

Wright, Richard. "How 'Bigger' Was Born." In *Native Son.* New York: HarperCollins, 1993.

———. "Joe Louis Uncovers Dynamite." *New Masses*, October 8, 1935, 18–19.

Wu, Frank. *Yellow: Race in America beyond Black and White.* New York: Basic Books, 2002.

Yamane, David. *Student Movements for Multiculturalism: Challenging the Curricular Color Line in Higher Education.* Baltimore: Johns Hopkins University Press, 2000.

Yoneyama, Lisa. *Hiroshima Traces: Time, Space, and the Dialectics of Memory.* Berkeley: University of California Press, 1999.

Young, Al. "Interview: Ishmael Reed." *Change*, November 1972.

Zamora, Lois Parkinson, ed. *The Apocalyptic Vision in America: Interdisciplinary Essays on Myth and Culture.* Bowling Green, OH: Bowling Green State University Popular Press, 1982.

Index

106 & Park, 135

2 Tongues. *See* I Was Born with Two
    Tongues

Aaliyah, 97

abjection, 119

Afro Asia, 37

Afro-Asians: bonds, 7, 30–34, 37–40,
    51; cultures, 6, 7, 8, 25, 26, 30, 43, 44;
    literary movement, 47–49, 50–51,
    53–54; mode of cultural production,
    41, 53–54; racialization, 10–11, 17, 78;
    radicalism, 26–29

Against Race (Gilroy), 65

*Aiiieeeee! An Anthology of Asian-
    American Writers*, 32, 35, 37, 40–42,
    43–54, 139, 140, 149n19, 150n23,
    151n43, 152n48

Alejandro, Roberto, 94

Alexander Global Productions, 55

Ali, Muhammad, 64

All-Star Game, 69, 70, 72

Althusser, Louis, 164–65n63

American Nervousness (Beard), 60

antiblackness, 12, 24–25, 29, 42, 45,
    51–52, 68, 141

Aoki, Richard, 24, 26, 28–29

Armstrong, Louis, 126

articulation, 68–69, 157n44

Asian American Left, 24, 26, 29

Asian American Literature (Kim), 43

Asian Americans: male sexuality, 135;

neoconservatives, 152n48; paneth-
    nicity, 27, 149n19; theater, 119–21;
    writing movement, 32–33, 35–55

*Asian Americans: The Movement and
    the Moment*, 26

Asian Improv, 124

Asian male body, 33, 45, 55–57, 67–68,
    75–77, 99–100, 116–19, 128, 133, 139,
    153n2, 158n58

Asian male sexuality, 101–2

AsianAvenue.com, 123

Asianness, 99, 127

assimilation, 6, 9, 20, 21–23, 32, 39, 42,
    44–45, 47–49, 51, 53, 57, 79, 87, 90,
    99, 108, 126–27, 141

"Avenging Women in Indian Cinema"
    (Gopalan), 102–3

Baer, Max, 63

Baldwin, James, 12

baseball, 33, 61–62, 63–64, 69–75,
    157n47

basketball, 33, 56–57, 75–83

Bederman, Gail, 58

Benjamin, Walter, 30, 116, 120–21

Beyond a Boundary (James), 62–63

Bhabha, Homi, 68

Bhaduri, Bhuvaneswari, 168n2

biological racism, 4, 56–57

Black Arts movement, 35

black male body, 57, 65–66, 68, 76,
    154n20

black male sexuality, 102

Black Panther party, 5, 26, 28–29

black pathology, 11, 18, 29

Black Power, 12, 16, 24–25, 84

"Black Power: A Scientific Concept
Whose Time Has Come" (Boggs), 26

black radicalism, 38, 41, 63

black revolution, 3, 10–11, 16, 24, 26,
29, 42

Black Skin, White Masks (Fanon),
156n33

blackface, 47–48, 151n43

Blackface, White Noise (Rogin), 47,
151n43

blaxploitation film, 84–85

"Bodies: The Exhibition," 117, 119

ballad hero, 93–94

boxing, 58, 61, 154n20

Brief History of Neoliberalism, A (Harvey), 13

Broken Speak, 115–16, 123–24, 127–28

Brooks, Gwendolyn, 49

buddy films, 33, 84–114, 162n47

Buenaventura, Stefi San, 23

capital imperative, 8–9, 17, 21, 30, 59

capitalism, 8–9, 13, 29, 59–61, 89,
132–33, 149n19

Chan, Charlie, 118–19, 153n2

Chan, Jackie, 86, 92, 97, 102, 103, 139

Chan, Jeffrey Paul, 37, 42, 50

Chang, Emily, 122

Chang, Jeff, 163n50

Chang and Eng, 117

Changes magazine, 35

Chin, Edward, 138–39

Chin, Frank, 32, 36–40, 42, 44, 45, 49,
50–52

China, 77, 82, 159n74

Chinatown, 22, 79–81

Chinese Exclusion Act of 1882, 160–
61n17

Chu, Louis, 50

cinematic citizenship, 91, 101, 105, 106,
110, 114

citizenship, 12, 94, 108, 128, 139, 141,
152n48, 160–61n17

Civil rights movement, 12, 18, 21, 26–27,
64

comparative racialization, 5–6, 8, 10, 11,
15, 21, 23, 38, 51, 92

Condition of Postmodernity, The (Harvey), 13, 150n23

conservative backlash, 10, 66, 155n28

corporate multiculturalism, 81

cricket, 62–63

crossover appeal, 130

cross-racial solidarity, 85

cultural nationalism, 38–40, 42

Daniels, Wayne, 49

Dead Prez, 96

Denizen Kane. *See* Kim, Dennis

Denning, Michael, 13, 38

dialogic criticism, 135

Diawara, Manthia, 91

Díaz, Junot, 27

differential racialization, 11

Doughball (Miyake), 121

Douglas, Carl, 85

Du Bois, W. E. B., 23, 31, 86, 89, 155n20

dual heritage, 44–45

Economic Citizens (So), 9

Edwards, Harry, 59, 65

Ellington, Duke, 50

Enter the Dragon (Clouse), 95

Epistemology of the Closet (Sedgwick),
104

Esguerra, Anida Yoeu, 115, 122, 124

Esguerra, Marlon, 115, 122, 123, 128–29
Everybody Was Kung Fu Fighting (Prashad), 39

Female Masculinity (Halberstam), 8
feminist theory, 59
Ferguson, Rod, 18–19
Fordism, 13, 150n23
Fordist Compromise, 13
Four Horsemen of Asian American literature, 37, 42, 50
Francis, Steve, 79
Free Labor Ideology, 89
Freedom Dreams (Kelley), 31–32
Fu Manchu, 118–19, 153n2
Fujino, Diane, 26
Fung, Richard, 67

Garvey, Marcus, 39
GenerAsian hip-hop, 129
George, Nelson, 132
Gilman, Sander, 19
Glazer, Nathan, 17
global multiculturalism, 73–74, 77, 105, 155n28
global sport, 30–33, 55–84
globalization, 9, 13, 33, 59, 72–75, 77, 88, 150n23
golden hour, 10, 14–15, 17, 19–20
Gopinath, Gayatri, 126–27
Gramsci, Antonio, 38, 87, 89, 90
Grey, Zane, 62

Hagedorn, Jessica, 115
Halberstam, Judith, 8, 58, 101
Hall, Stuart, 4, 13–14, 49, 67, 68, 92, 126
"Han" (Dennis Kim), 124–27
Harris, Charles, 37
Harris, Cheryl, 104, 164n58
Harris, William, 38

Hart-Celler Act, 12
Heart of Darkness (Conrad), 142
Himes, Chester, 36
hip-hop, 33–34, 71, 109, 115, 129–37, 139
hooks, bell, 91–92, 134
Horne, Gerald, 12, 16
Houston Rockets, 75, 76–77
Howard University Press, 44, 51
Howe, James Wong, 50
Hune, Shirley, 42
Hurston, Zora Neale, 36

I Was Born with Two Tongues, 33, 115–16, 122–29
Ice Cube, 163n50
Ichibobs, 55–56
Ichiro Suzuki, 33, 55–56, 68–74, 86
Iijima, Chris, 28
Immigrant Acts (Lowe), 8–9
imperialism, 23, 109–10, 165n66
Inada, Lawson Fusao, 37, 42, 50
influence of blackness, 43–44
Ingratitude (Ninh), 9
internment camps, 21, 140–42, 147n64
interracial mimesis, 42, 99, 100, 101, 112
Invisible Man (Ellison), 67
Isangmahal, 122
Ishii, David, 52
Iverson, Allen, 86
Iwamatsu, Mako, 119

James, C. L. R., 10, 62–63, 83
Japanese American Citizens League, 52
Japanese Americans, 19–20, 70–71, 142, 147n64
Jeffries, Jim, 154n20
Jet Li, 86, 92, 95, 97, 103
Jin, 135–36
Johnson, Jack, 58, 154n20

Jung, Scott (pseud. Chops), 129, 130, 132–33, 134, 135

Kaplan, Amy, 165n66
Keeling, Kara, 134
Kelly, Jim, 95
Kim, Claire Jean, 41
Kim, Daniel, 38, 46
Kim, Dennis, 33, 115–17, 122–29, 139
Kim, Elaine, 20, 43
Kimmel, Michael, 61
King, Martin Luther, Jr., 31–32
Kingston, Maxine Hong, 40, 45
Kochiyama, Yuri, 26, 31
Kondo, Dorinne, 121–22
Korea, 126
Korean American Grocers Association, 163n50
Korean Americans, 124–27
"Kung Fu Craze, The" (Desser), 95
kung-fu films, 95

Lawson, William, 49
Lee, Bruce, 33, 85, 96, 102, 103
Lee, Robert, 100, 118
leisure culture, 61–62
Leong, Russell, 54
liberal individualism, 132
Lim, Dennis, 92
Lin, Jeremy, 56–57
Lipsitz, George, 130, 135
Los Angeles Times, 16
Los Siete de la Raza, 29
Louis, Joe, 63
"Love Poetry" (Mountain Brothers), 136
Lowe, Lisa, 8–9, 24, 30, 151n44, 162–63n49
Lutz, Catherine, 15

Maeda, Daryl, 42
Mailer, Norman, 65
Major League Baseball, 63, 69, 72–73
Major League Baseball International, 73–74
Malcolm X, 28, 46
Manly Art, The (Gorn), 61
Mann's Chinese Theater, 106–7
market democracy, 5, 10–16, 19–22, 29, 32, 42, 87–90, 91, 102, 106, 160n10
masculinity: African American, 3–8, 10, 12, 18–19, 25, 32–34, 41–42, 43, 44, 48, 55, 63, 64–65, 76, 78–80, 86, 89, 112–13, 141, 155n28; Asian American, 3–8, 10, 32–34, 41–42, 45–47, 55–58, 69, 70–75, 76–77, 80–81, 86–87, 89, 92, 100–102, 108, 112–13, 116–19, 124–27, 129, 132–37, 139, 141, 151n40, 158n58; effect of industrial capitalism, 59–61, 89–90; popular sport's influence, 58–61, 63–64, 79; Victorian ideal, 60; white, 45–46, 60, 62, 64, 104–5, 107–8, 155n26, 155n27
martial arts: films, 33, 84–114, 162n47; heroes, 90, 93–95, 99, 101, 103, 105, 107–8, 110, 113
Marx, Karl, 59–60, 88
Masculinities (Connell), 8
materialism, 132–33
militarization, 15–16, 18, 155n28
minstrelsy, 118
model minority, 19–22, 25, 27, 39, 112; thesis, 20–21
modernity, 71, 139–42
Mountain Brothers, 33, 129–36, 139
Moy, James, 117–18
Moynihan, Daniel Patrick, 16–19
Moynihan Report, 16–19, 21
Mugdal, Hucheshwar G., 39
mythification, 113–14

NAACP, 79

Narrating Nationalisms (Ling), 47, 151n41

National Abjection (Shimakawa), 119–20

nationalism, 39–40, 59, 79, 157n47, 158n64

Native Speaker (Lee), 24–25

NBA, 75, 79, 82–83, 159n74; Draft Lottery, 75

Negri, Toni, 13–14, 15

"Negro Family: The Case for National Action, The" (Moynihan), 17

neoliberalism, 10–20, 22–23, 29, 31, 74

New Amsterdam News, 64

New Asian Immigration in Los Angeles and Global Restructuring, The (Ong, Bonacich, and Cheng), 13

New Left, 15, 26

New Line Cinema, 86

New York Times, 92

Nisei Daughter (Sone), 39

Nishio, Alan, 27

Nkrumah, Kwame, 13

No-No Boy (Okada), 21, 140–42

Noriega, Chon, 108

Okada, John, 21, 50, 140–42

Olajuwon, Hakeem, 75, 76

Oland, Werner, 119, 153n2

Omatsu, Glenn, 152n48

Omi, Michael, 64

O'Neal, Shaquille, 78–83

Ongiri, Amy, 96

oppositional gaze, 8, 33, 84, 91, 96–97, 100, 111

Order of Things, The (Foucault), 7

Otherness, 66, 68

Owens, Jesse, 63

Pacific Rim capital, 55–56, 72, 86

Pacifics, 123

Palm, Roberta, 44

Palumbo-Liu, David, 23

pansori, 125–26

"Paperchase" (Mountain Brothers), 132–33

Park, Ishle Yi, 40, 125

Parker, William, 15

Peterson, William, 16–17, 19–22

Pimpstrut Records, 131

Political Unconscious, The (Jameson), 30

Politics of Culture in the Shadow of Capital, The (Lowe and Lloyd), 30, 43

polyculturalism, 39–40

popular culture, 7

popular sport, 33, 55–83, 154–55n20, 156n33

Porter's Pub, 115

Possessive Investment of Whiteness, The (Lipsitz), 45

Prison Notebooks (Gramsci), 89

property ownership, 88, 90, 91, 103–4, 160n10, 161n17, 164n58

Psychic Life of Power, The (Butler), 30

psychoanalysis, 6–7

Pulido, Laura, 11

Race, Evolution, and Behavior: A Life History Perspsective (Rushton), 67, 156–57n37

Race and Resistance (Nguyen), 20–21

Race for Citizenship (Jun), 11

Race Rebels (Kelley), 145–46n46

race struggle, 56

Racial Castration: Managing Masculinity in Asian America (Eng), 6

racial fantasy, 95

racial fetishism, 65–66

Racial Formation in the United States
   (Omi and Winant), 6, 10–11
racial magnetism, 4–7, 11, 23, 25–26,
   27, 29–30, 32, 34, 36–37, 41, 47, 51,
   53–54, 55, 84–85, 91, 93, 116–17, 129,
   138–39, 142
racial stereotypes, 68–69
racialized labor stratification, 8–9, 29,
   59–61, 89–90, 142
racism, 5, 25, 46, 56, 65, 66, 81, 89–90
radical ethnics, 27
Rai, Lajpat, 30
Rawick, George, 118
Reddy, Chandan, 15
"Redressing the 'Natural'" (Straayer), 101
Reed, Ishmael, 32, 35–39, 49
reggae, 139
Revolutionary Action Movement, 26
Robinson, Jackie, 63–64, 74
Romeo Must Die (Bartkowiak), 86, 90,
   92–93, 97–99, 101–5, 112–13, 163n51
Rose, Tricia, 133
Ruffhouse/Columbia Records, 131
Rush Hour (Ratner), 86, 90, 92, 97–102,
   105–11
Rush Hour 2 (Ratner), 86
Rush Hour 3 (Ratner), 86

Safeco Field, 69, 71
San Francisco, California, 52–53
San Francisco Examiner, 92
Savage, Darius, 115–16
Saxon, John, 95
Saxton, Alexander, 118
Scale and Scope (Chandler), 59
Seattle, Washington, 52–53, 71
Seattle Mariners, 55–56, 70, 71, 73
Seize the Time (Seale), 28–29
Self: Volume I, 130, 131–34
self-marketing, 131

sexual boasting, 134–36
Sexual Neurasthenia (Mitchell), 60
shock effect, 120
Siamese twins, 117–18
slavery, 48–49
Smith, William Gardner, 50
social movements, 6, 10, 11–12, 16, 21,
   24, 35, 38, 53, 64, 85, 87–88, 96, 134
Society Must Be Defended (Foucault), 56
Souls of Black Folk, The (Du Bois), 89
Spalding, Albert G., 70–71
Speak It Louder (Wong), 120
Spivak, Gayatri, 168n2
spoken word, 33–34, 115–17, 122–29
*Sport, Men, and the Gender Order:
   Critical Feminist Perspectives* (Mess-
   ner and Sabo), 58–59
sport internationalism, 33, 72, 74, 75, 77,
   82–83
Sports Illustrated, 75
States of Injury (Brown), 47
Stern, David, 75, 79, 82
Stoler, Ann Laura, 23
Subculture: The Meaning of Style (Heb-
   dige), 69
Subject of Semiotics, The (Silverman), 91
Sui Sin Far, 39
Sumida, Stephen, 45, 70
suture, 91

*Taboo: Why Black Athletes Dominate
   Sports and Why We're Afraid to Talk
   About It* (Entine), 66–67
Takaki, Ronald, 160n17
Tampa's Museum of Science and Indus-
   try, 117
Tang, Irwin, 79–80, 81
Taylor, Peter, 52–53
Theory of the Leisure Class, The
   (Veblen), 61–62

third world liberation, 26–27, 150n23, 151n41

Tölölyan, Khachig, 126

Tony Bruno Morning Show Extravaganza, 78

"Tree City Anthem" (Kane), 127–28

Tucker, Chris, 92, 97, 139

TV Guide, 92

Two Treatises of Government (Locke), 160n10

Typical Cats, 117

urban culture, 84

Vietnam, 15

"Visual Pleasure and Narrative" (Mulvey), 98

Viswanathan, Gauri, 23

Wang, Chris (pseud. Peril-L), 129, 132, 136

Warner Brothers, 86, 95

Water Margin (Nai'an), 129

Watts riots, 12, 16

Wayne, John, 107–8

Wei, Steve (pseud. Styles), 129, 130, 131, 135

Welcome to the Jungle (Mercer), 66

West, Kanye, 139

"Whiplash" (Mountain Brothers), 135–36

White, Barry, 136

White Screens, Black Images (Snead), 113–14

white supremacy, 18, 23, 29, 38, 42–43, 46, 80, 85, 105–6, 117–19, 127, 138–39, 141, 150n30, 155n26, 164n58

whiteness, 8

Wiegman, Robyn, 66–67

Williams, Raymond, 152n46

Williams, Saul, 116

With His Pistol in His Hand (Paredes), 93

Wong, Deborah, 130

Wong, Shawn, 37, 42, 49, 50, 52

Wong Fei-hung, 94–95

"Work of Art in the Age of Mechanical Reproduction, The" (Benjamin), 120–21

Wretched of the Earth, The (Fanon), 43

Wright, Richard, 63

Writing Manhood in Black and Yellow: Ralph Ellison, Frank Chin and the Literary Politics of Identity (Kim), 7

Yao Ming, 33, 68, 75–83, 159n74

Yaomania, 76–78, 83

Yardbird Publishing Incorporated, 49, 53

Yardbird Reader 3, 32, 35, 37, 41–42, 49–54

Yellow Technicolor Tour, 123

yellowface, 100, 118–19, 153n2

Young, Al, 35, 38, 49

Zamora, Lois Parkinson, 18

CPSIA information can be obtained at www.ICGtesting.com
Printed in the USA
BVOW01*2144260215

389383BV00002B/2/P